Birth Marks

NEW CULTURAL STUDIES

Series Editors

Joan DeJean
Carroll Smith-Rosenberg
Peter Stallybrass
Gary A. Tomlinson

A complete list of books in the series is
available from the publisher.

Birth Marks

The Tragedy of Primogeniture in Pierre Corneille,
Thomas Corneille, and Jean Racine

RICHARD E. GOODKIN

PENN

University of Pennsylvania Press

Philadelphia

10 9 8 7 6 5 4 3 2 1

Published by
University of Pennsylvania Press
Philadelphia, Pennsylvania 19104-4011

Library of Congress Cataloging-in-Publication Data
Goodkin, Richard E.
  Birth marks : the tragedy of primogeniture in Pierre Corneille, Thomas Corneille, and
Jean Racine / Richard E. Goodkin.
    p. cm. — (New cultural studies)
  Includes bibliographical references and index.
  ISBN 0-8122-3550-9 (alk. paper)
    1. French drama (Tragedy) — History and criticism.   2. French drama — 17th century —
History and criticism.   3. Corneille, Pierre, 1606–1684 — Criticism and interpretation.
4. Corneille, Thomas, 1625–1709 — Criticism and interpretation.   5. Racine, Jean, 1639–
1699 — Criticism and interpretation.   6. Primogeniture in literature.   I. Title.   II. Series.
PQ563.G66   2000
842'.051209 — dc21   00-023390

For
Louise, Ira, and Mandel,
with love

Contents

Preface

> Sociological and ideological "models" tend to become forms of imperialism and to define new forms of orthodoxy. These models are necessary, because they delineate a process of research and thus make history intelligible. But for us, history must also offer resistance to these models; otherwise, all societies different from our own would appear to conform to our ideology or our experience. . . . Social history is . . . method, not truth.[1]

Michel de Certeau's observations about the difficulties and limitations of interpreting history set forth the central paradox of historical approaches to the study of French Classical tragedy. On the one hand, Classical scholars go to great lengths to emphasize the importance of contextualizing interpretations of texts which, in spite of their undisputed contribution to the Western literary tradition and hence to our present-day literary sensibility, are at a far remove from the lives and experiences of readers at the turn of the twenty-first century. On the other hand, the preoccupation with studying seventeenth-century texts in a carefully reconstructed historical framework belongs not to the seventeenth century, but to the present day. In other words, our desire to give our readings of French Classical tragedy authenticity and authority by reconstituting our best approximation of the sociopolitical and intellectual reality of the Versailles court tells us more about late twentieth- and early twenty-first-century ideas about seventeenth-century literature than it does about seventeenth-century literary texts. That our attempt at penetrating the complexities of a sociocultural context so different from our own conforms to the intellectual structures of the present can be a great source of frustration. It is my belief that it can also be a great source of creativity and inspiration.

It is in the spirit of what I see as the fruitful paradox of reading French Classical tragedy from a perspective that inevitably remains quite external to it — however painstaking one's efforts to immerse oneself in the context in which the plays were written and performed — that I have undertaken the present study of questions of birth order and inheritance in the works of

Pierre Corneille, Thomas Corneille, and Jean Racine. On the one hand, I have attempted to demonstrate that social issues like attitudes toward primogeniture, problems of dynastic succession, and the development of a capitalistic ethic based on competition in the present and a relative disregard for tradition are woven into the fabric of seventeenth-century French society, and that consequently the viewing public for whom these three playwrights wrote was highly sensitized to these issues. On the other hand, in my analyses of the plays themselves I have allowed myself to approach problems of birth order very much from a present-day perspective, not only because I believe temporal disjunction is to some degree inevitable, but also because I hope it can also be thought-provoking and productive. After all, what finer tribute can we offer to French Classical dramatists than to demonstrate that in spite of the vast cultural distance that separates us from their tragedies, these works continue to speak to us with a certain immediacy, indeed, intimacy?

To this extent one of my goals has been to find a happy medium between the two opposing viewpoints that characterize the polemic between supporters of traditional academic approaches to French Classical texts and proponents of more innovative, often more personal approaches, a debate set off by the 1963 publication of Roland Barthes' *Sur Racine*. Much of the firestorm of protest elicited by *Sur Racine* had to do with Barthes' insistence, through his structuralist, psychoanalytically informed analyses, on decontextualizing Racine's tragedies; he sought to point out the stark structures underlying the tragedies rather than the complex particularities of each individual play, character, or situation. In other words, while more traditional studies of Racine had emphasized Racine's difference — the various sociohistorical, esthetic, and intellectual factors that informed his works and purportedly needed to be understood before one could read them with any degree of understanding — Barthes attempted to reveal Racine's sameness, his approachability, his recognizability to the naked eye. It is as if the missing academic apparatus were actually a part of Barthes' text, our surprise at its absence foreseen and inscribed into the work by the author, like a masterful actor who knows to what devastating effect a long onstage silence can be put.

Here again, I believe that the recognition of a division — in this case the polarization of French seventeenth-century studies set off by the *affaire Barthes* — can lead to something productive. Although I have been much concerned in this book with the sociohistorical contextualization of the literary texts I have chosen to analyze, in my readings of the works themselves I have also tried to follow the spirit of Barthes' intimate reading of Racine by revealing the very personal way these texts speak to me, across the ocean and across the centuries. It is hardly controversial to believe that, like all great literature, French Classical tragedy teaches us both something very specific about the time and place that produced it and something much broader and more general, and that tragedy's larger truths are inseparable from its enduring value.

Finally, I hope to show that the very widespread interpretation of French Classical tragedy as a reflection of the increasing authoritarianism and repression of the Classical period, while it certainly has an element of truth, is partial and incomplete. A goodly number of scholars of the 1980s and 1990s, undoubtedly influenced by Michel Foucault's reading of the Classical period as a time of *renfermement*, have viewed the age of Louis XIV in the light of its oppression and intolerance; indeed, this picture of nascent absolutism may account for a certain resistance in recent years to the tragedy of the period, which has sometimes been considered, whether explicitly or implicitly, as an excessively ordered expression of absolutist esthetics. But we must not forget that the age of absolutism is also a time of increasing social mobility. Many of the policies Louis XIV formulates to undermine the position of his main opponents, the feudal aristocracy, have the indirect effect of opening society up to people of lower social standing, notably the bourgeoisie and the *noblesse de robe*, thus accelerating upward social mobility. The gradual questioning of primogeniture which I have discovered in my study of seventeen tragedies composed during the very years the absolutist state was consolidating its power represents a challenge of momentous proportions to an ancient and archconservative social structure. In our haste to condemn absolutism's social and political restrictiveness, we should not ignore that in other ways the period is characterized by an increased openness, which Tocqueville sees as the beginning of the social transformation that will lead to the Revolution a century later.

Introduction

And the Lord set a mark upon Cain, lest any finding him
should kill him. — Genesis 4:15

Meritocracy — rewarding members of society on the basis of the contributions they have made as individuals — as opposed to what we might call
"heritocracy" — a system of inherited privilege — is today hardly controversial. Its spirit goes to the heart of the cherished Western belief in self-
determination and self-improvement, the valuing of the freedom and openendedness of individual enterprise over the predetermination and rigidity
of inherited advantages.

The simple fact that things have not always been this way may help to
explain why the ideal of egalitarianism is so difficult to achieve. The feudalism that organized much of society in Western Europe during the medieval
period was founded on the basic principle of the transmission of land,
wealth, titles, and goods — in short, the very things that constituted power
and privilege — according to a predetermined criterion that had nothing to
do with merit: birth order. Primogeniture, the practice of passing along the
bulk of an estate to the oldest son, held sway in France, England, and
elsewhere for many centuries. It was legally abolished in France by the
Revolution, but did not die out completely there or in England until the
early twentieth century.

This book focuses on the issues of birth order and inheritance in
French Classical tragedy as examples of the complex evolution in mentalities that accompanied the transition between feudalism and capitalism.
The seventeenth century in France is widely held to be a time of particularly
vigorous interaction and confrontation between feudalism and capitalism,
so that it is not unreasonable to speculate that the body of literature to
which this period gave rise might be expressive of the conflicting attitudes
fostered by these two socioeconomic systems. The transition between them
was slow, complicated, and irregular; the impact of feudalism on the history
of mentalities far outlived its decline as an economic system. Its spirit lives
and breathes in the aristocratic circles described by Proust in the early

twentieth century, and as we shall see, the implications of a psychological form of primogeniture are with us to this day.

My goal in studying representative tragedies of the Classical period in France is to explore, on a small scale, the evolution of mentalities that underlies the large-scale socioeconomic shift transforming Europe at that time. To borrow the terms of the historian of science Frank J. Sulloway, I would like to use "microhistory," in this case a narrowly defined literary domain, to illustrate a problem raised by "macrohistory": "Macrohistory entails the interplay of historical forces over relatively long periods of time. In contrast, microhistory takes up the problem of individual lives. . . . The role of family dynamics, including its expression in the form of sibling differences in personality, elucidates questions about microhistory rather than macrohistory."[1] The relation between microhistory and macrohistory should be taken as analogous rather than causative, illustrative rather than comprehensive: no individual example perfectly embodies a large historical evolution, any more than the grand forces of history completely account for the events of an individual life. While the examination of a small number of interrelated concepts in the tragedy of this period cannot explain the larger historical movement from a feudalistic to a capitalistic society, such a study can allow us to observe that movement with the particularly keen perception that underlies any aesthetic (from the Greek *aisthesis*, perception) experience.

The body of literature I have chosen is a series of tragedies written and performed in France between the foundation of the Académie française in 1635 and the year Racine presented *Phèdre* as his theatrical swan song, 1677. The study of birth order and inheritance extends to other issues, such as the relations among siblings, the relations between siblings and parents, and siblings' access to power. I pay particular attention to the psychology of siblings, a field that has only recently come into its own. My undertaking has both a sociohistorical and a psychological component: in my approach to these Classical texts, I have drawn on both historical studies of early modern France and on psychological and sociological studies of birth order, the sibling bond, and the relations between the generations. I believe this heterogeneity of sources is justified for several reasons.

First and foremost, although primogeniture as a legal practice has gone the way of the dinosaurs, what I call psychological primogeniture — parents' tendency to treat their firstborn as a spiritual heir — has certainly not disappeared; probably no amount of legislation could take away the special status of the firstborn. In his recent monumental study of the effects of birth order within a huge sample of scientists, politicians, philosophers, and other thinkers from the sixteenth to the twentieth centuries, Frank J. Sulloway points out that the abolition of primogeniture around the time of the French Revolution had no significant impact on the very strong psychological birth-order effects he observes in his entire sample, spanning four hundred years:

> [Birth-order] effects have not tended to diminish over time in general. In other words, birth-order effects are just as substantial during twentieth-century disputes as they were four centuries ago. . . . [This] tends to rule out the possibility that birth-order differences owe themselves to the practice of primogeniture. Primogeniture — the custom of leaving whole estates to eldest sons — was abolished in most European countries in the wake of the French Revolution. This change in inheritance practices has had no measurable influence on the size of birth-order effects.[2]

Primogeniture is a particularly dramatic manifestation of societal attitudes toward birth order, but it is just one example of the more general pattern that often makes of firstborns their parents' spiritual legatees, with all the advantages and limitations that implies. Psychological primogeniture does not mean that firstborns get everything parents have to offer, but that whether consciously or not, parents very frequently expect firstborns to conform to their wishes and expectations to a greater extent than laterborns. If, as Sulloway posits, this is a consistent pattern demonstrable over a very long period of time, this basic cultural continuity may be one justification for using twentieth-century research on birth order in a study of seventeenth-century texts.

In addition to cultural continuity, the study of birth order raises questions that are so broad that they are transcultural as well as transsecular. Basic human needs like the older generation's eagerness to leave behind a spiritual legacy and the younger generation's wish both to belong to a tradition and to be able to rebel against tradition affect the relations between succeeding generations in most, if not all societies. According to Erik Erikson, "generativity" — guiding the next generation in anticipation of one's own mortality — is a fundamental human need:

> Generativity, then, is primarily concerned with establishing and guiding the next generation. In addition to procreativity, it includes productivity and creativity; thus it is psychosocial in nature.[3]

> Generativity, as the instinctual power behind various forms of selfless "caring," potentially extends to whatever a man generates and leaves behind, creates and produces. . . . The ideological polarization of the Western world which has made

Freud the century's theorist of sex, and Marx that of work, has, until quite recently, left a whole area of man's mind uncharted in psychoanalysis. I refer to man's *love for his works and ideas as well as for his children*, and the necessary self-verification which adult man's ego receives, and must receive, . . . emanating from what he has generated and from what now must be "brought up," guarded, preserved — and eventually transcended.[4]

Whether directly or indirectly, the older generation does its best to inculcate within the younger generation its own values, perspectives, and beliefs. It does this not only from a genuine concern for the younger generation — what Erikson calls "selfless caring" — but also from a selfish need for "self-verification," as if one had not fully existed without leaving behind a replica of oneself.

A final justification for my use of recent theories in social psychology in a study of seventeenth-century texts is that, as with psychoanalytical readings of early modern texts, the value of the conjunction resides in what it allows us to understand about the literary texts being scrutinized: the proof of the pudding is less in its confection than in its taste. Although what we call "psychology" did not exist as such in the seventeenth century, proto-psychological texts pepper the literature of the period, from the Corneille brothers, Racine, Molière, and Madame de Lafayette to La Rochefoucauld and La Bruyère. Psychological realism in tragedy is a much more recent phenomenon, but by comparison with the archetypal masked representations of ancient Greece, Classical French tragedy has already gone a long way toward creating individualized, idiosyncratic characters. And as thought-provoking studies like those of Francesco Orlando and Mitchell Greenberg have demonstrated, using psychological theories drawn from the nineteenth and twentieth centuries to study Classical tragedy can be highly illuminating.[5] My aim is thus to use concepts drawn from psychological studies of birth order, as well as from historical accounts of the reigns of Louis XIII and Louis XIV, in order to view in a new light problems of birth order and inheritance raised by French Classical tragedy.

During the reigns of Louis XIII and Louis XIV, the question of the transmission of power, both dynastic (who will be king?) and socioeconomic (who inherits land and titles?) was of such grave concern that literary themes like sibling rivalry, the choice of an heir, and inherited versus earned rewards undoubtedly had a resonance for audiences watching or reading the tragedies of the time that may well be lost on their twenty-first century counterparts. On a political level, the era preceding and leading up to the absolute monarchy is filled with dynastic disturbances and crises of succession. In terms of broader social practices and attitudes, the ramifications of allowing commoners to buy or otherwise acquire noble titles — a practice which was by no means new in the seventeenth century but which increasingly exposed the domain of inherited privilege to market forces — were endlessly revisited in one of the most hotly contested rivalries of the day, the long-standing struggle between nobles with ancient inherited titles (*noblesse d'épée*) and the upstarts who would join their ranks (*noblesse de robe*). Moreover the increasing influence, both economic and social, of the wealthiest stratum of the bourgeoisie brought with it a changing conception of family and lineage, with greater and greater emphasis placed on individual happiness and self-fulfillment at the expense of the demands of the lineage.

The socioeconomic changes that are gradually taking place over the course of the seventeenth century are reflected, I believe, in the two quite distinct generations of French tragedy. I see French Classical tragedy as a literary movement that does not attain its full expression until it has reproduced itself, that is, produced a second "generation," "as if an inheritance were clearly identifiable as such only by being passed on to the next generation."[6] The first generation of Classical tragedy, corresponding more or less to the last decade of the reign of Louis XIII (d. 1643), is dominated by Pierre Corneille, who writes his most famous tragedies during this period. The Regency, encompassing the years of Louis XIV's minority (1643–56), is a transitional period between the two generations of tragedy: the production of tragedies severely dwindles, and by the mid-1650s the form has virtually petered out. Its resurgence is partly due to the phenomenal success of *Timocrate* (1656), a play written by Pierre Corneille's younger brother, Thomas, who was a full generation (nineteen years) younger than his famous sibling.[7] The subsequent second generation of tragedy, which occupies the first two decades of Louis XIV's independent reign following the death of Mazarin (1661), is largely defined by the works of Jean Racine, and, to a lesser extent, Thomas Corneille; it also overlaps with Molière's most brilliant plays.

I have organized the book around these two generations and the transitional period between them to underscore an important shift that takes place between the generations in the dramatists' treatment of questions relating to birth order. As has been pointed out by literary critics and historians, Pierre Corneille's world is inhabited by figures who place honor above their own individual happiness, while Racine's universe is peopled largely by characters who continue to search for their own happiness —

generally in vain—even when it comes at the expense of their lineage. This may be one reason why Racine's view of siblings is quite different from Corneille's. In Corneille's works—or at least in those that have come to define him—a certain dignity and grandeur adhere to the position of heir, and the heir's relation to his name, his lineage, and his ancestors defines him fundamentally. In Racine's, questions of inheritance become more complex; while primogeniture is still apparently operative in a number of plays, the choice of an heir is often vexed, with the younger sibling tending to be given the *beau rôle*. And the relation between siblings in Racine's plays is frequently more important than the relation between parents and children. Finally, in keeping with the shift in values between the two generations, with individual fulfillment and preferences taking on a greater and greater importance, the younger-sibling characters in Racine are, as we shall see, more *lovable* than the more senior members of their cohort.

While the evolution I see between these two generations is subtle and gradual, the familial conflicts staged by each of the tragedies studied here are dramatic and sudden, although no less complicated for all that. It is my hope that the analyses of the conflicts in each individual play will alert the reader to patterns that had not previously been perceptible or seemed important. There are no final conclusions in the field of birth-order effects: those who study and write about them generally concede that no single position is advantageous from all points of view, for all entail trade-offs. My aim here is to sensitize readers to issues that can add depth to their understanding of plays considered in a particular sociohistorical context, and that can also bring an unexpectedly contemporary dimension to these tragedies.

PART I

THE TRAGEDY OF PRIMOGENITURE

I

Primogeniture and Its Discontents in Early Modern France

First Come, First Served

To see what a startling evolution the current-day apotheosis of competition and individual initiative represents, we must go back to the Middle Ages. Feudalism was the consummate system of inherited privilege; primogeniture — both a political practice governing the succession of monarchs and a socioeconomic practice regulating the transmission of lands, titles, and privileges between the generations — was one of its most basic principles. Let us begin by examining primogeniture as a socioeconomic law of material and social inheritance.

Starting in the twelfth or thirteenth century,[1] primogeniture, the inheritance of much or all of a fiefdom by the eldest son,[2] was adopted to protect against excessive division of familial lands, and this single practice had profound implications for social organization and social life. Frederick Greenspahn gives a clear explanation of this phenomenon in medieval England: "Large fiefdoms were more productive than those that were small. By limiting inheritance to a single heir, primogeniture . . . ensured that land parcels remained intact instead of being repeatedly divided over several generations."[3] As Philippe Ariès puts it, "The privilege of the child favoured by its primogeniture or by its parents' choice was the basis of family society from the end of the Middle Ages to the seventeenth century."[4] Ariès suggests that at times people were free to choose their heir among their children, a possibility that might introduce an element of merit into the question of inheritance, since parents would presumably select the most deserving of their children to oversee their lands. But although the specifics of the practice of primogeniture varied considerably — especially between northern

France, with its reliance on traditional law (*droit oral*), and the southern lands governed by a more formal code descended largely from Roman law (*droit écrit*)[5] — parents quite regularly had no choice in the matter, as Roland Mousnier explains: "Primogeniture [*droit d'aînesse*] was an absolute right. Fathers and mothers were allowed neither to leave their fiefdoms to their later-born children, nor to divide them up equally among all their children."[6]

Primogeniture was by no means a universal practice in France — although its use did extend to commoners,[7] it was most widespread among the aristocracy — nor did it systematically give everything to the eldest son and nothing to subsequent children. Sometimes, for example, the eldest son inherited a percentage of the family's land, one-half or two-thirds, after which the remaining land was divided among his siblings.[8] In one way or another the heir was often held responsible for the upkeep of his younger siblings, although not in the grand style that he would enjoy. But whatever the variations of practices might have been, the influence of primogeniture on French society was pervasive, its ramifications extending far beyond the realm of law and economics: "To modern eyes one form of privileged inheritance, primogeniture, stands for all that was unfair and arbitrary in the past. To be born to the position of sole heir can seem as unjust an advantage as to be born a noble or as unjust a disadvantage as to be born a slave. The way that people regarded primogeniture in the years between 1350 and 1800 is a clue to much of what they thought."[9]

First and foremost, primogeniture was a very conservative practice; indeed, it was conceived as such, since its main goal was to preserve the patrimony from the dangers of repeated divisions among siblings. Quite apart from the material inheritance involved in primogeniture, the practice also fostered a conservative mentality, one that tended to reinforce the status quo and to discourage enterprise. The eldest son knew that he could not be disenthroned from his coveted position as heir, the younger children that they could not take his place by showing talent or promise.

In terms of the relations among siblings, a system that according to our own lights seems terribly unfair might be thought to create endless discord between the heir and his Cinderella-like siblings. On the other hand, it might just as well act as a limit to sibling rivalry, since people generally reserve their energy for those fights that they have, if not necessarily a very good chance, at least a very firm right to win. The following plaintive text, quoted by René Pillorget in his discussion of primogeniture in England, gives us a good idea of the sense of passivity and fatalism that the practice must have cultivated in the minds of younger siblings: "The elder brother must have all; and all the rest (of the children) that which the cat left on the malt heap, perhaps some small annuity during his life or what please our elder brother's worship to bestow upon us if we please him, and my mistress, his wife."[10] Roland Mousnier gives the example in the eighteenth century of a younger brother of the illustrious Mirabeau family who writes these words of deference to his elder-brother heir, the economist Victor Riqueti, Marquis de Mirabeau: "I have learned from childhood on that you must have the entire heritage, except what I absolutely need to live, because you are the head of our lineage [*race*], because you are responsible for all things. I have learned that it is my duty to make a contribution rather than to take things into my own possession."[11]

Christian Biet sums up the sorry position of the younger sibling in his comments on the 1676 *Mémoires du sieur de Pontis*: "[The younger son] must leave the house, or else remain a bachelor as is the custom and stay with his older brother in their father's house, continuing to work for the growth and prosperity of the lineage. The oldest son has everything and gives nothing, with a clear conscience, a power recognized and accepted by the other children, whether they are younger sons or older or younger daughters destined to enter a convent or to live in the heir's house."[12]

Thus, ironically, a well-established practice of primogeniture is just as likely to deactivate sibling rivalries as it is to stir them up. Human sentiments cannot, of course, be legislated, and it would be beyond the realm of belief to imagine that younger siblings living under a system of primogeniture never resented or even detested the most senior member of their cohort. But precisely by formalizing the position of each sibling in the family, primogeniture could be seen as exercising a certain degree of control over the perennial jealousies inherent to the sibling bond. Might institutionalized favoritism not bring the balm of inevitability? Might a younger sibling not take comfort in the idea that rule by the eldest is simply the way things are?

The family relation that is most strongly brought into relief by primogeniture as it was practiced in the medieval and early modern periods is not the sibling bond, but rather the relation between father and eldest son. As Martine Segalen has written, "We may hypothesize that in [societies governed by primogeniture], the tensions within the family will be played out vertically, between parents and children."[13] It has often been pointed out that feudalism has a strongly hierarchical, "vertical" social organization, in which relations between the different strata of society are clearly delineated and are characterized by the notion of service between unequals. Primogeniture as the central preserving mechanism of feudalism creates an equally important diachronic vertical structure, a verticality across time that is no less crucial than the synchronic, social verticality of overlords, vassals, and serfs. Think of the branches of a family tree: primogeniture protects the vertical link, the relation between generations, from challenge or interference by the horizontal links, the relations between siblings. Primogeniture strengthens the heir's ties to his father, his grandfather, and all the previous heirs in whose footsteps he is following. From childhood on, primogeniture gives the heir apparent a connection to earlier generations of his family line stretching back toward the past; indeed, he is the representative of what in the Middle Ages is called a "lignée" or lineage. The term is obsolete by the sixteenth and certainly the seventeenth century, having been replaced in the aristocracy by *maison* and among commoners by *famille*,[14] but the image of a line that can be traced back across the generations is key to an understanding of the mentality of the feudal heir.

The heir inherits a direct connection with the traditions, the reputation, and the social standing of his lineage, not only as its representative in the present generation, but also as the defender of the very system which has given him his undisputed place of honor. Since he automatically inherits wealth and power, it is in his interest to uphold and perpetuate the practice whereby he himself and his descendants — or at least the fortunate circle of eldest sons among them — will continue to reap the benefits of his family's lands, properties, and titles.

Thus as a socioeconomic practice, primogeniture is a powerful force for assuring social order and continuity; as a political practice governing the succession to the throne, it has many of the same advantages. The Salic laws designated the king's eldest son as his successor: "This law is the foundation that assures the perpetuation of the French empire. The kingdom is conferred neither by election, nor by pure heredity, as in common law, for the king is not the owner of the kingdom and the kingdom is thus not hereditary. The kingdom is conferred by rights of succession. Males are called to the succession of the kingdom indefinitely by order of primogeniture."[15] This distinction between inheritance and succession[16] throws the power of primogeniture into even starker relief; it takes primogeniture to its logical limits. With the question of succession we are no longer dealing with property or material goods, which can be split up and distributed among siblings: "Because offices cannot be divided as easily as land and positions of authority must be clearly assigned to a particular individual, succession allows less room for the kinds of sharing and ambiguity sometimes tolerable in matters of ownership."[17] One either is king or is not king. Whatever their fantasies and secret machinations might be, the king's younger brothers are no more king than the humblest peasant is king.

If it is in the interests of all eldest sons to preserve primogeniture, it is absolutely essential for the king of France to do so: "As we know, hereditary succession to the throne has often been rejected because it makes descent and not ability the principle for selecting a ruler. From a sociological point of view, this way of selecting the ruler in the old France still heavily bound by tradition, certainly had a specific function. . . . It provided a certain guarantee that the king was maintaining the existing order."[18] This conservative nature of royal primogeniture may seem rather obvious, but it does provide an interesting point of comparison with democratic political systems, for example, which perennially struggle with the contradiction between coming to power and conserving power. Politicians routinely get elected by attacking the status quo only to find themselves in the position of having to defend it against their would-be ousters as soon as they are in power, which means that it is in their interests to change the status quo as quickly and as conspicuously as they can. Primogeniture as a law of succession encourages no such changes: like its economic counterpart, it too is an eminently conservative force.

An Idea Whose Time Is Passing

If feudalism is our starting point in tracing out the evolution of mentalities between the valuing of inherited privilege and the prizing of earned rewards, the seventeenth century is a great turning point, and this is true for primogeniture both as a socioeconomic and as a political principle. Let us first examine primogeniture as a law of material inheritance during the era of Louis XIII and Louis XIV.

By the seventeenth century a number of factors have begun to undermine primogeniture as a system of inheritance.[19] The most important is the development of capitalism and the concomitant rise of the bourgeoisie, which challenges not only the hegemony of the old landed aristocracy, but also some of the premises upon which primogeniture is founded. Among the numerous contrasts between feudalism and capitalism, perhaps the most important material difference from our perspective is that capitalism is not a land-dependent but rather an exchange-dependent system, one that does not necessarily require a given number of acres to maintain or to expand one's wealth. Now it is true that even under feudalism, improvements in farming techniques at times accounted for increased productivity in the absence of land expansion; this seems to have been the case in the tenth and eleventh centuries, and it has been claimed by some that this increased productivity, acting as a stimulus to markets for luxury items, encouraged the growth of trade and was one of the factors leading to the development of capitalism.[20] But whether or not agriculture plays a considerable part in the rise of capitalism, it is clear that the *haute bourgeoisie* does not depend upon farmland for their livelihood, even if they often buy land and titles once they have made their fortunes. And historians like Fernand Braudel, for example, seem to link early capitalism almost entirely with the realm of trade and commerce.

Expansionism, part of the very nature of capitalism with its emphasis on economic growth, is also in strong contrast to the mentality of feudalism. Feudal lords aim to live well, and living well generally means eating well, working little, and enjoying gentlemanly pastimes appropriate to their condition. They are adamant about maintaining and protecting their social standing and prosperity — about not losing ground literally or figuratively — and expand their lands when they can through military action or conjugal alliances. But the expansion of land — the basic source and measure of wealth in a system in which money does not play a very central role — is incidental to their way of life:

The aim of production [for the feudal lord] was consumption (including conspicuous consumption), not accumulation. As Marx put it, "the limits to the exploitation of the feudal serf were determined by the walls of the stomach of the feudal lord." . . . Contrast capitalism at its height. Urban life dominates, so that even owners of agricultural land are based in towns. . . . Money plays an absolutely central role. Everyone depends on selling something in order to get the means of livelihood — even if all most people have to sell is their labour power. Most importantly, there is no limit to the accumulation of wealth. Everything can be turned into money and members of the ruling class can own endless amounts of money. What drives the system forward is not the consumption of the ruling class, but what Marx called self-expansion of capital, the endless pursuit of accumulation for the sake of accumulation.[21]

While feudalism is contingent upon maintenance — the maintenance of land holdings in particular and of the status quo in general — capitalism is founded upon expansion, the premise that there is always room for improvement, whether in terms of one's business or the social standing of one-

self and one's family. In seventeenth-century France, the bourgeoisie generally value hard work, sobriety, and the conserving or expanding of resources
as much as the old aristocracy prize leisure and the pleasurable consumption of resources. Capitalism assigns no clear limits to the long-term growth
of economic well-being precisely because the accumulation of capital is
based not on something with clear physical dimensions, land, but rather on
intangibles like enterprise, competition, and the creation of markets.

This contrast between the conceptual underpinnings of feudalism and
those of capitalism is crystallized by Michel Foucault's analysis of the shift in
the conception of money that occurs in the seventeenth century:

Fine metal was, of itself, a mark of wealth; its buried brightness was sufficient
indication that it was at the same time a hidden presence and a visible signature of all
the wealth of the world. It is for this reason that it had a *price*; for this reason too that
it was a *measure* of all prices; and for this reason, finally, that one could *exchange* it for
anything else that had a price. . . . In the seventeenth century, these three properties
are still attributed to money, but they are all three made to rest, not on the first
(possession of price), but on the last (substitution for that which possesses price).
Whereas the Renaissance based the two *functions* of coinage (measure and substitution) on the double nature of its intrinsic *character* (the fact that it was precious),
the seventeenth century turns the analysis upside down: it is the exchanging function that serves as a foundation for the other two characters. . . . Gold is precious
because it is money — not the converse. . . . The value of things will no longer
proceed from the metal itself; it establishes itself by itself, without reference to the
coinage, according to the criteria of utility, pleasure, or rarity. Things take on value,
then, in relation to one another.[22]

From the perspective of feudalism, land — like precious metals which, as
Foucault points out, are extracted from land — is thought to have intrinsic
value, to constitute wealth in itself. And in the same way that seventeenth-
century mercantilism redefines the value of precious metals not as intrinsic
but rather as residing in their exchange value, capitalism defines itself, by
contrast to feudalism, as a system of impersonal exchange. The criteria of
value, the "utility, pleasure, or rarity" of goods and services, are as intangi-
ble and expandable as enterprise and markets. Thus exchange values — the
value of money itself as well as the values of the bourgeoisie whose livelihood depends on it — go hand in hand with the concept of unlimited
growth and improvability.

The importance of relativity in this new definition of value — "things
take on value in relation to one another" — finds its analogue in a reconcep-
tualization of family wealth and intrafamilial relations. When family wealth

is based not on land but rather on capital, strategies of distribution like diversification or the expanding of markets are available that are unfeasible in a strictly land-based system.[23] Consequently the problem of the repeated division of limited resources that was the initial goad to the institution of primogeniture does not necessarily pose the same kind of threat to the future well-being of a family of merchants, for example, as it does to a family of feudal landowners. Moreover, the emphasis which capitalism places on competition and which, for individuals growing up in capitalist societies, often finds its first expression in sibling rivalry, also sees competition as healthy and productive for all those who compete, not only for those who "win" a given contest. Capitalism thus "reactivates" the sort of sibling rivalry that inheritance by primogeniture keeps under wraps, but it also values the sense of competitiveness so stimulated. Finally, some of the greatest capitalist fortunes — those of the Astors, the Rockefellers, and the Rothschilds, to name only a few[24] — were amassed by family enterprises in which siblings were viewed not merely as potential contenders for the family's riches but as invaluable accomplices and allies in the expansion of the family business.

It would be grossly inaccurate to see capitalism as replacing feudalism in one fell swoop; on the contrary, the two systems coexisted to some extent for centuries. The transition between them was gradual, complicated, at times even vexed:

> There has been much debate about the character of western European society . . . from the 15th century onwards, with Dobb and Anderson, for instance, insisting it remained feudal, and Sweezy arguing it was based on a "petty commodity producing mode of production." But the important point was that it was a society in transition, with both feudal and capitalist forms of exploitation existing side by side, and in many cases intermingling.
>
> The two forms were both complementary . . . and contradictory. What is more, they operated according to different dynamics, . . . [so that] the balance between the two was continually changing.[25]

In her masterful study, *Ideology and Culture in Seventeenth-Century France*, Erica Harth sees the seventeenth century as the period of greatest confrontation between feudalism and capitalism: "The contradictions between a decadent feudalism and a nascent capitalism stand out with peculiar sharpness during the reigns of Louis XIII and Louis XIV."[26] In conflict during this period corresponding to the development and flourishing of Classical theater are not only two economic systems — or perhaps two economic components of a single social order — but also two divergent perspectives.

As we might expect, this same period sees a gradual shift in attitudes toward primogeniture; in fact inheritance practices throughout the seventeenth and eighteenth centuries varied widely according to socioeconomic status as well as geographical region. Primogeniture was not formally abolished until the Revolution, which correctly saw it as elitist and conservative and thus antithetical to the new egalitarian fraternal order it wished to usher in.[27] Its elimination was extremely controversial and was both hailed and abhorred; as Suzanne Desan writes in her analysis of the changes wrought by the abolition of primogeniture during the 1790s: "No aspect of family restructuring generated more contention in court or more outbursts of popular anger or approval than the new inheritance laws."[28] And yet a change in attitudes had already taken place long before 1789, as is documented by Philippe Ariès in his influential study of evolving notions of childhood under the Ancien Régime. In defense of his hypothesis that "it is public morality [*les moeurs*] rather than the Civil Code or the Revolution that got rid of primogeniture,"[29] Ariès cites the following passage from l'Abbé Goussault's *Portrait d'un honnête homme* (1692): "Not only is it foolish to hand over most of one's material goods to the eldest in the family so as to keep him in the limelight and perpetuate his name . . . ; it is also unfair. What did the younger children do to be treated in this way?"[30]

However much one agrees with this sentiment, it might be pointed out that primogeniture was no less unfair in the fourteenth century than in the seventeenth. If it was less likely to be thought of in those terms in that earlier time, this is probably because it served the purposes of the people who held power. In the late seventeenth century primogeniture still serves the same purposes and the same people, but those people no longer hold so much power. The bourgeoisie has made numerous inroads into aristocratic territory, the conflict between the *noblesse d'épée*, the old feudal military aristocracy, and the *noblesse de robe*, the administrative elite, descendants of individuals who bought or otherwise acquired titles and lands more recently, an ongoing one. The old landed aristocracy generally detest the *robins*, whom they consider glorified bourgeois, and, feeling themselves increasingly threatened by the growing power of these latecomers to nobility, they swell with the frightened pomposity of an old guard closing ranks to keep upstart newcomers from streaming in. "It is against this background — a high rate of infiltration across class boundaries, the old nobility's strong desire to sharpen the boundaries, and the recognition that the traditional marks of status were inadequate for this purpose — that we can begin to understand the intense, obsessive concern with honorific privileges. . . . These indicators of status were not new, but as the interclass boundaries became increasingly blurred they acquired heightened importance."[31] Chris Harman's analysis of the nobility's ineffectual reactions to early entrepreneurs rings equally true for the seventeenth century: "The ideology of the ruling class was less and less capable of coming to terms with the changes which were taking place. It increasingly came to reflect the pampered position which the feudal lords had attained, divorced from the world of production, concerned only with rank, honour and the defence of hereditary position."[32]

Margaret Mead's analysis of the ways that a society's openness or resistance to change is expressed by the nature of the relations between generations is quite applicable to the period in question. Here is how Mead describes what happens to a society undergoing a rapid transformation:

The idea that it is possible to incorporate in a society a very large number of adults, differently reared and with different expectations, introduces a significant change into the culture of that society. Behavior is no longer so firmly associated with birthright membership in the society that it appears to be essentially inherited, rather than learned. . . . [This situation] may produce a new flexibility and tolerance of difference. But it may also stimulate the development of countermeasures, such as a firmer drawing of caste lines to ensure that the newcomers will be prevented from attaining the privileges of birthright members.[33]

It is in the light of Mead's analysis of the ruling classes' counterreactions to social change that we may interpret the paradoxical fact that the practice of primogeniture continued to flourish, and in some cases to expand, during the very period it was coming under attack. As Mead points out, when an elite feels its rights and prerogatives threatened, it may just as well respond by retrenching as by accepting the changes taking place at its expense. Beatrice Gottlieb reveals this double aspect of primogeniture in the seventeenth century: "The practice grew and spread in the sixteenth and seventeenth centuries, displacing older patterns of inheritance, and reached its peak in the eighteenth century. . . . As it reached its peak, it came more and more under attack. At the end of the eighteenth century, the laws of the new American republic in North America, like those of the French republic in the same period, rejected it. To say that this was a welcome change for all Americans and Frenchmen would be far from the truth. Old habits die hard, and this habit was congenial to many."[34] A reversal of cause and effect would yield an equally true statement: as primogeniture came more and more under attack, it reached its peak, partly in reaction to those very attacks and the changes in society they exemplified.

Primogeniture is not only one of the central tools of feudalism; in the seventeenth century it can be seen more generally as emblematic of the relations between the *noblesse d'épée* and the various groups whose rise in society challenges their dominance: the *noblesse de robe* and the wealthiest stratum of the bourgeoisie, as well as, ironically, the king himself, who increasingly allies himself with these social upstarts in his quest to tame the unruly high aristocracy. The basic defensive strategy proferred by the old feudal nobility in its attempt to protect its position is identical to that of the eldest son: what they say, in effect, is not so much "we are more worthy," but rather "we were here first" — or rather, "we are more worthy because we were here first." And it is precisely this line of reasoning that comes under attack during the reign of Louis XIV.

The King and We

Thus while primogeniture remains a powerful force throughout the seventeenth century, it is also under assault on the socioeconomic front, encroached upon by an increasing emphasis on achievement and enterprise. It is also somewhat embattled on the political front, but for quite different reasons. As we shall see, in the first half of the seventeenth century, primogeniture as a law of royal succession causes Louis XIII a good deal of trouble. In the second half of the century, primogeniture as a socioeconomic principle impinges upon Louis XIV's absolutist ambitions; in a sense, what Louis XIV is waging a war against in his attempt to dominate the *noblesse d'épée* is the spirit of primogeniture.

The relative lack of power of the kings of France before Louis XIV's reign stems largely from the position of the king as nothing much more than the highest of the feudal overlords, a first among equals, a description evocative of a privileged eldest brother lording it over his younger siblings rather than of a powerful father figure keeping his children in line. This situation obtains as late as the reign of Louis XIII, who is seen by his own brother and by the princes of the blood not as a man of unassailable power, but rather as a figure perennially open to attack: "Monsieur, the king's brother, the princes of the blood, the heirs to the throne after him, saw in the king nothing more than the highest ranking member among them, a sort of president, and they often revolted against royal absolutism."[35]

Louis XIII's reign is a particularly acerbic example of several of the inherent limitations of primogeniture as a basic law of succession. Gaston d'Orléans, Louis' younger brother and the heir apparent until the birth of the future Louis XIV in 1638, frequently conspired against the king, allying himself with those next in line to the throne after him:

From the death of Henri IV until the end of the Fronde, for more than forty years we find a series of calls to arms, rebellions against royal authority, appeals to foreign powers and alliances with them, plots and conspiracies whose leaders are the king's own brother or the princes of the blood, such as the Prince de Condé or the Comte de Soissons.

[Gaston d'Orléans] was the most constant adversary of his elder brother, upon whose death he never ceased to base his hopes for the succession to the throne until the birth of the future Louis XIV, September 5, 1638.[36]

Indeed, while the endless plotting of Louis' covetous cadet is a dramatic example of one of the structural weaknesses of primogeniture as a principle of succession — the difficulty of assuaging the ambitions of younger brothers, especially if the king is childless — the much-anticipated birth of the future Louis XIII as well as the belated birth of the future Louis XIV illustrates yet another. One commentator attributes to the exultation felt upon the birth of Louis XIII after half a century during which no reigning king had produced a legitimate heir apparent the court's preoccupation with the infant-king's personified member — his *guilleri* — which his physician Jean d'Heroard called "what makes him the Dauphin": "the insistent enthusiasm of these practices in the case of Louis XIII probably derives from his unique status as heir to the throne."[37] History more or less repeated itself nearly forty years later when Louis XIII and Anne of Austria, who had remained childless during the more than twenty years of their marriage and no longer enjoyed regular conjugal relations, miraculously conceived an heir on a rainy night that the king chanced to spend with his wife. Their dynastic wishes were utterly fulfilled two years later by the birth of a "spare," Philippe. One of the clearest problems posed by primogeniture is that a king can no more guarantee that he will have a male heir than he can safely guard against having too many male heirs for comfort. The infant mortality rate being what it was — Louis XIV nearly died of smallpox at the age of nine[38] — the odds of raising an only child to adulthood were not favorable.

With the vivid memories of her combative brother-in-law still fresh in her mind, the mother of Louis XIV and Philippe did what she could to preclude the kind of ongoing fraternal challenge[39] that had plagued her husband's reign because of Philippe's uncle Gaston, whose title Philippe would in fact inherit upon Gaston's death in 1660. Anne, chosen as regent after the death of Louis XIII in 1643, took extreme measures to differentiate her two sons. Philippe was essentially raised as a girl, often dressed in female clothing until well past adolescence[40] (as an adult he was an occasional transvestite) and altogether reared "not to be the threat Gaston was to Louis XIII."[41] Whereas Gaston and Anne were repeatedly suspected of plotting to rid themselves of Louis XIII and to marry—when confronted by her husband about this, Anne is said to have responded wittily that she would have "gained too little from the exchange"[42]—it is Louis XIV himself who is rumored to have dallied with his brother's first wife, Henrietta Stuart, while Philippe's second wife, the Princess Palatine, fell in love with her brother-in-law, the king.[43] A recent biographer of Louis XIV says of Philippe that by contrast to Louis XIV's sons and grandsons, whose virtues are "seemingly drawn from a Corneille play," the king's brother "appeared more like a hero from one by Racine,"[44] a particularly astute observation given the fact that, as we shall see, the sibling bond is much more central to Racine's theater than to Corneille's.

Thus the structural limitations of primogeniture as a law of succession to the throne created considerable hardships for Louis XIII and contributed to his weakness as a figure of authority. By contrast, his heir enjoyed the luxury of having a single, harmless sibling who was no chip off the troublesome avuncular block. And while this cheerful state of affairs probably owed more to the Sun King's mother than to himself, Louis XIV also consolidated this already strong position by systematically empowering figures outside of his immediate family circle, as Norbert Elias observes:

The king always protects and allies himself most readily with people who owe him everything and are nothing without him. The Duc d'Orléans [Philippe], his nephew, the later regent, or his grandson the dauphin, amount to something even when not in his special favour. They are potential rivals. . . . High nobility conferred a limited degree of independence of the king which should never be allowed to degenerate into open opposition. All the more strongly, therefore, did Louis XIV support himself on people who owed their place at court to him alone and would fall into total oblivion if he dropped them, above all his mistress, the ministers and his bastard sons. He protected the latter above all, to the great vexation of the genuine nobility.

Under no circumstances would he permit any of his relations to receive a post that might give him influence. He never forgot, for example, the importance which the post of governor had had under his father as a basis for resistance to royal power. And he always vividly remembered the difficulties which his uncle, Gaston of Orléans, had caused the king on this basis. So when his own brother asked him for a *gouvernement* and a fortress, a *place de sûreté*, he answered, "La meilleure place de sûreté pour un fils de France est le coeur du Roi."[45]

The year before his death, Louis went so far as to issue an edict proclaiming that his illegitimate sons should be allowed to succeed to the throne in the absence of a prince of the blood; the edict was revoked in the end, but not until two years after Louis' death.[46] In stark contrast to the dynastic instability of much of his father's reign, Louis XIV's main problem in terms of the succession was that he outlived two dauphins, his son and his grandson; in the end he was succeeded by his four-year-old great-grandson.

On the whole, one might say that Louis XIV had a fairly easy time of it in terms of the laws of succession to the throne. Unlike his father, he produced numerous heirs from a young age, and if by the end of his reign death had ravaged his progeny and the laws of succession no longer suited him, he was allowed to believe that he could change even them. On the other hand, primogeniture as a mechanism for maintaining the feudal status quo created a serious obstacle to Louis' absolutist enterprise, and in a number of ways he indirectly worked to undermine it. The social and economic elites with which Louis allied himself were, like the individuals he relied upon in his circle of intimates, generally selected according to criteria other than birth and inherited privilege:

Society was evolving toward a society based on talent, in which classification within the social hierarchy increasingly depended on the role one played in the realm of the intellect, in law, science, art and literature, whether one was a creator, a teacher, or a practitioner in those domains. The basic, fundamental principle of society had apparently changed. The old hierarchy based on inherited military vocation had been modified in the sixteenth century by a new administrative hierarchy, which tended also to be or to become hereditary, and then, under Louis XIV, by a hierarchy based on intellectual achievement or talent. A slow, silent revolution was taking place.[47]

Numerous historians have followed Tocqueville's assessment of the absolutist monarchy as a tacit promoter of revolutionary social transformation.[48]

One of the most important reasons for the increasing stress on meritocracy and the concomitant deemphasizing of seniority as a necessary and sufficient condition for social prominence is quite simple: the king's perennial need for money. For while money may talk, it has no memory. Perhaps the single aspect of the capitalistic ethic that most clearly undermines the spirit of primogeniture is its impersonal, ahistorical nature: "The formation of the bourgeoisie . . . opened indeed, a new dimension and personal initiative became more important than birth for social prominence. In the towns, one exchanged goods and services of the same nature, as it were, without having to bind oneself to a specific status: the impersonal medium of money freed man from the bonds of mechanical solidarity. Thus, vassalage was losing its meaning. Equality and freedom had begun to bewilder the semantic universe that the cash economy would eventually shatter."[49] The spirit of capitalism, with its valuing of work, ongoing productivity, and earned recompense has certainly begun to penetrate the highest levels of society by the time of Louis XIV's reign: "The administrators level the social hierarchy to their own advantage, and by the same token we see [an ethic of] 'talent' insinuating itself into the nobility, by the will of the king who in this way introduces a third principle of social stratification that is . . . perhaps liable to open up the possibility of a society based on class [rather than orders or estates]."[50] The confrontation of the ethics underlying feudalism and capitalism is a complex interaction. It is clear that the rising bourgeoisie continue to covet noble lands and titles and to use their acquired wealth to purchase them. What is perhaps more difficult to quantify is the fact that the old landed aristocrats cannot help but be affected by the spirit of capitalism even as they continue to voice their disdain. This paradox is essentially that of the eldest sibling refusing to compete with the younger ones. Since primogeniture effectively sidesteps the heir's need to compete, accepting the validity — or at least the necessity — of competition can be a larger hurdle than finding ways of competing successfully. Before you can win the game, you have to agree to play.

This interaction between an old and a new ethic is apparent in the mechanisms of the court at Versailles. In his analysis of court etiquette, Norbert Elias makes clear that Louis' elaborate system of granting and withholding favors for services rendered (or not rendered) is essentially a type of economy:

In court society, social reality inhered directly in the rank and esteem granted to a person by his own society and, above all, by the king. A person with little or no standing in society was more or less worthless in his own eyes. . . . [Signs of status] were literal documentations of social existence, notations of the place one currently occupied in the court hierarchy. To rise or fall in this hierarchy meant as much to the courtier as profit or loss to a businessman.

It was not only in the sphere of bourgeois-capitalist competition that the idea of egoism as a motive of human action was formed, but first of all in the competition at court, and from the latter came the first unveiled descriptions of the human affects in modern times.[51]

The fact that the favors granted by the king are quite separate from any intrinsic value is precisely what makes courtly etiquette most closely resemble a capitalist economy. In itself, the action of changing from a nightshirt to a dayshirt has no particular interest. But the king makes this arbitrary action into a component of his economy:

> The king turned it into a privilege distinguishing those present from others. . . . Each act in the ceremony had an exactly graded prestige-value that was imparted to those present, and this prestige-value became to an extent self-evident. . . . Like the size of the courtyard or the ornamentation of a noble's house, . . . it served as an indicator of the position of an individual within the balance of power between the courtiers, a balance controlled by the king and very precarious. The direct use-value of all these actions was more or less incidental. What gave them their gravity was solely the importance they conferred on those present within court society, the power, rank and dignity they expressed.[52]

This is not to say that birth and hereditary position played no role in the establishment and maintenance of prestige at Versailles; quite the contrary. But they, too, were simply parts, albeit crucial ones, of the social equation:

> [The aristocrats'] rank within court society was, of course, determined first of all by that of their house, their official title. At the same time, however, permeating and modifying the official hierarchy, an actual order of rank which was far more finely shaded, uninstitutionalized and unstable established itself within court society. . . . There was, for example, an institutional hierarchy among dukes, based primarily on the ancientness of their houses. This order was legally enshrined. But at the same time the duke of a younger house might currently enjoy higher esteem, through his relations to the king or his mistress or any other powerful group, than one from an older house. The real position of a person in the network of court society was always governed by both moments, official rank and actual power position, but the latter finally had greater influence on behaviour towards him.[53]

Primogeniture itself becomes an element in a symbolic system of exchange; it is reduced to being a single criterion among many that may be used to establish and revise a pecking order that no longer changes slowly, across generations, but quickly and unpredictably, like the stock market, from day to day. At the outset the benefits of primogeniture were both material and social, consisting of property as well as titles. But what happens when land is no longer indisputably the primary source of wealth and power, when, like gold and silver, primogeniture detaches itself from its chthonic roots and becomes an exchange value rather than an intrinsic value? Under those circumstances, social standing may be used as a kind of commodity in a market that by its very existence undermines the system in which social standing was originally defined.

The Tragedy of Primogeniture

Seventeenth-century writers were not the first to question the relation between inherited nobility and earned nobility. As early as 1515, Erasmus identifies the highest form of nobility as "derived from virtue and good actions," and associates the lowest form with "an array of family portraits" and "genealogy or wealth." Erasmus cautions the seeker of fame not to "make a display of statues or paintings," but to rely on character as the benchmark of true nobility.[54] Nevertheless, the awareness of the potential conflicts between inherited and earned rewards becomes particularly acute during the reigns of Louis XIII and his son. Just as the attitude toward primogeniture shifts in the seventeenth century, so is the attitude toward the possibility of acquired as opposed to inherited nobility slowly beginning to change. "The authors of the seventeenth century emphasize the importance of blood and hereditary transmission. True nobility is race. . . . Acquired nobility is not true nobility, although it can eventually become true nobility. On the contrary, eighteenth-century authors . . . emphasize the role of the State, incarnated by the king, in the formation of nobility, its function as a reward for services rendered to the State, . . . and the fact that all people may work to achieve it."[55] These conflicting ethics that vie for hegemony throughout the last centuries of the Ancien Régime feed not only gradual social change—and, ultimately, violent social upheaval—but also the greatest period of French tragedy.

The clash between these two ethics is a particularly fertile terrain for the flowering of tragedy, and if this aspect of Classical tragedy has not received sufficient attention,[56] it is perhaps because one of the most cherished truisms about the form is its irrefutable "nobility," not only qualitative—it must have a certain grandeur, what Aristotle in the *Poetics* calls *megethos* or greatness—but also social—it is a theater for and about the aristocracy. The characters in tragedy are aristocrats, the positions they assume and the emotions they express of interest mainly to the privileged classes. I would not dispute this claim: the myths dramatized by French Classical tragedy are ostentatiously drawn from the cultural patrimony of the nobility. But in a more subtle and disquieting way, I believe that the plays may also express that group's own present conflicts with an ethic that is increasingly challenging their continued hegemony. It is true that Classical tragedy, with its historical and mythological subjects and its refusal to depict present-day social reality in any direct way, is certainly in strong contrast to Molière's comic stage, which is not only peopled by bourgeois as well as aristocratic characters but also represents contemporary mores much more overtly than its "nobler" counterpart. But even if tragedy cannot directly represent the developing confrontation between two opposing ethics, might it not give voice to the anxieties generated by such a confrontation?

In a fascinating study of the complexities and contradictions of aristocratic mores in seventeenth-century France, Jonathan Dewald analyzes the tragedians' staging of family conflicts in terms of what he views as "one of the central paradoxes of the age": "As family, state, and ethical ideals increasingly demanded renunciation of individual desires, men and women became increasingly absorbed in understanding themselves as individuals, and indeed in understanding personal desire itself. . . . Such deepening concerns with the personal offered one response to the oppressiveness of seventeenth-century expectations."[57] The conflicting demands of lineage and individual desire are the very stuff of tragedy, as Dewald writes:

The tragedians' recurrent interest in incest suggests the intensity of the emotions that familial competition mobilized. In the tragedies, family members long violently for the same objects, sexual as well as material. The tragedies teach that proper family life demands renunciation of such desire, ultimately under the threat of parental violence. In the tragedians' vision, the continuity of the race rests on a series of losses and conflicts that reach the bases of family itself. Parents sacrifice their children, heirs their younger siblings. . . . Self and inheritance cannot fully coexist.[58]

This same conflict between inherited values and duties on the one hand and individual self-definition on the other is observed by Jean Starobinski in his analysis of "an underlying conflict and an unresolved contradiction that permeate [Pierre Corneille's] theater, a conflict opposing the [aristocratic] ideology of his milieu to the psychology invented by the poet":

According to Corneille's psychology, as we have seen, the "great name" results from acts: the hero creates his fame from his high deeds. The glorious name serves the purpose of binding together discontinuous exploits. . . . And if it is all crowned with glory, it all begins with strokes of strength and will. But according to the ideology that Corneille shares with the nobles, who are to constitute the majority of his public, everything stems from having a great name, which inevitably results in great acts; this reverses the order of Corneille's psychology. For the nobles, all it takes is to be a prince or to be of high birth: the name anticipates and determines — guarantees — all exploits in advance. Greatness and generosity, which come from one's bloodline, are gifts received as a birthright. . . . The essence of glory . . . is not conquered, but rather inherited.[59]

French Classical tragedy developed and flourished at a time of rapidly accelerating social change, a time that saw the political and economic death throes of the feudal system and the rise of a more urbanized, centralized state that was less resistant to — and perhaps even to some extent a product of — social mobility and social change. Indeed, to borrow Margaret Mead's terminology, the seventeenth century in France can be viewed as a transitional period between a *postfigurative* culture and a *cofigurative* culture:

A postfigurative culture is one in which change is so slow and imperceptible that grandparents, holding newborn grandchildren in their arms, cannot conceive of any other future for the children than their own past lives. The past of the adults is the future of each new generation; their lives provide the ground plan. The children's future is shaped in such a way that what has come after childhood for their forebears is what they, too, will experience after they are grown.[60]

A cofigurative culture is one in which the prevailing model for members of the society is the behavior of their contemporaries. . . . In a society in which the only model was a cofigurative one, old and young alike would assume that it was "natural" for the behavior of each new generation to differ from that of the preceding generation. . . . Cofiguration has its beginning in a break in the postfigurative system. Such a break may come about . . . as a purposeful step in a revolution that establishes itself through the introduction of new and different life styles for the young.[61]

In terms of familial relations, a postfigurative system favors the vertical axis of the family tree by transmitting values intact from the older to the younger generation, while a cofigurative system relies more heavily on the horizontal axis: when parents cannot fully understand the experiences their children are going through, it makes sense that those children's bonds with others of their generation become especially important.

Mead's depiction of contrasting social organization is purposely schematic; probably few societies would exclusively correspond to either of these models. Nonetheless, in the seventeenth century, we find a particularly complex interaction between the two models. The feudal system was still sufficiently entrenched for power, position, and moral outlook to be transmitted to a certain extent by the mechanism of primogeniture. But with the increasing emergence of competition and market forces, the escalation of social change created a movement toward a culture in which the situation of children was at times so foreign to their parents that the younger generation had to learn — indeed, formulate — their values by collaborating with their peers as much as by listening to their elders:

[Richelieu] subordinated the "birth" of the nobility to the necessities of royal power. This distribution of power between the nobility and monarchy influenced the form which the court took on under Louis XIII. . . . No one will be impervious to the tragic aspects of this defunctionalization, whereby people['s] . . . existence and self-confidence are bound to a certain traditional attitude that has brought their fathers, and perhaps themselves in their youth, success and self-fulfillment, but which now, in a world that has changed for uncomprehended reasons, condemns them to failure and downfall.[62]

It is as an expression of the conflicting ethics of inherited privilege and individual enterprise[63] — the ongoing overlapping and interaction of these ethics — that I would propose to read issues of inheritance, sibling rivalry, and birth order in French Classical tragedy.[64] The court at Versailles, which was one of the principal venues for the performance of tragedy, was in fact an integral part of Louis XIV's scheme to undermine the feudal aristocracy by making it fashionable for them to live at court, far away from their fiefdoms, distracted by various *divertissements*, chief among which were the tragedies of Racine. It is a great irony of Classical tragedy that while it is a consummate example of upper-class aesthetics, it can also be seen as contributing to the breakdown of feudal values and the accelerating rise of the bourgeoisie, capitalism, and the centralized state.

Thus French Classical tragedy exemplifies Hegel's definition of tragedy as a confrontation between two value-systems: "The tragic destruction of figures whose ethical life is in the highest plane can interest and elevate us and reconcile us to its occurrence only in so far as they come on the scene in opposition to one another together with equally justified but different ethical powers which have come into collision."[65] Hegel sees tragedy not as the struggle of right and wrong, of justice and injustice, but rather as the collision of right with right, of two opposing and irreconcilable ethics or world views. A confrontation of this nature is one of the seminal forces generating French Classical tragedy.

2

Psychological Primogeniture

The Legacy of Primogeniture

For Western readers of today, primogeniture might appear to be nothing more than a distant, distasteful reminder of a less egalitarian time than our own. On the one hand, democratic societies are fond of the notion that all individuals can rise to the level their talents and achievements allow, and primogeniture places severe restrictions on one's ability to do so. On the other hand, in the past four centuries kinship and inheritance have come to play a less and less prominent role in social organization in the West. As Nancy Chodorow has remarked:

> In modern societies, ties based on kinship no longer function as important links among people in the productive world, which becomes organized more and more in nonkinship market and class relations. Moreover, the relations of material production, and the extended public and political ties and associations — the state, finally — which these relations make possible, dominate and define family relations — the sphere of human reproduction. Many aspects of reproduction are taken over by extrafamilial institutions like schools. Kinship, then, is progressively stripped of its functions and its ability to organize the social world.[1]

And yet one must not underestimate to what extent the beliefs, practices, and values of today are beholden to deeply embedded social structures of the past. Anne Gotman astutely observes that although "the principle of inheritance has lost ground in modern societies, it still remains operative and even quite active."[2] And as Pierre Bourdieu explains, even in this day and age the implications of inheritance are ethical as much as they are material:

> Properly speaking, there is not a single material heritage that is not also a cultural heritage, and *family goods* function not only as a physical proof of the seniority and continuity of the lineage — and consequently as a consecration of its social identity, which is inseparable from temporal permanence — but also as a factor that effectively

contributes to the ethical reproduction of the lineage, that is, to the transmission of values, qualities and abilities that legitimate individuals' claims to belonging to bourgeois dynasties.[3]

It is not difficult to accept Bourdieu's idea that material inheritance has a moral component; less obvious is the converse of his observation: that the "ethical reproduction" of each generation — the lessons parents inculcate in their offspring — retains vestiges of material inheritance practices like primogeniture which have largely disappeared from the material realm.

Indeed, primogeniture has ramifications that extend far beyond the sociohistorical reality of seventeenth-century France, for many of the underpinnings of primogeniture persist in our own society to this day, but shifted into the domain of psychology. It is only in the past two decades that the study of birth-order effects has come into its own, and the relative obscurity in which questions of birth order have remained until recently is partly a function of one of the invisible biases of a society obsessed by more conspicuous prejudices like race, gender, and religious belief. As higher achievers, on average, than their younger brothers and sisters, firstborns have been present in disproportionate numbers in many fields of intellectual endeavor, and those fields may well be affected by the predominance of oldest-sibling perspectives. Stephen P. Bank and Michael D. Kahn suggest that firstborns' overrepresentation in the field of psychotherapy has contributed to the relative disinterest in which the sibling bond has been viewed by the psychological establishment: "We should like to speculate about another factor that contributes to the avoidance of sibling issues by psychotherapists: their birth-order position. Many therapists are *first-borns*. Many studies point to the economic and educational advantages first-borns have over later-borns: psychotherapists, with their extensive schooling, have been the beneficiaries of their first-born position."[4]

Of course it is not inevitable that laterborns would be more interested than firstborns in studying the sibling bond, any more than it is inevitable that in countries whose power structures are dominated by Protestant white men, women and members of ethnic or religious minorities would be disproportionately inclined to raise questions of sexual, racial, or religious differences. Still, it is not unreasonable to expect that a particularly acute awareness of any kind of social difference might arise in individuals who feel that they have been placed at a disadvantage by that difference.[5]

The field of psychoanalysis, by far the most influential branch of psychology in psychological approaches to literary texts up to the present time, has overwhelmingly favored the study of the parent-child relation at the expense of the sibling bond. A number of researchers studying birth-order effects have speculated that this lacuna may be partly due to the fact that Sigmund Freud, the father of psychoanalysis, was an archetypal oldest child: "Freud, his mother's undisputed favorite and a typical firstborn, . . . valued authority and power over his fellowman. . . . Consistent with such attitudes, Freud assumed man to possess an innate evil component that must be constantly controlled by a higher authority (the superego)."[6] "Freud was the classic first-born who thrived by dominating: when he could not dominate, he tried to eliminate or ignore. . . . Sigmund considered himself superior to his siblings, with Alexander the single exception. In Freud's brief autobiography (1935), he mentions only his parents. . . . To Freud [his siblings] were something of a bother, people to be tolerated or who owed him admiration . . . [He] positioned himself at the head of a sibling group in which no one could question his dominance and special status" (Bank and Kahn, 213–14). As an oldest son, Freud largely dismissed his siblings.[7] Several commentators have pointed out that Freud's position within his own family may have been an important factor in the stress he laid on the parent-child relation as a determiner of personality, as well as his quite systematic overlooking of the sibling bond in his writings about the psychology of the family.[8]

As Bank and Kahn observe, Freud's struggles with several of his disciples, in particular Alfred Adler, a secondborn, may also be correlated to his position within his family:

[Freud's] personal autocracy in the psychoanalytic movement flowed naturally from the autocratic role that he had played out among his siblings. His younger brother, his only male rival, was his worshipful follower. In this light, Freud's struggles with his fellow psychoanalysts Alfred Adler and Carl Gustave Jung, his ruthless domination of one of his potential rivals, Victor Tausk, and his refusal to compromise intellectually or socially as leader of the psychoanalytic movement, all make more sense as a reflection of sibling dynamics than as simply one of his relationship with parents. (214–15)

Karl König sees the feud between Freud and Adler in particular as a latter-day version of the struggle between Cain and Abel: "A very typical example of this eternal struggle is the rift between *Sigmund Freud* and *Alfred Adler*. They were in close association for almost ten years, but gradually the domineering attitude of *Freud* who was a first-born child was unable to bear up with the carefree spirit of *Adler* who was a second son. Cain slew Abel and the latter accepted the blow. *Freud* in the end was the sufferer. He was never able to transform the bitterness in his mind and to turn it into forgiveness."[9]

While it cannot be proven that Freud's position as a firstborn influenced his theory of development, it would be difficult to dispute his relative disinterest in sibling relations. Freud based his theories of personality development almost exclusively on the triangle mother-father-child. His most important work about siblings, *Totem and Taboo*, is one of his most sociologically oriented writings, and in its postulation of a primordial horde of brothers in revolt, it is even more speculative than his recreations of the early psychic history of individuals. The very few times Freud mentions the sibling bond more directly, it is secondary to the parent-child relation, siblings seen as being in loco parentis, displaced objects of children's affection or hostility toward their parents. The privileged position in which Freud places the parent-child relation has greatly influenced subsequent psychoanalytic theory,[10] and has helped to set the tone for the study of family dynamics in other areas of psychology.[11] Judy Dunn and Carol Kendrick speak of "the focus on the mother-child relationship as the crucial feature of a child's emotional and social development in his first three years, a focus which has meant that the relationship between child and sibling has been seen *only* vis-à-vis the mother-child relationship."[12]

Lest we believe that the favoring of the parent-child relation is inevitable in theories of personality development, we need look no further than Freud's disciple, secondborn Alfred Adler, who developed a theory of envy and competition that makes sibling rivalry one of the fundamental forces determining an adult's outlook on life: "The second child is in a quite different position [from the oldest] . . . Throughout his childhood he has a pacemaker. There is always a child ahead of him in age and development and he is stimulated to exert himself and catch up. A typical second child is very easy to recognize. He behaves as if he were in a race, as if some one were a step or two in front and he had to hurry to get ahead of him . . . He trains continually to surpass his older brother and conquer him."[13] Adler views the position of laterborn children as potentially advantageous, but only insofar as their position of innate inferiority acts as a goad to achievement: "No child likes to be the smallest, the one whom one does not trust, the one in whom one has no confidence, all the time. Such knowledge stimulates a child to prove that he can do everything. His striving for power becomes markedly accentuated and we find the youngest very usually a man who has developed a desire to overcome all others, satisfied only with the very best . . . [But] if the older children are not to be excelled, the youngest frequently shies away from his tasks, becomes cowardly, a chronic plaintiff."[14] Although Adler's theories have been superseded in the last few decades by less speculative studies of birth-order effects, his abiding contribution to the field of developmental psychology is that he paid such close attention to birth order to begin with.

The bias toward parent-child relations in psychologists' descriptions of family dynamics has begun to be counteracted by the recent attention focused on the roles brothers and sisters play in each other's lives. The publication in 1996 of Frank J. Sulloway's *Born to Rebel: Birth Order, Family Dynamics, and Creative Lives* has gone a long way toward establishing the importance of birth-order effects. In Sulloway's study of the lives of four thousand scientists and their attitudes toward the controversies of their day, he discovers a consistent pattern: radical theories like those of Darwin were propounded and also supported by younger sons and opposed by more conservative eldest children. The psychological portrait that comes out of Sulloway's research belies conventional views of the good fortune of the oldest child: he finds oldest children to be more controlling, more conformist, more conventional, more respectful of authority, and less open-minded than their younger siblings.

A convinced Darwinian (and laterborn) himself, Sulloway sees the various roles taken on by siblings as adaptive strategies designed to maximize their allocation of a limited, precious resource: parental love, care, and sustenance. For example, infants have evolved the strategy of resisting weaning because breast-feeding acts as a natural contraceptive, delays the conception of the next child, and prolongs the period during which newborns get a high percentage of their parents' attention, thus making it more likely that they will survive into adulthood and reproduce. According to Sulloway, the oldest child, who has the advantage of growing up larger, stronger, and smarter than laterborns, naturally inherits the most desirable "family niche," the spiritual property closest to the parents. This forces subsequent children to move further afield and to diversify, which results in their greater openness to experience: "Faced with older siblings who are superior in age and expertise (and inclined to claim priority for good ideas), younger siblings do well to seek out interests of their own. The more interests, the better. . . . Broad interests are a prominent manifestation of openness to experience. . . . For laterborns, openness and versatility are tactical responses to firstborn priority, facilitating 'adaptive radiation' within the family system. . . . Everything about laterborns—their interests, their attitudes, and their cognitive styles—tends toward 'divergence'" (105). As

Bank and Kahn put it, "it appears that in most families there is only one person who can occupy a certain psychological space in a family at any one time" (23); since laterborns are generally born into families in which there is already a spiritual heir apparent in place, they must seek out other niches.[15] The fact that Sulloway finds laterborns to be greater travelers than firstborns can be seen as harkening back to primogeniture: just as in the early modern period laterborns often lived on the fringes of familial lands, or were banished from them altogether and forced to seek their fortune elsewhere, in contemporary families the spiritual equivalent of the family "lands" is often reserved for the firstborn and closed off, in effect, to those that follow.

One theme that recurs with some frequency in recent literature about the influence of siblings on identity is that children define themselves not only by what they get from their parents, but also by how much they get relative to other siblings: "The usual view is that it is the direct impact of how a parent relates to a child that influences that child's development. We argue that children are sensitive not only to how their parents relate to them, but also to how their parents relate to their siblings, and that children monitor and respond to that other relationship just as they monitor the relationship between their parents. This is a shift from viewing the child as child-of-the-parent to child-as-family-member."[16] In other words, the psychological parental heritage is not simply transmitted from parent to child. Rather, the ways in which children receive and perceive that heritage are very much affected by the ways in which their siblings have received and perceived it. "The process by which siblings become different . . . allows siblings to become 'opposites' in many major personality and interest areas. They thus avoid conflict, having divided up emotional territories and roles" (Bank and Kahn, 225).

Perhaps the most dramatic example of this fraternal and sororal division of labor is the distinction frequently made in psychological studies of siblings between the firstborn sibling and subsequent ones. The field of birth order deals simply with patterns, not thoroughgoing rules, but it would appear that the eldest child often receives the greatest direct impact of parental influence of various kinds: more attention, higher expectations, more projection on the part of parents.[17] As Bank and Kahn put it, "Eminence . . . appears related to one's being the oldest or the only child in a family, presumably because of the greater value and attention given to first-born children, both economically and psychologically" (205). The oldest child is the only one whose relation to parents is unmediated by a relation to siblings, at least until the birth of subsequent children. Thus while the oldest originally has only one familial role, that of son or daughter, younger children are from birth both offspring and sibling, a simple but far-reaching fact that is brilliantly dramatized by Simone de Beauvoir's description of her relation to her younger sister in *Mémoires d'une jeune fille rangée*: "Relegated to a secondary position, the younger daughter felt quite superfluous. For my parents, I was a new experience: my sister found it much harder to faze them or get their attention. I had never been compared to anyone, whereas she was constantly being compared to me."[18]

This particular view of the oldest child reconfirms received wisdom about birth order. But as we have seen, Sulloway suggests — and he is not alone in doing so — that being the oldest has drawbacks. Indeed, one of the most important themes in the literature of birth order is that of the oldest child as authoritarian, parent-identified, and conservative, as opposed to subsequent children, who tend to be iconoclastic, rebellious, and shrewd. Here is how Alfred Adler expresses it:

Oldest children generally show . . . an interest in the past. . . . They are admirers of the past. . . . Sometimes a child who has lost his power, the small kingdom he ruled, understands better than others the importance of power and authority. When he grows up, he likes to take part in the exercise of authority and he exaggerates the importance of rules and laws. Everything should be done by rule and no rule should ever be changed. Power should always be preserved in the hands of those who are entitled to it. We can understand that influences like these in childhood give a strong tendency towards conservatism.[19]

Even in present-day Western societies that have no explicit system of primogeniture, eldest siblings tend to be more conservative, more like their parents, and more respectful of authority than their younger brothers and sisters: "Parents tend to be more extreme and intolerant in their expectations for the conduct and achievement of their first child than they may be with later-born children. The impact of their personalities and standards seems to be maximum for that first child because he alone is the object of their attention for a period of time. Consequently older children and oldest children often seem to be more conforming to the standards of their parents than do later-born children."[20]

Is this conservatism of the firstborn not analogous to the essential conservatism of the heir apparent? In a society governed by primogeniture, when the eldest son knows he will automatically inherit his father's wealth and position, he tends also to replicate his father's value-system. When people grow up with the assumption and belief that they have a natural claim to something of great value — whether it is their parents' wealth or their attention — rather than being forced to fight for that thing, they are not likely to scrutinize the values they were raised with. The study of how placement within the family affects the mentalities of siblings shows to what extent primogeniture has survived in various ways long past its abolition as a legal practice. One of the greatest contributions of Sulloway's study is precisely its emphasis on the way birth order affects attitudes and mentalities: "For the past five centuries, the most consistent predictor of revolutionary allegiances turns out to be *birth order*. Compared with firstborns, laterborns are more likely to identify with the underdog and to challenge the established order. Because they identify with parents and authority, firstborns are more likely to defend the status quo. The effects of birth order transcend gender, social class, race, nationality, and — for the last five centuries — time" (356).

Primogeniture, whether legal or psychological, is not an unmixed blessing for the firstborns it designates as heirs. That studies of birth order do not come to a clear consensus about which position in the family is the best suggests that being a psychological heir, like being to the manor born, has both advantages and disadvantages. Knowing from birth that one will inherit a certain position gives one a sense of entitlement, but entitlements are only as stable as the social structures that award them; even in a very stagnant society, which ours is not, there are no guarantees in life. Being raised with a feeling of certainty as to the future, or with a clearly delineated, imposed sense of identity can cause problems when the future turns out to be different from what one expected. Moreover firstborn children are not always well suited to the heritage their parents thrust upon them. A sense of entitlement can be extremely limiting: it can be as much of a straitjacket as it is a protection: "The first child is a defender; a defender of faith, a defender of tradition, a defender of the family. The first child preserves the past against the onrush of any new ideas and actions. He has to maintain what has been achieved. The first child has to stand up for what is past whether he likes it or not. . . . There where law and order, tradition and continuity are needed, the first child has his place. It is the first child who is heir to the crown, the title, the leadership of the family, to the inheritance, be it spiritual or material."[21]

Conversely, "inherited" disadvantages can bring potential benefits to less favored siblings, thus compensating for the wear and tear on their psyches that comes from knowing they are not their parents' heirs. It can be quite useful to grow up with an understanding that things of value do not fall into one's lap but must be worked for and earned. The awareness that the status quo may not be the best of all possible worlds can open one's mind to the conception of other possible worlds. Finally, exclusion from power may bring with it a certain freedom that at least partially makes up for the disadvantages of being an outsider. Christian Biet sums up the pluses and minuses of the nonheir's position: "The younger child's . . . relation to power is fractured and must be constituted in some other way. Thus he is less subject to his family's fate, less marked by concerns over legitimacy of blood. His struggle is only partially undertaken in the name of his family, so that he must learn how to fight in the name of his own existence."[22]

A long literary tradition favors younger siblings as figures forced to overcome the natural advantage of elder siblings and thus to develop their intelligence. According to Bernard Barc, the account of human development in Genesis systematically favors the younger sibling:

God preferred the offering of Abel, the younger brother, over that of the elder, Cain. After murdering his brother, Cain, far from receiving a doubled inheritance, became a fugitive and a wanderer, while the place of the younger brother, left vacant by the murder of Abel, was occupied by a newborn son, Seth (Genesis 4:25). All of history before the flood confirms the curse weighing down on the elder branch, the descendants of Cain, which disappeared in the eighth generation, swallowed up by the waters of the flood . . .

Human history after the flood systematically confirms the domination of the younger brother over the older.[23]

Barc goes on to give numerous examples of this pattern, extending beyond Genesis to other books of the Hebrew Bible; among others, he cites Isaac's advantage over Ishmael, Jacob's over Esau, and Moses' over Aaron. The illustrious King David, a younger son, chose his youngest son, Solomon, to succeed him.

A history of younger siblings in literature is obviously beyond the scope of the present study, but aficionados of the French Classical period need go no further than Charles Perrault's *Contes de ma mère l'Oye* for two excellent examples of the phenomenon of younger-sibling domination. In "Le Chat botté," the eldest of three sons inherits his father's mill while the youngest is left nothing more than a cat, but the cat, a metaphor for both the dispossession and the shrewdness of the youngest child, is his ticket to success. Similarly, in "Le Petit Poucet," the youngest of seven brothers and the runt of the litter uses his wits to save his siblings and himself from destruction.

The come-what-may attitude that often develops in children in response to not being their parents' heir may be one reason why stories of siblings frequently portray the position of the younger (or youngest) sibling as more compelling than that of the firstborn. The future of an heir is clear, that of a nonheir anything but. Since storytelling invites us to upend the status quo—what would be the fun of a tale that simply maintained its initial situation in an unchanged form?—the come-from-behind victory of the laterborn is almost by definition more dramatic and compelling than the all-too-expected triumph of the firstborn.

The Curse of Primogeniture: Molière's *Les Femmes savantes*

As an example of psychological primogeniture, I would like to examine what I consider to be one of the most psychologically compelling plays of the Classical period, Molière's *Les Femmes savantes* (1672), one of Molière's few comedies in which an intact nuclear family—consisting of a mother, a father, and two full siblings—is portrayed. The mother, Philaminte, is the principal *femme savante*, an intelligent but pretentious woman enamored of philosophy and unbearable poetry. Chrysale, Philaminte's husband, is an unpretentious, down-to-earth type who proclaims without embarrassment: "Je vis de bonne soupe, et non de beau langage" (531) [I live on good soup, not fine language].[24] Armande, the couple's elder daughter, is like a carbon copy of her mother, while Henriette, the younger, finds her mother's airs and pomposity unpalatable without a large grain of salt. The relation between Armande and Henriette corresponds precisely to the psychological distinction between the idealistic, parent-identified older sibling and the practical, iconoclastic younger one.

It is clear from the very first scene that Armande is her mother's psychological heir: she has taken her mother's bait, hook, line, and sinker. Armande has gone as far as to reject marriage to Clitandre, a man who loves her and whom she loves, because she has taken literally her mother's discourses singing the praises of the spirit while belittling the lowly functions of the body. Armande, obviously still in love with Clitandre two years after having turned down his proposal, cannot reconcile her feelings of sexual attraction for him with her mother's disembodied spiritual discourse; taking to heart her mother's scorn for the body, she has fended Clitandre off so well that he has now turned his affections toward her younger sister (136–44). The initial situation of the play is complicated when Philaminte refuses to give Henriette permission to marry Clitandre. Instead, she proposes that the insufferable *précieux* Trissotin marry Henriette; Chrysale supports Henriette's desire to marry Clitandre but hasn't the moral fiber to stand up to his wife. Nonetheless, the play ends after a series of complications with the victory of the younger daughter, whose engagement to Clitandre is confirmed. This leaves Armande acutely disappointed at seeing her sister marry the man she herself still loves.

Armande's eagerness to be and remain her mother's daughter is apparent in her ambiguous use of the word "fille" in the very first line of the play: "Quoi! le beau nom de fille est un titre, ma soeur, / Dont vous voulez quitter la charmante douceur?" (1–2) [What! the fine name of daughter (maiden) is a title whose sweet charm / You would leave behind, my sister?]. "Le beau nom de fille" implies both meanings of the word "fille": "daughter" and "unmarried woman." To Armande, getting married means losing her title as a daughter worthy of Philaminte.

When Armande is confronted by the fact that Henriette intends to marry Clitandre, she covers her jealousy behind an abstract discourse worthy of her mother:

> Laissez aux gens grossiers, aux personnes vulgaires,
> Les bas amusements de ces sortes d'affaires.
> A de plus hauts objets élevez vos désirs,
> Songez à prendre un goût des plus nobles plaisirs,
> Et, traitant de mépris les sens et la matière,
> A l'esprit, comme nous, donnez-vous toute entière.
> Vous avez notre mère en exemple à vos yeux,
> Que du nom de savante on honore en tous lieux. (31–38)

> Leave to coarse folk, to vulgar people,
> The lowly diversions of that sort of business.
> Lift up your desires to higher objects,
> Develop a taste for nobler pleasures and, like us,
> Give yourself over wholeheartedly to the spiritual,
> Thus treating with scorn the sensual and the material.
> Look no further than your mother for an example,
> For everywhere she goes, as a learned lady she is honored.

Armande's espousal of the spiritual and her distaste for the physical mirror Philaminte's distinction between herself, ruler over the lofty domain of the spirit, and her husband, a lowly man of the flesh (1127–30).

If Armande is an archetypal firstborn, Henriette is a typical younger sibling. She makes no attempt to contest her sister's wholesale appropriation of the maternal heritage, but rather creates a distinct family niche for herself. From her first scene with her sister she makes clear her belief in a sororal division of labor: "Le ciel, dont nous voyons que l'ordre est tout-puissant, / Pour différents emplois nous fabrique en naissant" (53–54) [Heaven, whose order is, as we know, all-powerful, / Creates us for different tasks when we are born]. To this sentiment, echoing the passage in chapter 12 of Romans that explains that each of us is born with different gifts, current theories of birth order might add that once we are born, we choose which functions we will develop in order to avoid duplicating the roles already played by our siblings. This might help us to explain why Henriette has defined herself by contrast to both her mother and her sister, who closely resemble each other.

Henriette is not at all a *précieuse*; she is down to earth and quite eager to experience the pleasures of the body. One could of course interpret Henriette as simply her father's rather than her mother's daughter, and she certainly resembles Chrysale more than she does Philaminte. But the play suggests that Henriette defines herself by opposition to her sister and her mother rather than by resemblance to her father.

One of the play's central ironies is that while Henriette is utterly unlike her mother, she is a much keener reader of her mother's character than Armande, who resembles her. Although Henriette, too, echoes the terms "esprit" and "matière" used by Philaminte and mimicked by Armande, she correctly perceives that her mother, like everyone else, inhabits both realms. As she tells her sister, by accepting marriage she is imitating her mother no less than Armande is by rejecting it:

> Nous saurons toutes deux imiter notre mère:
> Vous, du côté de l'âme et des nobles désirs,
> Moi, du côté des sens et des grossiers plaisirs;
> Vous, aux productions d'esprit et de lumière,
> Moi, dans celles, ma soeur, qui sont de la matière. (68–72)

> We shall both be imitating our mother:
> You, in the realm of the soul and of noble desires,
> I, in the realm of the senses and of coarse pleasures;
> You, by producing spirit and light,
> I, by material productions, my sister.

Henriette's message, which Armande does not fully believe until the end of the play, is that their mother, too, is made of flesh and blood, matter as well as spirit.

Les Femmes savantes speaks volumes about the sororal division of labor, the different ways two sisters might relate to their mother's dictates, about sex or anything else. The older daughter accepts her mother's factitious self-presentation: she is her mother's best audience. The younger daughter, who arrives at the spectacle her mother stages too late to get a first-row seat, is reduced to the function of a critic of her mother's role. The elder sister has no need to think in terms of a division of labor; she has the luxury — which, as we shall see, is also the misfortune — of simply being her mother's heir. The younger sister sees things from a different perspective than her sister, which also means from a greater distance from her mother.

Thus when Armande sums up her matrophiliac position by enjoining her sister to show herself to be Philaminte's daughter — "Tâchez ainsi que moi de vous montrer sa fille" (39) [Try to follow my lead in showing you are her daughter] — we are justified in asking what precisely it means for Armande to be her mother's daughter. Although Armande tries to model herself completely on her mother, she is actually quite different from her, precisely because she models herself on a misinterpretation of her mother's discourse: she takes Philaminte's rejection of the body quite literally. But as a child of Philaminte's flesh as well as her spirit, Armande is living proof that her mother has not herself been systematic in scorning the body, as Henriette is quick to point out:

> Mais vous ne seriez pas ce dont vous vous vantez,
> Si ma mère n'eût eu que de ces beaux côtés;
> Et bien vous prend, ma soeur, que son noble génie
> N'ait pas vaqué toujours à la philosophie. (77–80)

> But you would not be what you are, and are proud to be,
> If my mother had had only those fine aspects;
> And you should be thankful her noble talents
> Did not always think about philosophy, my sister.

Henriette's suspicion that her mother is not the purely spiritual figure she would like to be is confirmed by the revelation late in the play that unbeknownst to Armande, Philaminte actually had nothing against her older daughter's marriage to Clitandre. When Armande informs her mother that

Chrysale and Henriette persist in opposing Philaminte's plan to marry Henriette off to Trissotin, Philaminte breezily comments that she was in favor of Armande's relationship with Clitandre:

> Je le trouvais bien fait, et j'aimais vos amours;
> Mais, dans ses procédés, il m'a déplu toujours.
> Il sait que, Dieu merci, je me mêle d'écrire;
> Et jamais il ne m'a prié de lui rien lire. (1135–38)

> I thought he was handsome, and I seconded [lit., loved] your love;
> But he constantly displeased me in his dealings.
> Good gracious, he knows how involved I am in my writing;
> And yet he never once asked me if he could read something I wrote.

"J'aimais vos amours": Armande has completely misread her mother, who now reveals that she was actually in favor of Armande's marriage with Clitandre. The marvelous ambiguity of the phrase suggests that at some level Philaminte has the power to love in her daughter's place ("I loved your loves"). Given the overpowering role Philaminte plays for Armande and the restrictions it places on her daughter's nascent sexuality, whatever the mother's conscious attitude toward her daughter's engagement might be, it is no wonder that Armande was reticent about going through with the marriage.

The narcissistic nature of the relation between the mother and her psychological heir is quite clear: the mother sees her daughter as a pure reflection of herself, and the daughter sees herself in the same light. We should not be surprised, then, to discover that Armande's error in reading her mother was essentially a failure at understanding her mother's need for attention and praise: Clitandre never asked her to read him one of her literary efforts, never flattered her. Once again Henriette, who models herself against her mother, shows a better understanding of her mother's character than her sister. She advises her lover not to ask for her hand in marriage from her father, but rather to curry her mother's favor (204–14).

Once we have understood this narcissistic aspect of Philaminte, we begin to see more clearly the advantages garnered by the younger sister's position of maternal dispossession. Armande tries to follow her mother's model so slavishly that she herself becomes redundant, reduced to living her life in a way that she believes conforms to her mother's strictures and expectations. Henriette, whose birth position gives her less importance in her mother's eyes and therefore places her at a greater distance from her, is better able to perceive her mother's contradictions. Henriette accepts her mother for what she is: a vain and powerful parent, but one who is not immune to being manipulated if only one observes her from a great enough distance to perceive her vulnerability.

Armande is the only one left out in the cold at the end of the play. Henriette gets Clitandre, along with the satisfaction not only of marrying the man she loves, but also, for once, of upstaging her sister. When Philaminte is tricked into believing that she and her husband have lost their fortune, she reacts with aplomb, revealing herself to be quite a well-adjusted, psychologically healthy woman. Chrysale, who favored the marriage between Henriette and Clitandre from the start, is allowed the luxury of believing that he actually has some measure of control over his family. Only Armande stands apart in this otherwise happily-ever-after ending, and her final exchange with her mother is all the more poignant in that it takes place in the midst of the general rejoicing that is going on around her:

ARMANDE:
Ainsi donc à leurs voeux vous me sacrifiez?
PHILAMINTE:
Ce ne sera point vous que je leur sacrifie;
Et vous avez l'appui de la philosophie,
Pour voir d'un oeil content couronner leur ardeur. (1770–73)

ARMANDE:
Does that mean you are sacrificing me to their wishes?
PHILAMINTE:
You are not the one being sacrificed here;
And you have the support of philosophy
To help you look upon their love with favor.

Is this Iphigénie *avant la lettre* not staging a timid revolt against the cruel parental sacrifice perpetrated at the end of the play? What is most cruel about Philaminte's final response to her daughter is that it is tantamount to a condemnation of her daughter for her daughter's gullible confidence in her. What Philaminte is saying here is: You actually believed me! You took my act seriously. You didn't realize this is a comedy.

Les Femmes savantes stages the tragedy of the older sister and the comedy of the younger. Perhaps the play's message is that in the end, being one's parents' psychological heir can be a curse as well as a blessing. Armande is portrayed as a highly idealistic and naïve young woman whose unquestioning and uncritical acceptance of her mother's self-presentation ultimately leaves her defeated and disillusioned. *Les Femmes savantes* is the story of how a firstborn daughter is taken in by her mother's belief-system, then painfully made to realize the unfortunate constraints she has placed upon her own life because she has internalized that belief-system without any degree of distance, analysis, or evaluation, functions that come more naturally to psychological nonheirs because they are outsiders from the start. To this extent, the play can be read as a cautionary tale about the drawbacks of psychological primogeniture.

PART II

THE FIRST
GENERATION

3

Médée

The Robe Is Mightier than the Sword, or The Clothier's Revenge

The tragedy of a betrayed woman who kills her children in order to take revenge on their worthless father, Pierre Corneille's *Médée* (1635) encapsulates the conflict between a value-system based on the inheritance of power and privilege and one in which individuals define themselves through personal enterprise. As Mitchell Greenberg has observed, Médée's murder of Jason's children is tantamount to an attack on a conservative social order that emphasizes the importance of progeny as a guarantor of intergenerational continuity.[1] It is thus not surprising that the character of Médée has often been interpreted as a purely malevolent, destructive being who defeats the forces of order structuring society. But to read the character in this way is to view the tragic conflict of the play purely from Jason's genealogicocentric perspective and to reduce Médée to the role of an underminer of that system. If, on the other hand, we consider Hegel's definition of tragedy as an expression of the conflict between two ethics, we may begin to understand that Médée's challenge upon the principle of continuity through inheritance is not purely negative, but rather includes within itself the kernel of a positive ethic of self-determination and freedom from inheritance.

Indeed, one of the most difficult and crucial issues in this, Pierre Corneille's first tragedy, is the profound ambiguity of the character of Médée. As an outsider to power and privilege, Médée is not only an attacker of the status quo. She is also the representative of a new value-system imposing itself at the expense of an older ethic whose demise, by the same token, it fosters.

One would be hard pressed to find a character in literature who more spectacularly undermines the notions of progeny and inheritance than Médée. Starting with her destruction of the autochthonous children of the

Earth whose blood soaks the very mother from which they have sprung (39–40, 904–6),[2] Médée not only kills children, but also displays their spilled blood: she specializes in exhibitionistic infanticide. When, upon murdering her own children by Jason, she vauntingly wields the bloody knife that accomplished the deed as a visual representation of the destruction of her husband's progeny (1539–42),[3] this most dramatic of all infanticides is merely the culmination of a career that consists largely of parading dead or dying children before the eyes of their fathers. As Médée herself mentions several times during the course of the drama (235–36, 795–804), while she was helping Jason pursue the golden fleece and the two were chased by her own father, she cut her brother into pieces and cast his severed limbs into the sea so that her father would be forced to stop and pick up his son's remains. In act 5, Jason's fiancée, Créuse, is with her father, Créon, as she is consumed by the lethal burning set off by Médée's poisoned robe; as we shall see, Créon, afflicted by the poison as well, escapes witnessing his daughter's death only by committing suicide (1419–23).[4]

Individualism Versus Inheritance

Given the limits imposed upon him by his use of a character with a long and well-known literary tradition, Corneille could hardly have avoided portraying Médée as a cruel infanticide — nor, presumably, would he have wanted to. By contrast, nothing forced him to give Médée the dynamism and power that are also apparent in his heroine and that combine with her destructive force to create the fascinating, complex character that she is. In her ambition, her drive, and her effectiveness, Médée is a worthy representative of an increasingly powerful, enterprising class whose challenge upon the feudal aristocracy is indeed seen as threatening, but whose talents and resources the nobles increasingly make use of even as they are refusing to stoop to compete.[5]

The double-edged value of Médée's attack upon the status quo is most clearly dramatized by another element of her story that is also traditional: Médée has the power not only to kill children, but also to make old people young again. Jason, feeling pity for his elderly father, Aeson, asks Médée to rejuvenate him, which she does (51–54). How can we reconcile Médée's two powers? How can the same woman destroy Jason's progeny and give his father new life?

Médée not only undermines the normative transmission of a heritage between the generations; by making Aeson young again, she also symbolically demonstrates the increased importance of each individual life span when the strict inheritance of values and social standing comes under serious attack.[6] Indeed, once we have understood the importance of leaving behind a posterity for someone like Jason ("M'enlever mes enfants, c'est m'arracher le coeur" [924] [Taking away my children is like tearing out my heart]) or Créon ("Et cet espoir si doux, qui m'a toujours flatté / De revivre à jamais en [ma] postérité" [1407–8] [And that sweet hope, which has always charmed me / For eternal rebirth through (my) posterity]), we might view Médée's two talents, destroying lineages and renewing individual life, as two sides of a single coin. If one cannot pass on one's name and power to one's progeny, accomplishing things during one's own lifetime takes on a greater value; by the same token inheriting nothing both obliges one and frees one to make something of one's own life. Médée proleptically solves with one wave of her magic wand the very problem she will later cause by the double stroke of her murderous dagger: she gives Jason's father a second chance at life to make up for seeing to it that he will leave no one behind to carry on his name.

Another textual example illustrates the same point, but from the opposite direction. Médée puts Jason's uncle, Pélie, the brother of Aeson, to death by claiming she can rejuvenate his blood and make him young again and then refusing to do so after she has duped his daughters into bleeding him (81–92). Jason's father, Aeson, is actually the rightful heir, but Pélie, Aeson's half-brother — the two men share the same mother — has usurped his power and tyrannized the hapless Jason. A significant difference between the rejuvenation of Aeson and the non-rejuvenation of Pélie is that Jason's father, who actually proved himself incapable of holding onto his birthright long before Médée happened along, has no power, which may account for the fact that unlike Aeson's heir, Jason, Pélie's heir, Acaste, who actually has something to inherit from his father, apparently has no desire to rejuvenate him. It is his sisters who wish their father to be young again, and while their motivation remains somewhat obscure — there is a hint that they harbor an incestuous desire for their father[7] — they certainly have nothing to lose by their father's rejuvenation precisely because they have nothing to gain by his death; their brother Acaste, not they, will inherit power. It is not a coincidence that Acaste does not participate in his sisters' scheme and is not even mentioned until after his father's death, when he besieges Jason's house to avenge Pélie's death (102–4). Acaste, a typical beneficiary of primogeniture, is only too happy to show his filial devotion — to his father's memory.

Unlike his cousin Acaste, then, Jason has no patrimony to inherit. One of the central ironies of the play is that the children whose passing Jason so keenly mourns as the continuers of his line would have inherited nothing from him except the crumbs from their adoptive mother's table; presumably Jason and Créuse would have produced an heir to Créon's throne, the very reason Créon is so eager to marry off his daughter, an only child, to Jason.[8] By the same token yet another irony of the play is that Médée has spent years of her life putting her considerable talents to use in order to assist a man who was in fact undeserving of her assistance even before he was unfaithful to her. As Jason's helpmate and confederate, Médée utilizes her power to prop up a man of little worth who has nothing left but a reputation — and a taste — for glory.

The Aristocrat as Nonhero

When Médée vows to take revenge for Jason's betrayal and Créon's order of banishment, she aims to get to the two men through their families, thereby undermining the system of power and inheritance they represent. This would appear to be a daunting task: how can a foreign woman get the better of the hero Jason, the leader of the Argonauts, and his future father-in-law, the king? But Médée's enterprise may not be as difficult as it might seem, for if Jason is the heroic representative of the order that Médée attacks, that order seems on the verge of toppling of its own accord. One of Corneille's most important modifications of his principal source for the drama, Seneca's *Medea*, is his increasing the importance of the character of Jason, but even if the expanded role succeeded in luring the illustrious actor Mondory into playing the part, having many lines to recite does not give Corneille's Jason greater majesty than Seneca's or, for that matter, Euripides'; this is a case in which familiarity breeds contempt.

With a few notable exceptions,[9] exegetes of Pierre Corneille's first tragedy have felt free to vilify the play's title character, and they have sometimes erred in the opposite direction by idealizing the character of Jason; perhaps his structural position as a man with some degree of power has blinded readers of the play to the irony of his would-be heroism.[10] Any dramatic hero, even one drawn from ancient mythology, inevitably incorporates certain aspects of contemporary images of heroism, but as a representative of the aristocracy of the sword, Jason embodies an ethic in decline, for he is portrayed as a latter-day Paris, a man devoid of resources other than his attractiveness to women. It is true, as André Stegmann points out, that

Jason astutely puts his masculine charms to good use and that his clever manipulation of women for political purposes prefigures the Machiavellian streak of many of Corneille's later characters.[11] Nevertheless, the text gives so many indications that Jason is cowardly and unworthy that his utter lack of merit, which cannot be spelled out explicitly without sending the character tumbling into the realm of comedy, becomes one of the play's most important subtexts.[12] By virtue of the seriousness of the genre Jason is less openly ridiculed than the Matamore figure in *L'Illusion comique*, Corneille's next play, but he is hardly less of a cut-out hero.

Jason's physical and moral cowardice is apparent throughout the play. When his fiancée, Créuse, asks him if she might have Médée's exquisite robe as a compensation for agreeing to adopt her children rather than exiling them, Jason readily agrees, but he declines to put the request to his ex-wife himself, preferring to delegate the task to her servant, Nérine, supposedly to protect Médée from the violence of his temper:

> Je vais chercher Nérine, et par son entremise
> Obtenir de Médée avec dextérité
> Ce que refuserait son courage irrité.
> Pour elle, vous savez que j'en fuis les approches,
> J'aurais peine à souffrir l'orgueil de ses reproches
> Et je me connais mal, ou dans notre entretien
> Son courroux s'allumant allumerait le mien. (594–600)

> I will find Nérine, and press her into service
> So as to obtain from Médée by guile
> What her angry heart would refuse.
> As for Médée, you know that I am avoiding her,
> For I would find it hard to swallow her haughty reproaches
> And if I know myself, her anger
> Would set me off if we were to speak.

It is through Nérine's "entremise" — a term that as early as the fifteenth century can be used as a synonym for "entreprise" in the sense of an occupation[13] — that the demand for the robe will be made. Jason does recognize that he has been avoiding Médée since he betrayed her, but the reason he gives — he would lose control of himself if his ex-wife criticized him — is not borne out by the action of the play. When Jason and Médée cross paths in spite of his attempts to run away — "Mais la voici qui sort; souffre que je l'évite" (769) [But here she is; please let me avoid her] — Médée lashes him with fifty lines of reproach (771–820), the longest speech addressed by one character to another in the entire play.[14] Her rage, far from setting off his, leads to a series of faint-hearted responses from Jason: "Ah! que n'as-tu des yeux à lire dans mon âme / Et voir les purs motifs de ma nouvelle flamme!" (821–22) [Oh, if only you had eyes to look into my heart / And see the pure motivation of my new passion!]; "Lassés de tant de maux, cédons à la fortune" (881) [Wearied by so much trouble, let us give in to destiny]; "Veux-tu que je m'expose aux haines de deux rois?" (888) [Would you have me be left open to the hostility of two kings?].[15]

Jason's fear of confrontation and competition is also apparent in his attitude toward his rival for the hand of Créuse, Aegée. Jason showers his fiancée with words of gratitude for choosing him over the far worthier Aegée, who is, after all, a reigning king: "C'est bien me témoigner un amour infini, / De mépriser un roi pour un pauvre banni! / A toutes ses grandeurs préférer ma misère" (547–49) [Scorning the favors of a king for me, a poor banished exile, / And choosing my miserable state over his grandeur, / What proof of boundless love!]. But at the end of the same scene, Jason not coincidentally decides to leave the stage just as Aegée is arriving; he attributes his abrupt departure to the business of getting Nérine to ask her mistress about the gift of the robe (605–8), and Créuse, possibly aware that the angry king in spite of his white hair would be too much for Jason to handle, gives her fiancé a convenient exit-line: "Allez donc, votre vue augmenterait ses peines" (610) [Go on your way, seeing you would only upset him]. This single moment well illustrates Jason's haplessness throughout the drama: he avoids a confrontation with his furious rival by going off to make sure he can avoid another confrontation with his furious ex-wife.

Nor does Jason acquit himself honorably when his fiancée is nearly carried off by the valiant Aegée, "Ce généreux vieillard" (1003) [That generous old man], himself a rather heroic figure. Upon hearing the news that Créuse has been rescued, Médée assumes that it is Jason who saved her, although her sardonic comment is no paean to valor: "Je devine la fin, mon traître l'a sauvée" (1022) [I can guess the ending, my traitor saved her]. And as we soon discover, the hero of the hour is not Jason himself, but rather his fellow Argonaut, Pollux, to whom Créon expresses his gratitude: "Invincible héros, c'est à votre secours / Que je dois désormais le bonheur de mes jours" (1059–60) [Invincible hero, from this day forward, / I owe my happiness to your assistance]. Here again, as is the case throughout the play, helpless Jason needs assistance; since Médée is no longer his ally, he mobilizes an entire cast of characters, Pollux and Nérine as well as Créon and Créuse, to rescue him. Even though Pollux, as modest as Jason is boastful, tries to brush off the praise (1065–84), we are left with the distinct impression that the leader of the Argonauts remained an inglorious bystander when it came to protecting the honor of his intended. According to William O. Goode, this episode encapsulates Jason's unheroic dependency throughout the entire drama: "[The incident] reminds us of the gulf that exists between the rhetorical image of Jason as 'homme de bien,' as 'vaillant,' . . . and the truth of his reliance upon others to shape for him this heroic identity. And it is this weakness that will deny him success in his final confrontation with Médée and that will underscore most strongly his failure to equal her."[16]

Other characters' evaluations of Jason reinforce his depiction as an unheroic figure. Pollux's admiration for the ease with which his friend attracts and uses politically well-connected women[17] carries a suggestion that Jason lacks other qualities that might give him more direct and glorious access to power: "Il est né seulement pour charmer les princesses" (22) [He was born to charm princesses, nothing more]; "en tous lieux, sans le secours de Mars, / Les sceptres sont acquis à ses moindres regards" (27–28) [Everywhere he goes, without resorting to the methods of Mars, / His slightest attentions garner him thrones].[18] Créuse herself never goes to great lengths to portray her lover as a hero. That Aegée attempts to change her mind by painting a dreary portrait of his rival—"un fugitif, un traître, un meurtrier de rois" (619) [a fugitive, a traitor, a murderer of kings]—is only to be expected. More surprising and significant is Créuse's response to Aegée, a damning of her lover by faint praise:

J'épouse un malheureux et mon père y consent,
Mais prince, mais vaillant, et surtout innocent:
Non pas que je ne faille en cette préférence,
De votre rang au sien je sais la différence.
Mais si vous connaissez l'amour et ses ardeurs,
Jamais pour son objet il ne prend les grandeurs. (627–32)

Although the man my father is allowing me to marry
Is down on his luck, he is a prince, he is valiant,
And, above all, he is innocent. I know I am foolish in my choice,
I know the difference between your rank and his.

But as you know, love and passion
Are never preoccupied with greatness.

Aside from one discreetly general word of praise for Jason's valor, "vaillant," Créuse does not really dispute Aegée's contentions about her fiancé's unworthiness.

Given this unheroic portrait of the Argonaut, Créuse's panegyric to her lover in the scene immediately preceding the one in which she concedes his worthlessness is ironic, indeed. This speech mixes a vocabulary of birth and privilege with one of merit:

> La fortune a montré dedans votre naissance
> Un trait de son envie ou de son impuissance;
> Elle devait un sceptre au sang dont vous naissez
> Et sans lui vos vertus le méritaient assez.
> L'amour, qui n'a pu voir une telle injustice,
> Supplée à son défaut ou punit sa malice
> Et vous donne, au plus fort de vos adversités,
> Le sceptre que j'attends et que vous méritez. (553–60)

> By your birth, fortune gave an example
> Of its envy, or its impotence;
> It owed you a throne because of your noble blood,
> And aside from your birth, your fine qualities were worthy of a crown.
> Love, which could not abide such injustice,
> Makes up for fortune's failure, or punishes its malevolence,
> And in your darkest hour gives you
> The throne that will be mine and that you deserve.

Créuse is here alluding to the important question of Jason's birthright. As we have seen, Jason's father, Aeson, the rightful heir to the throne of his own father, sees his power usurped by his half-brother, Pélie, who subsequently becomes Jason's tyrant—he sends Jason off to find the golden fleece—and ceases his persecutions only when he is killed by Médée's ruses. Thus Jason is and is not a rightful heir to power: he is the direct heir of someone who was himself outmaneuvered by a sibling who would not otherwise have inherited the throne, and only Médée's efforts have freed him from his cruel but enterprising uncle. Already in the previous generation we see a clash between the rights of inheritance and the power of individual enterprise; the enterprising sibling, Pélie, who by birth is excluded from power, can be outdone only by another, equally enterprising figure who is also excluded from power, Médée herself.

Thus Créuse's words of praise ring hollow not only because of Jason's worthlessness in the present generation, but also because his failings do not begin with him: his father already proved himself unable to hold onto his birthright. If Jason's "fine qualities" referred to by Créuse are not immediately apparent to the spectator, perhaps his lack thereof might be considered as a kind of ironic inheritance, as a capacity for failure passed on by his father instead of the power that neither man is capable of wielding. Jason is caught in the transition between two conflicting systems. Because of his father's bungling he has nothing to inherit, and yet he does not have the drive and ambition fostered by an expectation of noninheritance.

Clothes Make the Woman

It might be said that at some level Créuse actually understands the profound mediocrity of the man she loves. As her description of her first sighting of Médée wearing her spectacular robe suggests, Créuse is temporarily made to forget Jason and his golden fleece by Médée and her dazzling garment:

> [J]amais éclat pareil
> Ne sema dans la nuit les clartés du soleil,
> Les perles avec l'or confusément mêlées,
> Mille pierres de prix sur ses bords étalées,
> D'un mélange divin éblouissent les yeux;
> Jamais rien d'approchant ne se fit en ces lieux.
> Pour moi, tout aussitôt que je l'en vis parée,
> Je ne fis plus d'état de la Toison dorée
> Et dussiez-vous vous-même en être un peu jaloux,
> J'en eus presques envie aussitôt que de vous.
> Pour apaiser Médée et réparer sa perte,
> L'épargne de mon père entièrement ouverte
> Lui met à l'abandon tous les trésors du Roi,
> Pourvu que cette robe et Jason soient à moi. (579–92)

> Never has such brilliance
> Sown lights bright as the sun across the night sky,
> Pearls indiscriminately mixed with gold,
> A thousand precious stones spread out along the edges
> Dazzle the eyes with a divine mixture;
> Never has anything like it been seen in this place.
> As for me, as soon as I saw her wearing it,
> I no longer cared about the golden Fleece
> And even if telling you this makes you a bit jealous,
> I wanted it almost as instantly as I wanted you.
> To placate Médée and make up for her loss,
> My father's treasury is at her disposal,
> Giving her the choice of the King's treasures,
> Provided that this dress and Jason are mine.

Médée's gaudy, overstated robe, all shimmer and glitter, may be taken as a metaphor for herself. Insofar as *Médée* is a tragedy, we may fairly assume that Corneille's goal here is not social realism; indeed, the play's fantastical mythological setting in itself precludes direct social representation. Nonetheless, the robe can, I believe, effectively function as a social metaphor without becoming in any way a social artifact, a representation of the way women dressed in the 1630s.

Médée's robe has several characteristics that apply to its wearer as well. While it is undeniably spectacular and valuable, it is also immodest, excessive, and ostentatious. And yet the fact that Créuse envies Médée the gown she is wearing might well be an indication of her secret admiration for the woman herself: she seems to covet Médée's style nearly as much as she wants her husband, the similarity in her mind between Jason and the robe as objects of desire something she is unembarrassed to admit: "I wanted it almost as instantly as I wanted you." Médée's robe is a metaphor for her mercurial resourcefulness, precisely the dynamic quality that is lacking in both Jason and Créuse. The description of the robe emphasizes not only its great worth—"A thousand precious stones spread out along the edges"—but also its heterogeneous, haphazard nature: "Pearls indiscriminately mixed with gold," "divine mixture." The repetition of forms of "mêler" [mix] suggests that the robe is adorned with a hodgepodge of precious stones thrown together without any apparent central design. The garment is not the result of a singlemindedness of vision; on the contrary, its unprecedented richness and brilliance are the result of the very sort of brash innovation that stimulates a demand for goods no less today than it did in the year 1635. What Créuse is saying, in effect, is that she has never seen anything like Médée's robe before and that she simply must have one like it.

The difference between the enterprising Médée and the complacent, haughty Créuse is crystallized by Créuse's offer of all her father's money for Médée's robe. Médée did not inherit this robe, but rather snatched it away from her father's house when she fled his wrath: "Des trésors dont son père épuise la Scythie, / C'est tout ce qu'elle a pris quand elle en est sortie" (577–78) [Of the Scythian treasures her father carried off, / This is all she took when she left]. Another facet of the robe's complex metaphorical value is thus its "illegitimacy." By contrast, Créuse appears to have full access to her father's wealth and few qualms about spending it all on whatever catches her eye: "My father's treasury is at her disposal, / Giving her the choice of the King's treasures."

For a seventeenth-century audience, the brilliant, treacherous robe with which Médée prepares her final victory over the lackluster Jason may well have had associations with the "noblesse de robe," the very class that occupied an intermediary position between the feudal aristocracy and the rising bourgeoisie. This is the class that considerable numbers of rich bourgeois buy their way into, the class that the old landed nobility have all the more scorn for in that the *noblesse de robe* are beginning to eclipse their own power quite seriously. Médée's robe is a single image that is the knotty meeting point of several strands of signification, a signifying node. It is clearly a figure for the enterprise of the bourgeoisie, and particularly of the merchant classes who procure pleasures and luxuries for the nobility. But it may also be interpreted as an emblem of the *noblesse de robe* toward which that very same bourgeoisie sets its sights as the reward for their efforts, the new nobility that will in fact never be fully accepted by the old. However well Médée dresses, she will always be a social outcast: "Sa robe, dont l'éclat sied mal à sa fortune / . . . n'est à son exil qu'une charge importune, / . . . une vaine parure, inutile à sa peine" (761–65) [The splendor of her dress, ill suited to her condition, / . . . is nothing but a bothersome burden to her exile, / . . . an empty adornment, unable to relieve her suffering]. These lines echo the scorn felt by a declining class of idle privilege toward a rising class defined by enterprise and productivity. What Jason is saying is that it is perfectly acceptable for a woman like Médée to dirty her hands by offering various and sundry forms of assistance, financial and otherwise, to those who feel themselves to be above her. But once she has helped them as much as she can, all that remains for them to do is to snub her. In other words, Médée's role is procuring rich clothes, not wearing them.

Good Help Is Hard to Find

Médée's status as helpmate to Jason and his complete inability to do anything for himself are apparent in the fairly frequent repetition of the words "aider" [help], "secourir" [assist], and "entreprendre" [undertake], associated mainly with Médée. Indeed, in her first words onstage, Médée uses the verb "aider" in such a way as to suggest that the idea of helping is part of her very name: "Souverains protecteurs des lois de l'hyménée . . . / Voyez de quel mépris vous traite son [Jason's] parjure / Et m'aidez à venger cette commune injure" (201–6) [Sovereign protectors of the laws of marriage . . . / See with what scorn Jason's betrayal treats you / And help me avenge this insult to you and to me]. In Médée's opening soliloquy, she names herself indirectly: "m'aidez" [help me], the second verb Médée utters in the play and a homophone of her name, might be taken as an instance of heroic self-naming as well as tragic reversal, since Médée, who has spent many years helping Jason, now must turn to the gods to ask for their assistance in exacting her revenge.

Since it is repeatedly made clear that Jason is helpless on his own, the worst thing Médée can ask the Furies so as to get back at her husband is that he not receive the help he needs, a fate that for Jason is worse than death:

> Quelque chose de pis [than death] pour mon perfide époux:
> Qu'il coure vagabond de province en province,
> Qu'il fasse lâchement la cour à chaque prince,
> Banni de tous côtés, sans bien et sans appui,
> Accablé de frayeur, de misère, d'ennui,
> Qu'à ses plus grands malheurs aucun ne compatisse. (220–25)

> Something worse [than death] for my perfidious husband:
> May he wander as a vagabond from province to province,
> May he court princes like a coward,
> Banished from all lands, without wealth or support,
> Burdened by fear, deprivation, torment,
> May his greatest misfortunes inspire no compassion.

This might seem like a mild curse coming from a woman with powers as extraordinary as Médée, but it shows how well she knows her husband. For Jason, being "without support" is a dire state, since he can do nothing for himself.

The wordplay "Médée"/"m'aidez" is all the more appropriate in that Médée sees the assistance she brings others as essential to her reputation. As she tells Créon, she has bailed out not only Jason, but also an entire class of heroes: "Je ne me repens point d'avoir par mon adresse / Sauvé le sang des Dieux et la fleur de la Grèce: . . . / Tous vos héros enfin tiennent de moi la vie" (437–41) [I have no regrets at having skillfully saved / The blood of the Gods and the flower of Greece: . . . / Why, all your heroes owe their lives to me]. Since Médée defines herself as the helper of others, she can ask for assistance only from the gods: "Mais pour exécuter tout ce que j'entreprends, / Quels Dieux me fourniront des secours assez grands?" (255–56) [But in order to carry out all I've undertaken, / What Gods will provide me with great enough help?]. When Aegée offers his assistance, she turns him down:

> Je veux une vengeance et plus haute et plus prompte;
> Ne l'entreprenez pas, votre offre me fait honte:
> Emprunter le secours d'aucun pouvoir humain,
> D'un reproche éternel diffamerait ma main.
> En est-il, après tout, aucun qui ne me cède?
> Qui force la nature a-t-il besoin qu'on l'aide? (1241–46)

> I want a greater and a swifter revenge;
> Do not undertake it, your offer shames me:
> Accepting the help of a human agent
> Would stain my hands with an eternal reproach.
> After all, is there anyone who does not give in to me?
> Does one who forces the hand of nature need assistance?

The word "entreprendre," along with the related noun and adjective "entrepreneur," has begun by the seventeenth century to take on an economic sense; two of the examples given by the dictionary of the Académie française fall into this category.[19] Although it is unlikely any of the words in this speech had primarily economic connotations for an audience of the 1630s, they undoubtedly created a network of associations: aside from "entreprenez," we find "offre," "secours," and "aide."

The association of Médée with a vocabulary of helping reaches its climax in the scene that portrays Médée's current oppressor, Créon, being burned by her robe. Créon, like his daughter, is burned by Médée's clothing, but unlike her he recognizes (symbolically) that his position of privilege has contributed to the destruction of himself and his progeny. Appropriately, although he is unable to fight Médée, who is not within his grasp, he lashes out at the nameless characters who stand in for her in this scene, his servants, or to be precise, his (un)dressers:

> Loin de me soulager, vous croissez mes tourments:
> Le poison à mon corps unit mes vêtements
> Et ma peau, qu'avec eux votre secours m'arrache,
> Pour suivre votre main de mes os se détache:
> Voyez comme mon sang en coule à gros ruisseaux.
> Ne me déchirez plus, officieux bourreaux:
> Votre pitié pour moi s'est assez hasardée;
> Fuyez, ou ma fureur vous prendra pour Médée.
> C'est avancer ma mort que de me secourir,
> Je ne veux que moi-même à m'aider à mourir. (1359–1368)

> Far from relieving me, you are increasing my torments:
> The poison is fusing my clothing to my body
> And my skin, which your help is causing to rip away,
> Is separating from my bones as your hands pull on my clothing:
> See how my blood streams forth from the wound.
> Stop tearing me apart, solicitous executioners:
> Your pity for me has done quite enough;
> Begone, or in my fury I will mistake you for Médée.
> Helping me is hastening my death,
> I want only myself to help me to die.

The word play that once again, as at the beginning of the play, associates the name "Médée" (1366) with the action "m'aider" (1368) is reinforced by the synonymous "me secourir" (1367).

Médée wins out in the end not only because in her struggle to get the better of her three enemies she is the only character left alive,[20] but also because the death of Créon, her most powerful adversary, coincides with the symbolic defeat of his privileged position. When, in his refusal of his servants' sartorial assistance, Créon disdainfully names Médée and the homonymic action of helping or serving that characterizes her power, his words are among the most ironic of the entire drama. By declaring his wish to rid himself of his servants and of Médée and to act alone, without assistance, he unintentionally gives voice to the very ethic of self-determination and enterprise that she represents. Even if the full irony of the king's action escaped Corneille's courtly public, in a less violent context they would have scoffed at the idea of a king undressing himself. Créon's subsequent suicide punctuates his ultimate inability to free himself from Médée's power: the only way he finds to escape her usual punishment of witnessing the death of his children is by abdicating his paternal role and denying his daughter's final wish to die in his arms (1411–14). If this is any kind of victory at all for Créon, like Médée's robe it is not worth the price.

4

Horace, or How to Kill
Friends and Influence People

In none of Pierre Corneille's tragedies does the sibling relationship play a more prominent role than in *Horace*, a tale of divided allegiances featuring a Roman brother and sister romantically paired off with an Alban sister and brother. The ferocious Roman hero Horace meets his match in his equally ferocious sister, Camille, while Horace's timorous Alban wife, Sabine, shares the stage with her mild-mannered brother, Curiace. The symmetry of the two sets of siblings is complemented by the parallel relations between the two sets of in-laws: the singleminded Camille and Horace run roughshod over the conflicted Sabine and Curiace. As we shall see, Camille's and Sabine's competition of misfortune in the drama's opening acts paves the way for Horace's and Curiace's fight to the death, a confrontation between a decorous, doomed older-brother figure and a driven younger-brother figure. But ultimately the fierce competitiveness that allows Horace to win the battle against his brother-in-law and friend is turned against him when Camille, as determined a contender as her brother, tricks him into killing her, thereby sullying the victory he has just won over Curiace.

Questions of birth order and seniority remain beneath the surface in *Horace*, but they are nonetheless essential to an understanding of the dynamics of the sibling relations portrayed. Corneille's principal source for the drama is the historian Livy's account of the war between Rome and Alba, averted when each side selected three champions to go head-to-head in a smaller battle intended to decide the outcome of the distressing conflict between these two traditional allies. Livy's narrative, the pertinent chapters of which Corneille had published as a prelude to his drama, tells the story of a battle between two sets of triplets, the Roman Horatii and the Alban Curiatii, who are said to be more or less of the same age and strength

(*History of Rome* 1:24). Corneille never says his combatants are triplets, nor does he give any direct information about the relative ages of Curiace and Horace, but I submit that Curiace, by virtue of his nationality, his social position, and his character, is the representative of an ethic depicted as prior to that of his Roman adversary, and that consequently Horace plays the kind of upstart, challenging role that is associated with the figure of a younger sibling.

Older and Wiser

Curiace's position of seniority is suggested first of all by his nationality: historically and dramatically, Alba is presented as prior to Rome. The fact that the two Alban protagonists appear onstage before their Roman counterparts[1] may be seen as a reenactment of the relation of priority between Alba and Rome which Livy makes clear, since Rome originated from the royal family of Alba (*History of Rome* 1:23). In her apostrophe to Rome in the first scene of the play, Sabine emphasizes this relation between the Alban mother and its Roman offspring:

> Ingrate, souviens-toi que du sang de ses [Albe's] rois
> Tu tiens ton nom, tes murs et tes premières lois.
> Albe est ton origine: arrête et considère
> Que tu portes le fer dans le sein de ta mère.
> Tourne ailleurs les efforts de tes bras triomphants;
> Sa joie éclatera dans l'heur de ses enfants;
> Et se laissant ravir à l'amour maternelle,
> Ses voeux seront pour toi, si tu n'es plus contre elle. (52–60)

> Ungrateful [Rome], remember that you owe your name, your
>   ramparts,
> And your earliest laws to the blood of Alba's kings.
> Alba is your origin: pause and reflect
> That you are about to plunge your sword into your mother's breast.
> Seek triumph through your exploits, but turn your arms elsewhere,
> And you will see her rejoice in her children's good fortune;
> And giving free rein to her maternal affection,
> She will be on your side if only you are not against her.

If Alba is Rome's metaphorical mother, Curiace, by virtue of his association
with this older civilization, is an older-brother figure for Horace.

Curiace's and Horace's relative social standing is another factor that
gives the Alban warrior an implicit seniority over his Roman counterpart.
One of the play's most important subtexts, and one that has generally been
overlooked, is the difference in status between Curiace and Horace. The list
of characters tells us that Curiace is a "gentilhomme d'Albe," while Horace's
father, le Vieil Horace, is a "chevalier romain." This indicates that the Curiatii are patricians, the highest group in the social hierarchy, while the
Horatii are knights, as is Valère, Camille's Roman admirer whose suit has
perhaps been passed over by her father in order that his daughter might
marry a man of higher birth. As the representative of a prior order, and of
the highest echelons of the aristocracy, Curiace evokes the scion of a family
belonging to the old feudal aristocracy, Horace a nobleman from a more
recent family for whom the establishment and consolidation of a newfound
prominence is crucial. Rome's need to affirm its autonomy by having its
finest fighter do violence to the civilization that it sees as its origin but that it
now does its best to supersede must have had a very clear resonance for a
seventeenth-century French audience.

Horace's and Curiace's positions within their respective families also
bespeak a considerable difference of power. However brash and arrogant
Horace may be, he is still subordinated to his father, whereas there is no
"Vieux Curiace" to complete the symmetry between the two families. If
Curiace's father is still alive, he is never mentioned in the play, so that
Curiace, unlike Horace, at all times speaks for himself. The fact that Curiace's father is not mentioned also reinforces the impression that Curiace
and Horace are not only brothers-in-law, but also brother figures, especially
since Horace's father seems as fond of Curiace as he is of his own son.

Curiace finds himself playing a most peculiar role: although he is not
related to Horace's father either by blood or by alliance — he is only engaged to Camille, not married to her — Curiace functions as the favorite
"son" of le Vieil Horace, a man who does not show any particular affection
for his own son until he is victorious and in the fifth act may well be
defending him mainly out of a sense of familial duty and paternal despera-
tion; he has no other children left (1706–8). Contrary to what some critics
have claimed, Horace is not portrayed as his father's psychological heir, that
is, as a son merely carrying on a patriarchal tradition;[2] le Vieil Horace is far
less a caricature of a stiff, unfeeling Roman soldier than is his son. In the first
three acts of the play, le Vieil Horace essentially sides with Sabine and

Curiace over the crucial issue of whether one should be allowed to cry in misfortune or to fear for one's enemies if they are also one's friends. In act 3, le Vieil Horace is nearly as tearful as his daughter-in-law, Sabine: "Loin de blâmer les pleurs que je vous vois répandre, / Je crois faire beaucoup de m'en pouvoir défendre" (951–52) [Far from blaming the tears I see you shed / It is all I can do to keep my own eyes dry].

Voltaire finds a moist-eyed paterfamilias outside the realm of *vraisemblance* (or perhaps *bienséance*) and goes as far as to claim that Horace's father is simply "pretending to be as weak as the women,"[3] but one wonders how he would explain the scene in which a tearful Vieil Horace bids his son-in-law-to-be (not his son) goodbye. Le Vieil Horace first addresses a generic, businesslike dismissal to Horace and Curiace together: "Allez, vos frères vous attendent; / Ne pensez qu'aux devoirs que vos pays demandent" (703–4) [Off with you now, your brothers await; / Think only of the duties your countries ask of you]. But as soon as the emotional Curiace scratches the surface of this formal farewell, le Vieil Horace allows himself a personal, heartfelt adieu to his daughter's fiancé, a man whose departure seems to upset him more than his own son's:[4]

CURIACE:
Quel adieu vous dirai-je? et par quels compliments . . .
LE VIEIL HORACE:
Ah! n'attendrissez point ici mes sentiments;
Pour vous encourager ma voix manque de termes;
Mon coeur ne forme point de pensers assez fermes;
Moi-même en cet adieu j'ai des larmes aux yeux. (705–9)

CURIACE:
How can I bid you farewell, and what words of respect . . .
LE VIEIL HORACE:
Oh, please don't try to soften me up;
My voice is bereft of words to urge you on;
My heart cannot find the resolve that it needs;
Saying goodbye has brought tears to my eyes, too.

If this is the father of the man who bid farewell to this same beloved family friend, Curiace, by saying "Albe vous a nommé, je ne vous connais plus" (502) [Alba has named you, you are no longer my friend], then it is clear

Horace has not simply inherited his ferocious, singleminded competitiveness from his father; that he has not "inherited" it, from his father or anyone
else, is precisely the point. Horace's role is not to live up to his father's
heritage, but rather to go beyond it.

Like Sister, Like Brother

A similar difference in seniority distinguishes the two female protagonists,
Sabine and Camille. Octave Nadal writes, "Camille's conflict implies the
same givens as Sabine's; all one has to do is to replace a woman's love for her
husband with a young girl's love for her fiancé."[5] Indeed, the relation between the two sisters-in-law establishes the pattern for the relation between
the two brothers-in-law, and the fact that Sabine's and Camille's characters
are developed at greater length makes the portrayal of the older- and the
younger-sister figures indispensable to an understanding of the relationship
between the two brother figures. Like their male counterparts, Sabine and
Camille are faced with a conflict of allegiances. Like the two men, their
quite distinct reactions to their dilemma reveal fundamental differences in
their characters. Sabine's reaction demonstrates that she is so traumatized
by the idea of contentiousness between friends that she cannot win whatever the outcome of the battle, while Camille's reaction is evidence of her
strength as a contender: whether Rome or Alba is victorious, she will not
allow herself to lose.

Sabine's refusal of the very terms of the conflict is expressed in the way
she views the outcome, which is clear in her address to Rome:

> Quand je vois de tes murs leur armée et la nôtre,
> Mes trois frères dans l'une, et mon mari dans l'autre,
> Puis-je former des voeux et sans impiété
> Importuner le Ciel pour ta félicité? (35–38)

> When I see their army and ours from your ramparts,
> My three brothers in one army, my husband in the other,
> What can I wish for? Is it right for me to disturb the Gods
> By asking them to favor your efforts?

> Je ne suis point pour Albe, et ne suis plus pour Rome;
> Je crains pour l'une et l'autre en ce dernier effort,
> Et serai du parti qu'affligera le sort. (88–90)

I will not side with Alba, and can no longer side with Rome;
I fear for both cities in this final confrontation,
And I will be on the side of whoever is destined to lose.

While rooting for the underdog can be an exhilarating position, refusing the joy of victory is tantamount to not accepting the terms of the battle.[6] Sabine's implication that the outcome is in the hands of fate ("le sort") is a way of distancing herself from the upsetting uncertainty of competition. In the face of an unprecedented contest between the older, established order to which she once belonged and the unsettling new ethic which she admires and does her best to adhere to, Sabine simply covers her eyes.

By contrast Camille translates the potential internal division that rips Sabine apart into terms that, far from undermining her own integrity, allow her to conserve a complete singlemindedness of purpose by projecting onto the Albans the irresolvable contradiction of the situation. Jacques Scherer characterizes the distinction between the two sisters-in-law in this way: "Sabine, a veritable cultural halfbreed, is in the uncomfortable position of being able to live only in ambiguity, the very position that Camille refuses."[7] The way Camille avoids being destroyed by the conflict at hand is that she displaces its contradictions onto Curiace, thereby putting him, not herself, in an impossible position. Rather than fretting over the question of which side to root for, Camille focuses her lament on the contradictory position of Curiace:

Soit que Rome y succombe ou qu'Albe ait le dessous,
Cher amant, n'attends plus d'être un jour mon époux;
Jamais, jamais ce nom ne sera pour un homme
Qui soit ou le vainqueur ou l'esclave de Rome. (229–32)

Whether Rome is forced to yield or Alba goes down to defeat,
Dear lover, you may no longer expect ever to become my husband;
That title will never, ever belong to a man
Who is either the conqueror of Rome or its slave.

Sabine views the conflict in terms of her own loyalty impossibly divided between two groups: does she favor her husband or her brothers, her birth family or her marriage family?[8] Camille dwells on the conflicting roles of another: as either the victor over her country or the citizen of a state it has subjugated, Curiace cannot expect to marry her.

If the psychological differences between the older- and the younger-

sister figures that we have observed also apply to Curiace and Horace, it is
largely because of the similarity between Sabine and Curiace on the one
hand, and between Camille and Horace on the other. Sabine and Curiace
are nearly identical in their distaste for competition and their inability to
muster any kind of enthusiasm even for a potential victory, as if the very fact
of having to fight with peers they have always thought of as confederates
overshadowed any imaginable benefit. A number of the lines pronounced
by one of the siblings could easily be spoken by the other. Sabine's declara-
tion, quoted above, that she cannot allow herself to wish for the victory of
either side is clearly echoed by Curiace's cry of despair: "Quels voeux puis-je
former, et quel bonheur attendre? / De tous les deux côtés j'ai des pleurs à
répandre; / De tous les deux côtés mes désirs sont trahis" (395–97) [What
wishes can I make, what happiness can I expect? / Whichever side wins I
will have tears to shed; / Whichever side wins my desires are betrayed].
Serge Doubrovsky summarizes this similarity of the two Alban siblings:
"Torn apart in the fiber of his being, . . . Curiace is presented from the start
as the *masculine analogue* of Sabine."[9]

The similarity of the Roman siblings is less obvious but no less compelling. Even if they have completely dissimilar allegiances—Horace wholeheartedly embraces the cause of patriotism while Camille espouses her love
for Curiace as her only motivating force—Camille and Horace closely resemble each other in their psychological makeup. What obscures their similarities is their complete disagreement over the issues at hand, but their
intransigent approach to those issues makes them similar: they are extre-
mists with no capacity for compromise. This paradox is not an uncommon
one within families: Camille and Horace suffer from a typical too-close-for-
comfort antagonism between two siblings who cannot abide their essential
similarity.[10]

For this reason my reading of the relation between the Roman siblings
differs considerably from that of David Clarke, who describes the final
confrontation between Camille and Horace in this way: "Nowhere else in
the play is the balance of argument given more effective and morally dis-
turbing scenic expression than here [in the scene leading up to the murder
of Camille], as the triumphant Roman ethos embodied in an armed and
exultant Horace is brutally contrasted with appalled humane values represented by the tearful and defiantly despairing figure of his sister."[11] I do not
see Camille's values as humane: Horace's cause is his brutal devotion to
Rome, and what she is fighting for is her savage, defiant love for Curiace,
but she is as fierce a combatant as her brother. Harriet Stone's recent inter-

pretation of the play corrects numerous misreadings that have portrayed the opposition between Horace and Camille as one between a brother's power and a sister's despair: "It is in the very double aspect of the final tribute, paid first to Horace and, in the same speech, to Camille, that the 'putting to rest' — the entombing or enclosing of her revolt within the frame of representation — achieves its full stature. I submit that of the two images that close the play — the brazenly Roman Horace and the frustrated revolutionary Camille — hers is the more remarkable."[12]

In the final analysis, the psychology of birth order is more central to a study of the two sets of in-laws in *Horace* than to the two pairs of blood siblings who are cut from the same cloth, the differences in their attitudes and positions largely a function of their gender differences. Indeed, birth-order effects are often stronger between siblings of the same sex, whereas an oldest son and an oldest daughter, for example, may each demonstrate certain qualities of an oldest sibling. That *Horace* stages a struggle between sibling figures as much as one between siblings makes it no less a masterpiece of insight into the sibling bond.

"Alba Has Named You, You Are No Longer My Friend"

The difference in Sabine's and Camille's perspective prepares us for a similar difference in the perspectives of their male counterparts. Curiace, the figure of the older brother, feels a genuine conflict between his allegiance to his heritage — his country, his family, in a word his *name* — and his affection for his friend and brother. Horace, the figure of the younger brother, has so much to gain by his competition with the older-brother figure that what he has to lose by it — his friendship with Curiace, which may in fact not be as warm and tender from Horace's side as it is from Curiace's — seems trivial by comparison. Curiace is so preoccupied with reconciling himself to the idea of fighting his brother that he ends up battling with himself more than with Horace. By contrast, Horace knows from the start that it is only through competition that he can hope to come out a winner.

This fundamental difference in perspective affects not only the attitudes of the combatants, but also the way they fight. One of the main reasons Horace wins is that Curiace and Horace play by different rules. Emerging victorious from the battle is not Curiace's highest priority. Curiace's division is the division of the oldest son: he remains attached to a certain respect for tradition that is the very basis of primogeniture, and that attachment keeps him from being the kind of all-out competitor that Horace is. Horace, on the other hand, not only wants to win the battle at all costs, he also uses the difference between his own singlemindedness and the divided perspective of his opponent, a difference he perceives only too well, to weaken Curiace by betraying the latter's feelings of affection for him.

Horace claims he wants Curiace to imitate him, to act like a Roman and recognize victory and glory as a single all-encompassing value, but the play allows of quite another interpretation: Horace purposely undermines his brother-in-law's confidence and sense of honor by refusing to fight the battle in a way that Curiace would term honorable. What defeats Curiace is not that he has to fight his brother, but rather that he is made to fight a brother who refuses to fight him as a brother. The drama of two brother figures forced by circumstance to fight each other might well lead to a story of shared heroism, the bilateral upholding of a code of honor making even the loser of the battle into a kind of winner who goes to his death nobly fighting a man he loves. But a very different story results when one of the combatants fights this kind of battle, while the other one finds a resolution to his internal conflict by breaking all ties with his adversary and fighting him as he would fight any other enemy.[13]

Horace wins an anonymous battle of pure competition by a psychological betrayal of his older-brother figure: by making him believe he is no longer his brother. It is certainly harder to fight a battle against someone you love than against someone you hate. But it is also more difficult to fight a battle against a friend you feel has betrayed your friendship — in this case by viewing the need to fight you to the death as simply a heroic opportunity to demonstrate his strength and self-mastery — than against a friend who feels the same kinds of reservations about fighting you as you feel about fighting him. It is the very anonymity of the conflict, the faceless competition it is turned into by Horace, that hurts and ultimately defeats Curiace.[14]

From a dramatic point of view it might appear that Horace is given a certain priority over Curiace by virtue of being chosen as the representative of his country before Curiace is chosen by his, but this is not the case.[15] If Horace is named by the Romans more quickly than Curiace is named by the Albans, even though the latter remain in their tents to confer while the Romans go back to the Senate (326–27), this is because as a younger-sibling figure Horace is from the very start a competitor. In fact the only way Horace is named first is as a competitor; as the younger sibling all that he "inherits" is a realization that in order to get anything at all he must compete.

Tragedy is often about the injustice of the universe, but it can also be about its inevitable trade-offs, the sobering fact that you cannot have it all. Horace gets something Curiace does not, victory, because of having something that Curiace does not have: a willingness to win at all costs that makes him unbeatable. But it might also be argued that Horace has an unbridled need to win precisely because of what Curiace has that he himself does not have and never will have: a sense of abiding value without extraordinary merit. Curiace may share many of Horace's (and Rome's) values; he may recoil from the idea, suggested by the impetuous Camille when she sees he has left the battle, that he might in any circumstance become a deserter, even as a result of what she believes is his absolute love for her (243–52). But one has the sense that he will still be a Curiace and an Alban even if he does not win the fight:

> Ce triste et fier honneur m'émeut sans m'ébranler:
> J'aime ce qu'il me donne, et je plains ce qu'il m'ôte;
> Et si Rome demande une vertu plus haute,
> Je rends grâces aux Dieux de n'être pas Romain,
> Pour conserver encor quelque chose d'humain. (478–82)

> This sad, proud honor touches me but leaves me unshaken:
> I value what it offers me, and I regret what it takes away from me;
> And if Rome demands a higher virtue than that,
> I thank the heavens that I am not a Roman,
> So that I may still preserve a shred of my humanity.

In his recognition that fighting for his country but against his brother is a mixed blessing rather than a simple source of glory, Curiace may appear lackluster and indecisive by comparison to the firebrand who is his opponent: Robert Brasillach quips that unlike Horace, Curiace has not enlisted but rather has been drafted.[16] But this speech also illustrates Curiace's maturity and lucidity; he is clearly a man whose wisdom and self-knowledge go beyond Horace's.[17] And while that in itself may be quite obvious, the underlying reason for it is not: it is impossible to come to know oneself at the same time as one is intent on proving oneself,[18] for if one is proving oneself one can allow oneself to recognize only what one is trying to prove oneself to be.

Curiace goes to his death a martyr to his self-knowledge. He competes with his younger-brother figure, but he refuses to make competition and victory his single value, as the description of his death, recounted by Valère to le Vieil Horace, suggests:

> Horace, les [the three Curiace brothers] voyant l'un de l'autre écartés,
> Se retourne, et déjà les croit demi domptés.
> Il attend le premier, et c'était votre gendre.
> L'autre, tout indigné qu'il ait osé l'attendre,
> En vain en l'attaquant fait paraître un grand coeur;
> Le sang qu'il a perdu ralentit sa vigueur. (1113–18)

> Horace, seeing that the three Curiace brothers have become separated,
> Turns around, and already thinks the battle is half-won.
> He awaits the first one, your son-in-law.
> The other, quite indignant that he has dared to lie in wait for him,
> Vainly shows great courage in his attack;
> But the blood he has lost saps his energy.

Is the only thing holding Curiace back in this final battle the loss of blood, as Valère assumes, or is the outcome of the battle not a foregone conclusion resulting from the beliefs of both adversaries expressed earlier in the play? "Qui veut mourir ou vaincre est vaincu rarement" (385) [A person who would rather die than be defeated is rarely defeated], says Horace, and indeed he is not defeated, while Curiace proleptically states: "Je vous connais encore, et c'est ce qui me tue" (503) [You are still my friend, and that is what kills me]. The younger-brother figure has such a strong need to prove himself that he would rather die than lose; the older-brother figure has such a strong revulsion at the idea of forgetting that his contender is his best friend that he would rather die than win. There, in a nutshell, is the conflict between Horace and Curiace.[19]

Camille and the Name of Curiace

In typical tragic fashion, the same quality that leads to Horace's greatest victory, his exaggerated need to prove himself, also brings him down. It is precisely because Horace does not understand his fundamental insecurity — in spite of his bravado, in spite of his victory, and in spite of his rhetoric — that his sister is able to defeat him.

If the play's four protagonists can be classified according to their intolerance for ambiguity and contradiction, there is no doubt that Horace is at the top of the heap — which turns out to be the bottom when the heap is upended by his sister. As we have seen, Camille's advantage over Sabine is that the Roman woman projects the contradictions of the situation onto Curiace, while Sabine internalizes them. Analogously, Curiace allows the conflict to become his own, that is, he internalizes it, while Horace does not; but Horace goes even further than his sister in his attempt to erase any sense of divided allegiances. Horace's potential conflict, which is not so much resolved as it is sublimated by his heroism,[20] cannot be rendered completely harmless until Curiace himself, the object of the battle, is transformed into a pure enemy: "Alba has named you, you are no longer my friend" (502). Horace thus takes Camille's projection of contradictions onto the Alban one step further, which is perhaps necessary for winning the battle but turns out to be one step too far from the point of view of reintegration into the world of nonheroism after the victory. Camille has it easier than Horace: the man she makes into the locus of her paradox, Curiace, is simply eliminated after she has evacuated onto him her own inner divisions. All that Horace has eliminated by his victory is his "pure" enemy; the inner contradictions remain, his claims notwithstanding.[21] Camille understands this and uses it to defeat her brother.

Camille does to Horace what Horace did to Curiace; she "outsiblings" him by making him feel betrayed by her attitude and position, which are as artificial as his own, for she no more simply despises Rome than her brother simply embodies it:

Rome, l'unique objet de mon ressentiment!
Rome, à qui vient ton bras d'immoler mon amant!
Rome qui t'a vu naître, et que ton coeur adore!
Rome enfin que je hais parce qu'elle t'honore! (1301–4)

Rome, sole object of my loathing!
Rome, in whose name you have just sacrificed my lover!
Rome, which saw your birth, and which your heart adores!
And yes, Rome, which I despise because it honors you!

In the play's most famous tirade, Camille lauches a vicious attack on Rome, proleptically countering its nascent expansionist ambitions with a vision of its destruction, also starting from the center and moving outward.[22] But her monophobic hatred of Rome cannot be taken seriously. After claiming Rome as the sole object of her loathing, she explains that she detests her country because it honors Horace; we must then conclude she also hates Horace. Camille may indeed hate Rome — although given her Roman temperament this is debatable — but if there is a "sole object" of her hatred, it is certainly not Rome, but Horace. Camille is merely presenting Horace with a mirror image of his own artificially univalent vision, according to which Rome is his only object of devotion. Harriet Stone writes of Camille and Horace, "Negating the singularity of perfection with which he identifies (Rome as universal), she refuses the sufficiency of his one act."[23] To this I would reply that Camille does not negate her brother's singular vision but replicates it, like a photographic negative, in reverse.

Just as Horace destroys Curiace psychologically by finding his point of greatest vulnerability, Camille has no difficulty zoning in on the fraternal jugular: Horace's jealousy of Curiace. Numerous exegetes have taken Horace's complete identification with Rome at face value, but the play gives us reason to believe that even this consummate Roman is jealous of his brother-in-law. As we have seen, le Vieil Horace expresses the kind of affection for Curiace that he likely never allows his own son to see, and Horace might well feel slighted when his father chooses an Alban aristocrat as Camille's fiancé rather than Valère, a Roman knight like Horace himself. Camille uses Horace's unrecognized jealousy to bring her brother down.[24]

If Horace ushers in an era of unprecedented competition by saying to his brother "Alba has named you, you are no longer my friend," Camille gains victory over her brother by reestablishing the name of Curiace suppressed by Horace's battle strategy. In the climactic confrontation between brother and sister (4:5), the siblings' first wary responses dance around the name Curiace; it is as if the name, like "Hippolyte" in Racine's *Phèdre*, had been expressly forbidden:[25]

HORACE:
Vois ces marques d'honneur, ces témoins de ma gloire,
Et rends ce que tu dois à l'heur de ma victoire.
CAMILLE:
Recevez donc mes pleurs, c'est ce que je lui dois.
HORACE:
Rome n'en veut point voir après de tels exploits. (1255–58)

HORACE:
Observe these marks of honor, these witnesses to my glory,
Do your duty, show the proper feelings at my victory's good fortune.
CAMILLE:
If I must, here are my tears, that is what I owe to it [or to him].
HORACE:
Rome is not interested in tears after such great acts.

The antecedent of "lui" is taken by Horace to be "l'heur de ma victoire" [my victory's good fortune], while Camille is thinking of Curiace, but she does not actually say the name until some lines later.

CAMILLE:
Mais qui me vengera de celle [the death] d'un amant,
Pour me faire oublier sa perte en un moment?
HORACE:
Que dis-tu, malheureuse?
CAMILLE:
                O mon cher Curiace!
HORACE:
O d'une indigne soeur insupportable audace! (1265–68)

CAMILLE:
But who will avenge me for my lover's death,
Who will make me forget his loss in a single moment?
HORACE:
What are you saying, wretched woman?
CAMILLE:
                Oh, my dear Curiace!
HORACE:
I will not stand for that kind of audacity from my worthless sister!

Camille's audacity consists, in part, of saying the name "Curiace," which up to now Horace himself has said only once in the entire play, in his first onstage line to his sister—"Avez-vous su l'état qu'on fait de Curiace, / Ma soeur?" (515–16) [Have you heard of the honor that has been paid Curiace, / Sister?] — as if Curiace's name existed for Horace only in relation to his sister and his jealous feelings toward her.[26]

Once Camille has pronounced the name "Curiace," the real battle begins. She points out to Horace that his barbarous action has deactivated her previous relation to him: "Ne cherche plus ta soeur où tu l'avais laissée; / Tu ne revois en moi qu'une amante offensée" (1283–84) [You'll not find your sister waiting in the place where you left her; / When you look at me, you see nothing but a wronged lover]. Is this not Camille's way of turning the tables on Horace by saying, "You have killed Curiace, you are no longer my brother?"

Just as Horace's first onstage line to his sister ends with the word "Curiace," his last line to her before he stabs her to death with his sword also ends with the word "Curiace," which is consequently the last word Horace says to his sister before executing her, as if Camille's crime were that she has perpetrated upon Horace this renewed recognition of who Curiace is:

CAMILLE:
Puissé-je de mes yeux y [on Rome] voir tomber ce foudre,
Voir ses maisons en cendre, et tes lauriers en poudre,
Voir le dernier Romain à son dernier soupir,
Moi seule en être cause et mourir de plaisir!
HORACE:
C'est trop, ma patience à la raison fait place;
Va dedans les enfers plaindre ton Curiace! (1315–20)

CAMILLE:
If only I could see lightning strike Rome with my very eyes,
See its houses reduced to ashes, your victory wreaths to dust,
See the last surviving Roman drawing his last breath,
If only I alone could bring that about, I would die from the pleasure!
HORACE:
You've gone too far: I've been patient long enough. Now reason takes over.
Go snivel over Curiace in hell!

At the beginning of this scene Camille responds to Horace's complete identification with Rome by expressing her allegiance to Curiace's memory. At this, the climactic moment, Horace ironically follows his sister's example: he responds to her complete disidentification with Rome by expressing his hatred and jealousy of Curiace, the very personal and private motivations that have underlain his public stance from the beginning. Horace kills his sister not as a Roman, but as a jealous brother who erroneously believed that his victory over a much-loved brother figure would win him instantaneous, permanent, and universal esteem, even from those who once preferred his brother to him.

What spoils it all for Horace is that Camille does to him what he did to Curiace, just as artificially but no less effectively: she claims to be opposing him in an anonymous battle that treats him not as kin but as a faceless, nameless adversary. She, of course, knows that this Armageddon between siblings is anything but anonymous. But if her brother ever puzzles that out, it is not until he has been outmaneuvered and humiliated into killing his most formidable adversary of all. And when Camille's bloodied corpse is pitifully laid out in full view of her father and her sole surviving brother at the beginning of act 5, even to Horace's bellicose eyes it must less resemble a dangerous threat to Rome's future than a young, unarmed woman who happened to be his sister, a sister who, just before she died, got him to say the name of the brother she will always love.

5

The End of an Era, or
The Death of Pomp(ey)

It is particularly appropriate that *La Mort de Pompée* was written and produced when it was, during the period that saw the death of Louis XIII in
1643 closely following Richelieu's demise the previous year: what has often
been overlooked by critics focusing on the drama's Roman theme is that
this play is actually about a royal succession, that of the Egyptian throne.
More than any of Pierre Corneille's earlier plays—with the possible exception of *Cinna*—*La Mort de Pompée* is about the transition between two
political eras;[1] Michel Prigent is quite right to call it a "dynastic tragedy."[2]

In fact, while the play has been linked by a number of scholars to the
death of Richelieu,[3] it marks not only the tumultuous end of a historical
epoch,[4] but also a turning point in Corneille's treatment of familial relations. If Corneille's early tragedies, *Médée*, *Le Cid*, *Cinna*, and *Polyeucte*—
Horace is a notable exception—generally focus on the power of parental
figures, *La Mort de Pompée*, the last tragedy he wrote during the reign of
Louis XIII, is about the death of the father and the squabbling that follows
when the deceased leaves behind no clear-cut inheritance, moral or material. While most of Corneille's tragedies up to this point deal with the
question of an ethical heritage, none addresses the transmission of power
between the generations as explicitly as *La Mort de Pompée*.

Pompée himself, who never appears onstage, is much more than Julius
Caesar's adversary in a power struggle culminating in the disastrous battle
of Pharsalus which precipitates the action of the drama. Corneille makes
him into a representative of a dying ethic of familial honor and continuity
that is increasingly undermined by a new political reality. The death of
Pompée does not signal the breakdown of his own family continuity; his
final words to his wife, Cornélie, ask her to avenge his death (472–76), and
once his assassins have all died, she vows to avenge his defeat at Pharsalus as
well (1701–16). What Pompée's death marks is rather a much broader

failure: the undermining of an entire system by which values are passed on from one generation to the next.

The action of the play is quite simple: all the components of the plot are unified by their relation to Pompée's death, which takes place very early in the drama. *La Mort de Pompée* opens with the decision by the Egyptian king, Ptolomée, to follow his counselors' advice and curry César's favor by putting to death Pompée, who is seeking refuge in Egypt after his defeat at Pharsalus. Although César benefits politically from Pompée's death, when he learns of it he claims that if his archrival had not been assassinated he would have forgiven him and re-allied himself with him. In addition to this feigning of a *générosité* reminiscent of Auguste in *Cinna*, César hypocritically blames Ptolomée and his advisors for Pompée's death and goes after his deceased rival's assassins. The climax of the play comes with the death of Ptolomée and the crowning of his elder sister, Cléopâtre, the latter event made to coincide with the proper funeral rites accorded to Pompée.

This is one of Corneille's most brilliant and thought-provoking plots, one that makes the play into a kind of *Waiting for Godot* in reverse: we stop waiting for Pompée to arrive early in the drama, but his presence continues to be missed so sharply that his absence becomes the tragedy's moving force. The invisible Pompée, like Godot, comes to represent something much greater than an individual character, his death resonating with all the solemnity of the passing of an era. David Clarke writes: "Corneille risks an extraordinary dramatic effect: the hero of his play never appears on stage. All we are permitted to witness are the sordid calculations of those who betray Pompée, and the equivocal reactions of others to his ignominious death. His physical absence and looming moral presence dominates the play's illustration of the irreparable consequences of Ptolomée's betrayal of the one man who embodied an indisputable moral integrity."[5]

The two major events to which the tragedy's concatenation of events ultimately leads, Pompée's funeral carried out with "la pompe d'un beau jour" (1808) [the pomp of a fine day] — the pun "Pompée" / "pompe" has been commented on by at least one critic[6] — and the crowning of Cléopâtre, implicitly link Pompée's death to the crucial problem of the transmission of power. César's final speech makes the relation between the two ceremonies explicit:

Cependant, qu'à l'envi ma suite et votre cour
Préparent pour demain la pompe d'un beau jour,
Où dans un digne emploi l'une et l'autre occupée

Couronne Cléopâtre et m'apaise Pompée,
Élève à l'une un trône, à l'autre des autels,
Et jure à tous les deux des respects immortels. (1807–12)

In the meantime, let those in my entourage vie with those in your
    court
In preparing the pomp of a fine day for tomorrow,
Solemn ceremonies that your people and mine will carry out
To crown Cléopâtre and to lay Pompée to rest,
To raise up a throne for one, and funeral altars for the other,
And to pledge eternal respect for both of them.

Cléopâtre is crowned at the same time Pompée is "appeased" ("apaise"); it is as if the crowning of the right successor to the late king were as necessary to the repose of Pompée's soul as his funeral, the throne and the ritual altar the two sites of a single ceremony. Even though Pompée is not himself a king, his funeral, which properly restores him to a position of respect, is concomitant with the transmission of power to an older sibling.

The Will of the Father

If Pompée's ignoble demise is a figure for the undermining of the values he represents, the most important of those values is intergenerational continuity. *La Mort de Pompée* differs from its main source, Lucan's *Pharsalia*, in that Pompée is the executor of the Egyptian king's will, which protects the rights of the older sibling, Cléopâtre, by dictating that her younger brother, the reigning king who has refused to grant her any power, should share the throne with her. Not only is Pompée the archenemy of the powerful Roman emperor, but his role as holder of the elder Ptolemy's will poses an additional threat to the younger Ptolemy: this is a case when a Roman bearing a will is as dangerous as a Greek bearing a gift. Just as Pompée was instrumental in placing the elder Ptolemy back on the throne after the king had been deposed by a popular revolt (289–303), Pompée is now charged with assuring that the late king's political legacy is respected. The elder Ptolemy's will, which at the beginning of the play is presumed to be in Pompée's possession, names Cléopâtre as heir to the throne on an equal footing with her brother in recognition for the role she played in recapturing the throne for her late father (313–20).

The dangerous connection between Pompée's arrival and the carrying out of the late king's wishes does not escape the notice of the youthful usurper, as he admits in speaking to one of his advisors:

> Photin, ou je me trompe ou ma soeur est déçue:
> De l'abord de Pompée elle espère autre issue.
> Sachant que de mon père il a le testament,
> Elle ne doute point de son couronnement. (213–16)

> Photin, unless I am mistaken, my sister will be disappointed:
> She expects a different outcome from Pompée's arrival [i.e., not his death].
> She knows he has my father's will,
> And she has no doubt that she will be crowned queen.

The paternal legacy, which in Corneille's early tragedy had a straightforward spiritual value, now becomes problematized at the same time as it becomes politicized. If the main action of *La Mort de Pompée* is the reinstatement of Cléopâtre as her father's heir, the transmission of Cléopâtre's inheritance is difficult to separate from the power struggle going on between César and Pompée, as well as from the conflicting political positions voiced by Ptolomée's advisors and the two siblings themselves.

In this light, Ptolomée's decision to do away with Pompée is far more complex than has generally been assumed.[7] It is not only that Ptolomée hopes Pompée's death will put him on good terms with the powerful César, but also that he does not trust Pompée who, were he allowed to land in Egypt, would instruct him to respect his father's final request and share power with his sister. Photin, the principal advisor of Ptolomée who favors Pompée's death, recognizes this threatening aspect of Pompée:

> Seigneur, c'est un motif que je ne disais pas,
> Qui devait de Pompée avancer le trépas.
> Sans doute il jugerait de la soeur et du frère
> Suivant le testament du feu Roi votre père. (223–26)

> Sire, this is another reason, one I hadn't mentioned,
> To hasten the decision to do away with Pompée.
> Surely he would follow the will of your late father, the King,
> In judging the rights of the sister and the brother.

Cléopâtre's defense of Pompée and her indignation at the idea of his being put to death may be interpreted in a similar vein, as her brother states: "Confessez-le, ma soeur, vous sauriez vous en taire, / N'était le testament du feu Roi notre Père: / Vous savez qu'il le garde" (281–83) [Sister, admit it, you would say nothing about Pompée's death / If it were not for the will of our Father, the King: / You know he is in possession of it].

Thus one of the most important motivating factors in the drama of allegiances and betrayals surrounding the death of Pompée is the Roman general's role as an enforcer of intergenerational continuity. It is true that the elder Ptolomée's will is not carried out exactly as stated, since Corneille's dénouement has the death of Pompée lead to the death of the younger Ptolomée, leaving Cléopâtre on the throne alone.[8] Nevertheless, because of Pompée's heroic death, the spirit of Ptolomée's will is indeed executed, and the play ends with the victory of the elder sibling over the younger.[9]

Age Before Beauty

The relation between the siblings in Corneille's play is modified a great deal from the historical sources. In Lucan's *Pharsalia*, Cleopatra and Ptolemy are about to fight a war over the crown when Pompey arrives in Alexandria; Corneille tones down this dispute, probably to streamline the plot. Historically the siblings were destined to be married, as the 1660 "Examen" mentions, but presumably *bienséance* ruled that element of the story out. In Corneille's drama, then, Ptolomée and Cléopâtre are neither about to kill nor to marry each other, but this does not mean the sibling relation is underplayed in this work. *La Mort de Pompée* is the first drama we have encountered in which two siblings confront each other directly over the question of the inheritance of power. Moreover the siblings' gender difference is not highly developed. The theme of César's love for Cléopâtre is not prominently featured, as is Antony's love for Cleopatra in Shakespeare's drama.[10] In Corneille's play Cléopâtre's beauty is reduced to a political asset that gives her a potential power which her brother lacks, a point made clear by Corneille in his 1660 "Examen": "Cléopâtre's personality is recognizable [from the historical sources], [but] is made nobler by the development of the more illustrious characteristics it might have had. I have made Cléopâtre a lover by ambition and ambition alone; she apparently falls in love only insofar as love can be put to the service of her greatness" (*Oeuvres complètes*, 316). The gender difference between Cléopâtre and Ptolomée is merely a useful distraction that allows Corneille to explore the extremely sensitive issue of the power struggle of two royal siblings, one elder, one younger, over who is to inherit the kingdom.

If we accept this greater importance of the siblings' age difference over their gender difference, *La Mort de Pompée* can be read as the drama of a conservative older sibling whose claim to power, based on her father's intentions, is undermined by a younger sibling who embodies a new ethic whereby the younger generation feels free of the constraints of its elders.[11] In the context of an emerging political order, the Egyptian queen, presented as a traditionalist disapproving of her freewheeling younger brother, must have reminded the audience of the old feudal aristocracy looking down on the upstarts whose increasing power it alternately views with distress and condescension.

From her first appearance onstage, Cléopâtre is a stickler for the rules:

CLÉOPÂTRE:
Seigneur, Pompée arrive, et vous êtes ici!
PTOLOMÉE:
J'attends dans mon palais ce guerrier magnanime,
Et lui viens d'envoyer Achillas et Septime.
CLÉOPÂTRE:
Quoi? Septime à Pompée, à Pompée Achillas! (236–39)

CLÉOPÂTRE:
Sire, Pompée is arriving! What are you doing here?
PTOLOMÉE:
I am awaiting that noble warrior in my palace,
And I have just sent Achillas and Septime to meet him.
CLÉOPÂTRE:
What? Septime to meet Pompée, Pompée met by Achillas?

Cléopâtre has very clear notions of what is and is not done. When she discovers that her brother has not gone to meet Pompée's ship, her first concern is, precisely, with the pomp of Pompée's arrival. In her first two lines she manages to say Pompée's name three times, as if she herself were grandly announcing his arrival to make up for her brother's paltry reception of him. Cléopâtre states that some things never change, that Ptolomée owes allegiance and respect to Pompée — "Si vous en portez un [crown], ne vous

en souvenez / Que pour baiser la main de qui vous le tenez" (243–44) [If
you are wearing a crown, remember that only / To kiss the hand you got it
from] — even if the latter has suffered a recent defeat: "Fût-il dans son
malheur de tous abandonné, / Il est toujours Pompée, et vous a couronné"
(247–48) [Were he to be abandoned by everyone in his misfortune, / He is
still Pompée, and he gave you your crown].

Cléopâtre's pridefulness in contrast to her brother's lowly demeanor is
apparent throughout the drama. She claims Ptolomée has treated her like a
slave — "Vous m'avez plus traitée en esclave qu'en soeur" (328) [You have
treated me more like a slave than a sister] — but that particular family dynamic actually seems to go in the opposite direction. Cléopâtre scorns the
lowly birth of her brother's advisors to their faces. She lumps together
Photin, the king's chief advisor and a character often associated with Richelieu, with others "of his kind": "Je ne le vois que trop, Photin et ses pareils /
Vous ont empoisonné de leurs lâches conseils. / Ces âmes que le ciel ne
forma que de boue . . ." (263–65) [I see it only too well, Photin and his
kind / Have poisoned you with their cowardly advice. / These souls that
the heavens fashioned from pure mud . . .]. The phrase "Have poisoned
you" may well have had a particular resonance for those who thought Louis
had been mysteriously poisoned by Richelieu before his own death. Cléopâtre goes so far as to say she herself has feared that Photin and his cohorts
might try to poison her (330–31).

Cléopâtre returns repeatedly to this theme of the baseness of the king's
cabinet. A believer in socioethical determinism, she views those of low birth
as unsuited to hold power, those of high birth "always" endowed with high
virtue and debased only by associating with underlings:

> Les princes ont cela de leur haute naissance:
> Leur âme dans leur rang prend des impressions
> Qui dessous leur vertu rangent leurs passions.
> Leur générosité soumet tout à leur gloire,
> Tout est illustre en eux quand ils daignent se croire,
> Et si le peuple y voit quelques dérèglements,
> C'est quand l'avis d'autrui corrompt leurs sentiments. (370–76)

> What high-born nobles receive from birth
> Is that their souls draw upon their rank to form impressions
> That subordinate their passions to their virtue.
> Their nobility places their glory above all else,

When they keep their own counsel, they are illustrious indeed,
And if the common people see them leading misguided existences,
It is only because their noble sentiments have been debased by others.

Is there not a glimmer of the past glory of earlier Corneille heroes and
heroines in this vision that subordinates all things to concerns for one's
name and reputation? From the heights of her glorious name, Cléopâtre
continues to look down her royal nose at all those around her (1193–1200,
1347–48) until the very end of the drama. When asked by her brother to
help protect Pompée's murderers from César's punishment, she agrees to
try to help, but out of pure disdain, refusing to sully her hands with the task
of exacting revenge from the likes of them: "Si j'avais en mes mains leur vie
et leur trépas, / Je les méprise assez pour ne m'en venger pas" (1227–28) [If
the question of their survival were in my hands, / They are so far beneath
me that I would not seek revenge].

Another way Cléopâtre is associated with a conservative ethic is that
her superciliousness is accompanied by a sense of decorum and propriety
that tempers her ambitions. Cléopâtre has two possible paths to power, one
a well-charted path of legitimacy — her reinstatement as queen according to
her father's will — the other a more or less unlimited path of opportunism —
her possible marriage to César. That she chooses the former indicates that
she is portrayed as ambitious, but not at any cost. Cléopâtre dreams of
marrying César (428–30) but refuses to seek power in a way that might
compromise her (431–38). Indeed, she is the first to point out to César the
main obstacle to their possible marriage, Rome's mistrust of kings and
queens (1293–1302).

Whatever Cléopâtre's ambitions might be, one thing is clear: in the
battle between César and Pompée, she sides with Pompée when it would
have been advantageous to side with César. Cléopâtre's choice of Pompée is
as central to the play's subject matter as her brother's rejection of him, the
tug-of-war over the Roman general suggesting that the most important
conflict of the play is not the dispute between Ptolomée and César but
rather the polarization of the two siblings.

King for a Day

When Cléopâtre confides that she wishes she could be the queen of the
world for a single day, Corneille may be putting into the sister's mouth

words that are more applicable to the brother: "Achevons cet hymen [with César], s'il se peut achever, / Ne durât-il qu'un jour, ma gloire est sans seconde / D'être au moins un jour la maîtresse du monde" (428–30) [Let us carry out this marriage to César, if that is possible, / Even were it to last a single day, my glory would be without comparison / For being the mistress of the world, at least for a day]. While Cléopâtre has not married César and become queen of the world by the end of the play, at least her assumption of the Egyptian throne is a stable state of affairs. By contrast, Ptolomée's attempts to occupy the throne never seem more than an embarrassingly flawed dress rehearsal for a production destined to be cancelled before opening night.

If Cléopâtre is associated with an ethic of conservatism and decorum, her younger brother is ready to try anything to further his ambitions. Although Corneille admits he has made the Egyptian boy-king somewhat older than his historical sources suggested so that a courtly audience would believe him capable of ruling, Ptolomée is still presented as a bumbling, ineffectual younger brother.[12] The characterization of the two siblings makes it impossible to forget that Ptolomée is younger than Cléopâtre.

Ptolomée is a naïve, easily manipulable ruler and a fearful one to boot. In his first meeting with César he is described as being so terrified that Cléopâtre's squire, Achorée, is embarrassed for him:

Dès le premier abord notre prince étonné
Ne s'est plus souvenu de son front couronné.
Sa frayeur a paru sous sa fausse allégresse,
Toutes ses actions ont senti la bassesse.
J'en ai rougi moi-même, et me suis plaint à moi
De voir là Ptolomée, et n'y voir point de Roi. (747–52)

As soon as he saw César, our thunderstruck prince
Forgot he was wearing a crown.
His fear showed through his façade of joy,
All his actions betrayed his lowliness.
It made me blush, and I silently fumed
That my eyes could see Ptolomée, but could not see a king.

After one excruciating meeting between the Egyptian king and César (3:2), Ptolomée — like the trembling Sabine in *Horace* escaping from her formidable sister-in-law[13] — flees at the emperor's sight (1237–40).

Of equal importance in Corneille's portrayal of the young king is his attitude toward the past and the present, which is diametrically opposed to Cléopâtre's. This is apparent from the very first confrontation of the royal siblings (1:2). Cléopâtre points out her brother's obligations to the past, that is, what he owes Pompée because of the latter's assistance to their late father. Ptolomée counters by making a distinction between the generations that would make Rodrigue's blood run cold in *Le Cid*—and, more to the point, would have a similar effect on Don Diègue:

CLÉOPÂTRE:
Fût-il dans son malheur de tous abandonné,
Il est toujours Pompée, et vous a couronné.
PTOLOMÉE:
Il n'en est plus que l'ombre et couronna mon père,
Dont l'ombre et non pas moi, lui doit ce qu'il espère.
Il peut aller, s'il veut, dessus son monument
Recevoir ses devoirs et son remercîment. (247–52)

CLÉOPÂTRE:
Were he to be abandoned by everyone in his misfortune,
He is still Pompée, and he gave you your crown.
PTOLOMÉE:
He is no longer more than a shadow of himself, and if he crowned my
    father,
My father's shade, not I, owes him repayment.
If he wishes, he can go to my father's tomb
To receive the gratitude that is owed him.

Ptolomée's position is a shocking reversal of the ethic of intergenerational continuity embodied by a character like Rodrigue, for example.[14] The single phrase, "My father's shade, not I," marks a break between father and son, thereby going against a whole set of assumptions about the obligation of the younger generation to represent the older. In Ptolomée's mind there is no continuity between the generations or within a single individual's lifespan: Pompée is but a shadow of his former self.

While this last concept is not new to Corneille's theater—Don Diègue and Horace, for example, both lament how difficult it is for heroic individuals to remain at the pinnacle of their glory[15]—in Ptolomée's discourse it is no longer presented as a heroic source of anguish but rather as a natural, matter-of-fact state of affairs:

CLÉOPÂTRE:
Après un tel bienfait, c'est ainsi qu'on le traite!
PTOLOMÉE:
Je m'en souviens, ma soeur, et je vois sa défaite.
CLÉOPÂTRE:
Vous la voyez de vrai, mais d'un oeil de mépris.
PTOLOMÉE:
Le temps de chaque chose ordonne et fait le prix. (253–56)

CLÉOPÂTRE:
After all he did for you, this is how you treat him!
PTOLOMÉE:
Sister, I remember what he did, but now I see he has been defeated.
CLÉOPÂTRE:
You have good vision, but your eyes are full of scorn.
PTOLOMÉE:
Time rules all things and establishes their value.

Ptolomée's last statement quoted above sums up Corneille's characterization of the Egyptian youth. Nothing is stable in his ethical universe; everything is open to negotiation. His father's debts are not his own, and his father's moral creditors, including Pompée, can simply leave their threatening demands for payment on the elder Ptolemy's grave. While Cléopâtre exercises the older sibling's prerogative of looking down on those of more lowly birth, Ptolomée has scorn ("mépris") for Pompée's latest defeat, which he finds more important in establishing his current attitude toward Pompée than the Roman's earlier "bienfait," which Ptolomée sees as ancient history. "Time rules all things and establishes their value": this statement of moral relativism sounds strangely close to a capitalistic article of faith alluding to the power of markets and the fluctuations of prices according to the whims of supply and demand. Serge Doubrovsky explains the debased position occupied by Ptolomée and his advisors in this way: "'Machiavellianism' originates in the degradation of the aristocratic project, when it is taken up by *plebeian* minds. For the Slave . . . any road to success is considered acceptable."[16]

Ptolomée is not portrayed as a monstrous ruler along the lines of Néron in Racine's *Britannicus*; rather, he is what one might call a majoritarian, a ruler who plays not by the book but by the numbers. When he is trying to determine whether to grant asylum to Pompée, his decision is based not on conviction, but rather on mathematics:

N'examinons donc plus la justice des causes,
Et cédons au torrent qui roule toutes choses.
Je passe au plus de voix, et de mon sentiment
Je veux bien avoir part à ce grand changement. (189–92)

Let us no longer examine what is right,
We must yield to the current that drives all things.
I go with the majority, and with enthusiasm
I am eager to be a part of this great change.

Two of Ptolomée's advisors are in favor of putting Pompée to death, one is opposed; he goes with the flow. Quite the opposite of his sister, Ptolomée has no real opinions.

Ptolomée's death is in keeping with his laissez-faire attitude toward life, which becomes easily "overloaded" because it rejects nothing on principle. Ptolomée, fleeing what he fears will be César's wrath, jumps into a boat that is simply too full:

Il voit quelques fuyards sauter dans une barque,
Il s'y jette et les siens, qui suivent leur monarque,
D'un si grand nombre en foule accablent ce vaisseau
Que la mer l'engloutit avec tout son fardeau. (1653–56)

He sees several men getting away in a boat,
He jumps in, and so many of his own men,
Following their king, weigh down the vessel
That the sea swallows it up, along with its cargo.

The physical overflow of bodies in the getaway boat leads to a humiliating, anonymous death by drowning worthy of Odysseus' obscure companions.[17] If Ptolomée listens to too many people during his brief reign, his death is a reenactment of his political life: he is literally sunk by his weighty entourage.

Talking Heads

La Mort de Pompée, unlike dramas such as *Le Cid* and *Cinna*, has no "head," no single *chef* or point of reference: in their opposition to César, Pompée and Ptolomée are each called "chef" (15, 1434), and while César has the greatest political power of any character in the play, his political positions are not much clearer than Ptolomée's. Like Auguste in *Cinna*, César alludes to a generous, post-civil war world in which family feuds would be neutralized by a new political order. But this idealized order, in which "mes plus dangereux et plus grands adversaires, / Sitôt qu'ils sont vaincus, ne sont plus que mes frères" (917–18) [My most dangerous and formidable opponents / Become my brothers as soon as they are defeated], is unconvincing, not least because fraternity is a doubtful figure of noncombativeness. César later confesses that his most cherished hope is to found a bloodline of new little Césars with Cléopâtre (1317–26), a goal that is not consistent with a postfamilial order. César also worships Cléopâtre but opines that the humblest Roman lady is worthier than the Egyptian queen (1069–70). All in all, he does not stand for the same sort of coherent value-system that Auguste comes to represent by the end of *Cinna*. As Michel Prigent states: "There is no longer a hero, but rather heroes: affairs of State have exploded a single value-system into several characters. The entire attempt at conversion that takes place in *Cinna* goes for nought."[18]

   This dispersion of perspectives, a kind of figurative decapitation of the unified value-system supposedly put in place by the end of *Cinna*, becomes literalized in *La Mort de Pompée* by the decapitation of the play's titular hero. Pompée is in fact the real "chef" of the play: the two terms most closely associated with him are "tête" and "testament."[19] Pompée's head is cut off after he is put to death, and if Corneille is following his historical sources in this, his almost fetishistic treatment of Pompée's head, which Louis Marin underscores in his extremely perceptive analysis of the play,[20] is his own: Pompée's severed head is so extensively referred to and described that one might be tempted to rename the play "La Tête de Pompée." Even Pompée himself speaks of his own head; in the only direct speech of his reported in the entire play, as he leaves his ship to go face his death at the hands of the Egyptians, Pompée tells his wife that his head must be sacrificed in order to spare anyone else who might be tempted to help him: " 'N'exposons,' lui dit-il, que cette seule tête / A la réception que l'Egypte m'apprête" (469–70) ["Let this head be the only one," he tells her, / "Exposed to the reception that Egypt is preparing for me"]. The head of Pompée, once it is truncated, becomes both a figure for the undermining of the old system of inheritance embodied by this bearer of a king's will and a figure for the residual admiration for that system that is one of the strongest components of the atmosphere of nostalgia and regret created by the play's conclusion.

The image of Pompée's severed head draws much of its power from the way it harkens back to Don Diègue's metaphor of family relations in *Le Cid*. In that play, Rodrigue's father, speaking to the king after the death of Chimène's father, defends his son in this way:

> Si montrer du courage et du ressentiment,
> Si venger un soufflet mérite un châtiment,
> Sur moi seul doit tomber l'éclat de la tempête:
> Quand le bras a failli, l'on en punit la tête.
> Qu'on nomme crime ou non ce qui fait nos débats,
> Sire, j'en suis la tête, il n'en est que le bras. (*Le Cid*, 719–24)

> If showing that one has heart and spirit,
> If avenging an insult deserves punishment,
> The storm should break over me and me alone:
> When the arm has acted wrongly it is the head that is punished.
> Whether or not you call this matter a crime,
> Sire, I am the head of it, he is nothing but the arm.

Just as the question of inheritance remains largely figurative in *Le Cid*, whereas it becomes literal in *La Mort de Pompée*, the father-figure's head — which in *Le Cid* is a metaphor for his vital connection to and control over his heir ("bras") — becomes literalized in the later play, but without losing its metaphorical value. If Pompée is the legal representative of the feuding siblings' late father, his severed head is a powerful figure for his ultimate inability to enforce the paternal will directly — it is not Pompée himself who will bring Cléopâtre to power, but rather César's elimination of Ptolomée. The true power of the image of Pompée's head is that we are made to perceive its nobility at the same time as it is an emblem of Pompée's downfall at the hands of the mediocre forces of the present. A sign of defeat, it is also, paradoxically, a locus of admiration, the last refuge of honor and of a certain kind of grandeur in a debased world.

After Pompée's death, the trunk of his body is thrown into the sea, but his head takes an extraordinarily long time to lose its vital force; Louis Marin observes that once the ritual murder of Pompée has taken place, "the tragic 'head,' the dead man's head continues, by the very power of its image, to spur on and trouble the main characters' various confrontations leading up to Ptolomée's death."[21] As he knowingly faces his death in the skiff sent by Ptolomée to meet his ship, Pompée is stoic and self-possessed; his heart lets out no complaint, and his face remains unexpressive:

> D'un des pans de sa robe il couvre son visage,
> A son mauvais destin en aveugle obéit,
> Et dédaigne de voir le ciel qui le trahit,
> De peur que d'un coup d'oeil contre une telle offense
> Il ne semble implorer son aide ou sa vengeance. (514–18)

> He covers his face with a fold of his robe,
> Blindly obeying his cruel fate,
> And will not stoop to look at the traitorous heavens,
> Lest his glance seem to be asking for help or revenge
> For the offense committed against him.

But once Pompée is dead, his severed head takes on a life of its own:

> Sur les bords de l'esquif sa tête enfin penchée,
> Par le traître Septime indignement tranchée,
> Passe au bout d'une lance en la main d'Achillas,
> Ainsi qu'un grand trophée après de grands combats. (529–32)

> And his head, drooping over the edge of the skiff,
> Is ignobly cut off by the traitor Septime,
> And skewered onto a spear in Achillas' hands,
> Like some great trophy after a great battle.

Pompée's severed head has a gruesome, uncanny power. As Ptolomée's advisor, Achillas, carries it through the streets of Alexandria at the end of a spear, the people of the city turn their own heads away, as if Pompée's head had some mystical power to stare down theirs: "Cependant Achillas porte au Roi sa conquête [Pompée's head], /Tout le peuple tremblant en détourne la tête" (549–50) [Meanwhile Achillas carries his conquest (Pompée's head) to the King, / The terrified population all turn their heads away from Pompée's]. When César arrives and Cléopâtre sends her confidante, Charmion, to find out how he reacted to being presented with Pompée's

head, "ce beau présent" (731), she discovers that the head continues to produce surprising and unexpected effects: "La tête de Pompée a produit des
effets / Dont ils [Pompée's assassins] n'ont pas sujet d'être fort satisfaits"
(735–36) [Pompée's head produced effects / That his assassins would be
foolish to welcome].

The culmination of the macabre role of Pompée's truncated head comes
when César discovers that his rival has been put to death. César's reaction is,
as one might expect, complex, the relief of being rid of one of his most
serious contenders for power—"L'aise de voir la terre à son pouvoir sou-
mise" (777) [The pleasure of seeing the whole world subordinated to his
power]—mixing with the horror of seeing him betrayed and degraded
rather than fairly and nobly defeated: "S'il aime la grandeur, il hait la per-
fidie" (781) [If he values greatness, he despises betrayal]. But whatever
feelings César might be hiding inside of himself, his reaction at seeing
Pompée's decapitated head is nothing as compared to the reaction of the
head at seeing him:

> A ces mots [the announcement of Pompée's death] Achillas découvre
>   cette tête:
> Il semble qu'à parler encore elle s'apprête,
> Qu'à ce nouvel affront un reste de chaleur
> En sanglots mal formés exhale sa douleur,
> Sa bouche encore ouverte et sa vue égarée
> Rappellent sa grande âme à peine séparée,
> Et son courroux mourant fait un dernier effort
> Pour reprocher aux Dieux sa défaite et sa mort. (761–68)

> Once Pompée's death has been announced, Achillas uncovers the
>   head:
> It is as if, at this fresh insult, the head were ready
> To speak again, as if a vestige of life
> Were breathing out its grief in ragged sobs,
> The mouth, still agape, the eyes, bewildered,
> Call back the great soul, barely severed from the body,
> And the head's dying wrath musters a last reproach
> To the Gods for this defeat and this death.

Whereas the living, breathing Pompée avoided reproaching the gods for his
impending death, after his murder his head gains a strange, poignant ex-

pressiveness. By a series of synecdoches, attributes of Pompée himself—
grief, bewilderment, wrath, and defeat—are displaced onto his decapitated
head. The referent of the long series of possessive pronouns ("sa douleur,"
"sa grande âme," "son courroux," etc.), halfway between the English "his"
(if the referent is "Pompée") and "its" (if the referent is "la tête de Pompée"), is unwontedly ambiguous for a Classical text.[22]

Like his severed head, Pompée's headless trunk excites more interest
than do the surviving characters of the drama. When the old Roman, Cordus, happens upon Philippe, one of Pompée's freed slaves, who has re-
covered his master's trunk from the sea and is about to carry out hasty
funeral rites, Cordus recognizes the headless corpse of Pompée rather than
Pompée's living servant:

> Et n'y voyant qu'un tronc dont la tête est coupée,
> A cette triste marque il [Cordus] reconnaît Pompée.
> Soudain la larme à l'oeil: "O toi, qui que tu sois,
> A qui le ciel permet de si dignes emplois [the funeral rite],
> Ton sort est bien, dit-il, autre que tu ne penses;
> Tu crains des châtiments, reçois des récompenses." (1501–6)

> And seeing nothing but a headless trunk,
> At this sad mark Cordus recognizes Pompée.
> Suddenly, with tears in his eyes, he says, "Whoever you are
> Whom heaven allows to carry out such a worthy act [the funeral rite],
> Your fate is nothing like what you believe;
> You fear punishment for your actions, but you will be rewarded."

Pompée, "a headless trunk," is identifiable; Philippe, "Whoever you are," is
not.[23] Obviously this contrast makes sense on a purely rational level—
Cordus knows Pompée's trunk has been cast into the sea, and why would he
recognize one of Pompée's attendants?—but Corneille seems to be going
out of his way to stress this opposition and to suggest to us that its significance goes beyond the immediate context. Even if Cordus does not recognize the salvager of Pompée's trunk, there is a certain irony in the fact that
he considers heroic the man's action of rescuing the illustrious corpse from
the waters of oblivion in which Ptolomée will subsequently meet an unheroic death.

Unlike the decaying trunks lying on the battlefield of Pharsalus described in the play's opening scene, Pompée's trunk is ultimately avenged,

reunited with his head and reduced to ashes, as custom requires (1678–90). The horrifying description of those unburied corpses opens the play:

> Le destin se déclare, et nous venons d'entendre
> Ce qu'il a résolu du beau-père [Pompée] et du gendre [César],
> Quand les Dieux étonnés semblaient se partager,
> Pharsale a décidé ce qu'ils n'osaient juger.
> Ses fleuves teints de sang, et rendus plus rapides
> Par le débordement de tant de parricides,
> Cet horrible débris d'aigles, d'armes, de chars,
> Sur ses champs empestés confusément épars,
> Ces montagnes de morts privés d'honneurs suprêmes,
> Que la nature force à se venger eux-mêmes
> Et dont les tronc pourris exhalent dans les vents
> De quoi faire la guerre au reste des vivants,
> Sont les titres affreux dont le droit de l'épée,
> Justifiant César, a condamné Pompée. (1–14)

> Fate has spoken, and has just informed us
> Whether it favors the father-in-law [Pompée] or the son-in-law
>   [César],
> While the bewildered Gods seemed to hesitate,
> Pharsalus decided what the Gods could not judge.
> Its rivers stained with blood, and quickened by the flow
> Of so many men murdered by their kin,
> The broken remains of weapons, chariots, eagles,
> Lying horribly scattered over its putrid fields,
> The mountains of corpses, deprived of the last rites,
> Forced by nature to take their own revenge
> By wafting the stench of their rotting trunks
> On the winds that assault the survivors' nostrils,
> Are the dreadful reasons the mighty sword gives
> To justify César and condemn Pompée.

Paul Valéry gives this passage as an example of Corneille's verse that would seem shocking even in Shakespeare;[24] this is as unclassically gory a description as the famous *récit de Théramène* detailing Hippolyte's grisly death in *Phèdre*. Quite aside from the irony whereby Corneille might be said to mark the death of the founder of the Académie française by opening his next play with a *malséant* description of putrid, rotting corpses, these lines are crucial to an understanding of the impact of the burning of Pompée's head and trunk at the end of the drama.

La Mort de Pompée opens with an image of patricide: not only the internecine violence of a bloody civil war, but the decay of an entire system of inherited debts and benefits. If it ends with the funeral of a figure of the past betrayed by the forces of the present, that funeral can be read as a tribute to a dying ethic as much as to a fallen individual. At the beginning of the play, the heaped-up, abandoned cadavers of Pompée's troops are forced to take their own revenge via the smell of their rotting flesh which they fan into the nostrils of the survivors. And at the end of the drama, when the ashes of Pompée's head and trunk are reunited with all due ceremony, we might believe we are witnessing a return to the rituals of intergenerational continuity, in the same way that Cléopâtre's accession to the throne appears to carry out her father's will. But in neither case is the return complete. As we have seen, the circumstances in which Cléopâtre assumes power can hardly be said to be a direct execution of the older Ptolemy's wishes. As for Pompée, his funeral is conducted not by his family, but by his enemy.

Nevertheless, Pompée's remains are treated honorably by an enemy who mourns his passing. It would be easy to call César's final actions hypocritical, even easier than it would be to concur with Napoleon's characterization of Auguste's generosity at the end of *Cinna* as hypocritical. And yet the dignity and power of the defunct Pompée are such even in death that his funeral should not be seen as an utterly empty ceremony.[25] Can one not imagine César shedding a tear as he contemplates the ashes of his enemy, a silenced figure of the passing of an era?

PART III

BETWEEN THE
GENERATIONS

6

A Sibling Rivalry over
Sibling Rivalry

Pierre Corneille's *Rodogune* and
Thomas Corneille's *Persée et Démétrius*

Rodogune (1644), written when Pierre Corneille was thirty-eight years old, and Thomas Corneille's *Persée et Démétrius* (1662), written at the age of thirty-seven, are the two plays in which the brothers, each in his turn, deal most directly with the question of sibling rivalry. In Pierre's play, although the relative ages of the twin brothers, Séleucus and Antiochus, are never definitively established, it is Antiochus, whom I believe to be the younger brother, who gets the throne. Nevertheless, as we shall see, *Rodogune* ultimately glorifies the rigid, dispossessed Séleucus as the noble, doomed resister of the degrading compromises of the present to which Antiochus has no apparent difficulty adapting. Thomas Corneille's tragedy, by contrast, portrays the older sibling and heir, Persée, as a weakling and Démétrius, his younger brother, as far worthier to inherit the throne. Thus, Pierre Corneille destabilizes the law of primogeniture—his play stages the younger brother's fantasy of being named as heir—only to reaffirm the greater worth of the man who is apparently passed over because of his inflexibility. Thomas Corneille, on the other hand, wholeheartedly sides with his younger-brother hero, thus mounting a full-scale attack on primogeniture.

Séleucus: The Older Brother Who Would Not Be King

The action of *Rodogune* is set off by the question of which brother is, in fact, the elder, but Pierre Corneille focuses our attention on the issue of birth order without ever resolving it.[1] In his 1660 "Examen," Corneille admits that the brothers' birth order is never established because of the unreliability of their mother, Cléopâtre: "Séleucus' death spared me the trouble of developing the secret of the two brothers' birth order [droit d'aînesse], which at any rate would not have been believable, since it could be revealed only by somebody [Cléopâtre] in whom not enough sincerity has been seen to lend any assurance to her testimony" (*Oeuvres complètes*, 418).[2] This apparent undecidability of the twins' birth order is not the end of the story, but rather the beginning.[3] In the same "Examen" Corneille also makes it clear that Séleucus is the older of the two brothers according to his principal source for the play, Appian of Alexandria.[4] And there are several elements of the drama that support the theory that in Corneille's mind, Séleucus remains the older son whose birthright is withdrawn and bestowed upon Antiochus as a reward for the latter's compliance. While the *coup de théâtre* whereby Cléopâtre first tells Antiochus that he is the elder—"Rendez grâces aux Dieux qui vous ont fait l'aîné" (1357) [Thank the Gods who have made you the elder] — only to change her mind two scenes later does technically leave the issue unresolved, the order of the revelations suggests that she first suppresses the truth and then reveals it to Séleucus to punish him for his rebellious nature:

CLÉOPÂTRE:
Le trône était à toi [Séleucus] par le droit de naissance,
Rodogune avec lui tombait en ta puissance,
Tu devais l'épouser, tu devais être roi!
Mais comme ce secret n'est connu que de moi,
Je puis, comme je veux, tourner le droit d'aînesse,
Et donne à ton rival ton sceptre et ta maîtresse.
SÉLEUCUS:
A mon frère?
CLÉOPÂTRE:
                    C'est lui que j'ai nommé l'aîné. (1419–25)

CLÉOPÂTRE:
The throne was yours according to your birthright,
And along with it Rodogune would have been in your possession,
You were to marry her, you were to be king!
But since that secret is mine and mine alone,
I can do as I wish with the elder's birthright,
So I'm handing over your crown and your mistress to your rival.

SÉLEUCUS:
To my brother?
CLÉOPÂTRE:
    He is the one I have named the elder.

Since the matter of the brothers' birth order is not brought up again, we are left with the impression that the truth was revealed the second time around. Moreover, in Séleucus' relation to his brother, he is portrayed as dominant. Although Antiochus appears onstage first (1:2) and states that if he were named the elder he would gladly yield the throne so long as he could marry Rodogune, Séleucus takes the initiative in the brothers' first scene together (1:3) by making the very same offer before Antiochus has a chance to. When Antiochus confesses that Rodogune is all he cares about as well, the following exchange between the brothers ensues:

SÉLEUCUS: Quoi? l'estimez-vous tant?
ANTIOCHUS: Quoi? l'estimez-vous moins?
SÉLEUCUS: Elle vaut bien un trône, il faut que je le die.
ANTIOCHUS: Elle vaut à mes yeux tout ce qu'en a l'Asie.
SÉLEUCUS: Vous l'aimez donc, mon frère?
ANTIOCHUS: Et vous l'aimez aussi.
    C'est là tout mon malheur, c'est là tout mon souci. (134–38)

SÉLEUCUS: What? I she that important to you?
ANTIOCHUS: What? Is she less important to you?
SÉLEUCUS: She is worth a throne, I must confess.
ANTIOCHUS: She is worth all of Asia, to my eyes.
SÉLEUCUS: You love her then, brother?
ANTIOCHUS: And you love her too.
    That is my whole misfortune, that is my whole concern.

The repetitions within this short exchange, which are clearly meant to emphasize the resemblance between the two brothers by the triple use of anaphora, have Séleucus speaking first and Antiochus echoing him three times; even when Antiochus breaks out of the pattern in his last response, it as if he had internalized his role as his brother's echo, for he assumes both parts and echoes himself. How typical of a younger brother's frustrating dilemma; whatever he thinks of, his brother seems to have come up with the idea first, as Antiochus goes on to say: "Et dans ce juste choix vous m'avez prévenu" (142) [And in this wise choice you have beaten me to it].[5]

Séleucus not only dominates his brother, he also idealizes the fraternal relation, a pose typical of oldest sibling-heirs, whose natural advantage often allows them to view their younger counterparts with magnanimity. While Antiochus' position is that each brother should go after the throne, and that whoever gets it should be allowed to marry Rodogune — "Souhaitons-le tous deux, afin de l'y placer" (166) [Let us both wish for the throne, so that we can place her upon it] — Séleucus anticipates the potentially disastrous outcome of the sort of rivalry Antiochus espouses. Drawing upon the ancient examples of Oedipus' warring sons in Thebes who kill each other for power and the Trojan War fought for the love of Helen — "Thèbes périt pour l'un, Troie a brûlé pour l'autre" (179) [Thebes perished for one, Troy burned for the other] — Séleucus speaks of the necessity of repressing envy and jealousy:

> Malgré l'éclat du trône et l'amour d'une femme,
> Faisons si bien régner l'amitié sur notre âme,
> Qu'étouffant dans leur perte un regret suborneur,
> Dans le bonheur d'un frère on trouve son bonheur.
> . . . .
> Ainsi notre amitié, triomphante à son tour,
> Vaincra la jalousie en cédant à l'amour. (191–98)

> In spite of the throne's attraction and our love for the same woman,
> May our friendship so govern our souls
> That we stifle any dangerous regret at losing them,
> And find entire happiness in our brother's.
> . . . .
> In this way our friendship, triumphant in turn,
> Will conquer jealousy and yield to love.

This is an extraordinary speech, a rare example of a character not only revealing an idealistic position he is about to assume, but also recognizing the base emotions — regret, jealousy — to be kept in check by that pious stance. Séleucus' idealized fraternal alliance openly uses repression and artifice: the fury of losing out to one's brother is "stifled" by an appearance of happiness at his good fortune.

Antiochus' devastating, understated response to Séleucus' dream of fraternal solidarity is a powerful example of a sibling's doubts as to the possibility of ever going beyond fraternal competitiveness: "Le pourrez-vous, mon frère?" (201) [Can you really do that, brother?]. The best Antiochus can do is to express his doubts tactfully, by demanding that Séleucus' "nobles sentiments" (205) be shored up by an oath, "le secours des serments" (206). When the infinitely desirable Helen chooses a husband, her many suitors swear an oath to uphold her choice by attacking anyone who refuses to respect her marriage; this is, of course, the entire premise of the Trojan War. But the Achaians swear only to refrain from killing Helen's mate, not to pretend to be happy for him. The fraternal oath between Séleucus and Antiochus demands that the brothers not even recognize envy. No wonder Antiochus feels a need to call upon the gods' assistance.

The Heir as Yes-Man

Given the fact that Séleucus dominates his brother, we might wonder why he does not simply win out. But this is no longer a world in which inheritance is a straightforward question of entitlement. Rodrigue must uphold his position as his father's heir, but he does not fight for it; rather, he must be worthy of it.[6] Inheritance becomes a very different notion when it is confused with the need to be pleasing, to satisfy the older generation: Shakespeare's *King Lear*, a story about a favorite — in this case youngest — daughter who balks at her father's request that she praise him to win her inheritance, is about this very phenomenon. The idea of making the status of heir contingent on fulfilling certain conditions is a startling development that goes to the heart of the changing nature of society and the court in mid-seventeenth-century France. In *Rodogune*, rather than a predetermined formula for the transmission of the family heritage, what is still called primogeniture ("droit d'aînesse") has become subject to the whims of individuals. As Michel Prigent writes, "Primogeniture is no longer inscribed in nature, but rather will simply reward Rodogune's killer."[7] Cléopâtre does not mince words: "Embrasser ma querelle est le seul droit d'aînesse: / La mort de Rodogune en nommera l'aîné" (644–45) [The elder's birthright means taking up my fight, / The death of Rodogune will name the elder son]; "Point d'aîné, point de roi, qu'en m'apportant sa tête" (672) [No elder son, no king, unless I am brought her head]. Nor, in his appeal to Rodogune, does Antiochus: "Notre seul droit d'aînesse est de plaire à vos yeux" (914)

[The only elder's birthright is for us to please you]. Indeed, the greatest asset of Antiochus has nothing to do with strength or entitlement; he is simply more pleasing to his mother than Séleucus.

As astonishing as this may appear, the most serious challenge upon Séleucus' idealization of his brother comes not from his desire for Rodogune or for the throne, but rather from his impatience at his brother's refusal to treat their mother as a usurper. Séleucus cannot tolerate his brother's inability to judge or criticize Cléopâtre: "Ah! que vous me gênez / Par cette retenue où vous vous obstinez!" (1053–54) [Oh! how you upset me / With your stubborn restraint!]; "Lorsque l'obéissance a tant d'impiété, / La révolte devient une nécessité" (1061–62) [When obedience is so wrong, / Revolt becomes a necessity].

In addition to their diverging attitudes towards sibling rivalry, what distinguishes Séleucus from Antiochus is not their overall worth — Corneille stresses the equal merit of the two brothers[8] — but rather their attitude toward their mother. The main impediment to Séleucus' being "named" as the older twin is that he refuses to satisfy Cléopâtre — and, ultimately, Rodogune. When the princess shows herself to be a worthy rival of her future mother-in-law by explaining to the brothers that she will marry the one who kills Cléopâtre, Séleucus has no more patience for her demands than he does for his mother's (1083–86). Perhaps the murder of Cléopâtre to avenge the death of the twins' father, Nicanor, would be just in itself, for not only would Cléopâtre be punished for killing her husband, but also the brothers would no longer need to abide by her conditions for becoming the heir. "Cléopâtre's successor would not be a king, but a slave";[9] killing Cléopâtre would simultaneously mean not having to please her and gaining access to the throne by avenging the death of the late king. But murdering Cléopâtre to satisfy Rodogune is quite another story; her conditions are no less degrading to Séleucus than his mother's. Thus Séleucus refuses to "earn" the throne by giving in to his mother's ultimatum, but he also refuses to kill her, the murderer of his father, because he sees that action as being contaminated by a lover's motivation.

By contrast, Antiochus completely idealizes his mother, from his first appearance onstage to his last. We first see Antiochus' excessive reverence for Cléopâtre when her inventory of all she has done for the brothers culminates in an allusion to the murder of their father, for which she strongly implies she was responsible (575–80). Antiochus's reaction is not one of shock and moral indignation, as one might expect, but one of gratitude and filial discretion:

Le récit nous en charme, et nous fait mieux comprendre
Quelles grâces tous deux nous vous en devons rendre;
Mais afin qu'à jamais nous les puissions bénir,
Epargnez le dernier [the murder of Nicanor] à notre souvenir.
Ce sont fatalités dont l'âme embarrassée
A plus qu'elle ne veut se voit souvent forcée.
Sur les noires couleurs d'un si triste tableau
Il faut passer l'éponge ou tirer le rideau.
Un fils est criminel quand il les examine,
Et quelque suite enfin que le ciel y destine,
J'en rejette l'idée, et crois qu'en ces malheurs
Le silence ou l'oubli nous sied mieux que les pleurs. (587–98)

All your efforts on our behalf, it makes quite a tale,
And shows us all we have to thank you for;
But spare us the knowledge of your final action [the murder of
    Nicanor]
So that we can forever bless the others.
There are often these things that souls in trouble
Are forced to do against their wishes.
Let's wipe the slate clean, let's pull the curtains
Over the somber hues of that gloomy picture.
A son is a criminal if he looks at them too closely,
And however the heavens make things turn out,
I will not do such a thing. I find in these hard times
It is better to be silent and forget than to lament.

Antiochus' reaction is not merely one of acceptance of the maternal crime, but one of censorship of its clear knowledge. He quickly excuses his mother's actions by saying that her hand was surely forced by fate ("fatalités"), but most of his speech concerns not the crime itself, but covering it up. He wants to "wipe the slate clean," to "pull the curtains." Silence and forgetfulness are his tools of choice in dealing with his father's murder, not remembrance and revenge.

It is not so much Antiochus' actions as his reactions that are shocking: faced with the dilemma of having to side with one parent against the other, Antiochus might well decide not to take up arms against Cléopâtre, but he will not even examine his mother's conduct. His failure to avenge his father is systematically presented not as a well-thought-out decision, but rather as an abdication: "Je tâche à cet objet [Cléopâtre's crime] d'être aveugle ou stupide, / J'ose me déguiser jusqu'à son parricide" (719–20) [I am trying to be blind, unaware of her crime, / I even dare to put her husband's murder out of mind]. Antiochus' inability to rebel against his mother extends to her ultimatum concerning Rodogune. In response to Séleucus' stunned condemnation of Cléopâtre when she demands the death of Rodogune in exchange for the honor of being named the heir to the throne — "O femme, que je n'ose appeler encor mère!" (680) [Woman I can no longer call my mother!] — Antiochus remains the obedient, respectful son: "Gardons plus de respect aux droits de la nature, / Et n'imputons qu'au sort notre triste aventure" (687–88) [We must have more respect for nature's rights, / Fate alone is to blame for these sad events]. The only strategy Antiochus can conceive of mustering against his mother is activating her love, that is, arousing her pity: "Elle est mère, et le sang a beaucoup de pouvoir, / Et le sort l'eût-il faite encor plus inhumaine, / Une larme d'un fils peut amollir sa haine" (726–28) [She is a mother, and blood is powerful, / And even if fate had made her more inhuman, / A son's tears can melt her hatred].

Indeed, Antiochus' attachment to his malignant mother is so exaggerated that it nearly reaches the comic proportions of a caricature. After the news of Séleucus' murder interrupts the wedding of Antiochus and Rodogune and the report of his dying words suggests the murderer is Cléopâtre or Rodogune, Antiochus staunchly defends his mother against his bride's accusations. This is, in fact, what ultimately saves his life. While Cléopâtre savagely downs the poisoned wine intended for Antiochus in a desperate ploy to get him to follow suit, he spends so much time trying to smooth things over that the poison starts to work on her before he has had a chance to drink it. The sight of his mother bathed in sweat, her throat swollen and her eyes glazed, convinces Antiochus of his mother's murderous intentions, and still he won't give up: "N'importe, elle est ma mère, il faut la secourir" (1810) [I don't care, she's my mother, I have to help her]. To Cléopâtre's dying curse, he responds, "Ah! vivez pour changer cette haine en amour!" (1825) [Please live, and change your hatred into love!].

How can we explain Antiochus' stubborn need for love from an untrustworthy, tyrannical mother? Is it not that he has learned how to gain power indirectly by endearing himself to others who wield power themselves?[10] Gordon D. MacGregor bluntly characterizes the opposition between the two brothers: "Antiochus's perpetual servitude is the sole alternative to his brother's gloriously doomed revolt."[11] This is a strategy typical of those who for various reasons have no direct access to power.

This aspect of Antiochus' character is clearly revealed in the scene in which Cléopâtre names him the elder son (4:3). The queen goes from accusing Antiochus of being a rebellious son by virtue of his love for Rodogune (1331) to naming him the heir to the throne and Rodogune's future husband: "C'en est fait, je me rends, et ma colère expire" (1355) [That does it, I give up; I am no longer angry]. What makes Cléopâtre "surrender" is not any kind of counterattack inspired by her unreasonable demands, for Antiochus makes none, but rather his tugging at her maternal heartstrings:

> Madame, commandez, je suis prêt d'obéir:
> Je percerai ce coeur qui vous ose trahir,
> Heureux si par ma mort je puis vous satisfaire,
> Et noyer dans mon sang toute votre colère!
> Mais si la dureté de votre aversion
> Nomme encor notre amour une rébellion,
> Du moins souvenez-vous qu'elle n'a pris pour armes
> Que de faibles soupirs et d'impuissantes larmes. (1341–48)

> Madam, I await your orders, I shall obey:
> I'll stab this heart that has dared to betray you,
> I'd die happy if only that were enough for you,
> If I could drown all your anger in the shedding of my blood!
> But if you are so unyielding in your hatred
> That you still call our love a rebellion,
> At least remember this: its only weapons
> Were meek sighs and powerless tears.

In effect, Antiochus' unswerving allegiance to his mother takes the place of his fulfilling of the conditions she has set forth: even if he cannot bring himself to kill Rodogune for her, he makes her believe that he does not love her any the less for asking him to do so.

Antiochus' expression of devotion is apparently sufficient, as Cléopâtre indulges in a rare outpouring of affection that she herself may later proclaim (and believe) is feigned, but that nothing prevents us from taking seriously:

> Ah! que n'a-t-elle [your rebellion] pris et la flamme et le fer!
> Que bien plus aisément j'en saurais triompher!
> Vos larmes dans mon coeur ont trop d'intelligence,
> Elles ont presque éteint cette ardeur de vengeance,
> Je ne puis refuser des soupirs à vos pleurs,
> Je sens que je suis mère auprès de vos douleurs. (1349–54)

Oh, if only your rebellion had been armed with flames and swords!
How easy it would be to cut it short!
Your tears see all too well into my heart,
They have nearly doused my passion for revenge,
I can but sigh in the face of your tears,
My motherhood revives when I see your grief.

It is true that Cléopâtre later claims that her seeming reconciliation with Antiochus is false — as soon as he has turned his back she apostrophizes him as gullible — "crédule" (1392) — but it may be that Cléopâtre is a character who fools herself as well as others. Throughout the play Cléopâtre stresses her utter disregard for love, whether conjugal or maternal, but her pose of hardheartedness cannot necessarily be taken without a grain of salt any more than her virtuous ploys.

Might it not be the case that what Cléopâtre has done she has done for the sake of a son that at least pretends he loves her? In her dying speech to Antiochus, Cléopâtre says: "Règne: de crime en crime enfin te voilà roi. / Je t'ai défait d'un père, et d'un frère, et de moi" (1817–18) [Reign: one crime has led to another, and now you are king. / I have rid you of a father, of a brother, of myself]. Antiochus walks away scot free; he has done nothing and obtained everything. The final irony of the play is that Cléopâtre's obvious irony turns back on itself, that there is some truth to Cléopâtre's thumbnail description of what even a tyrannical mother is capable of doing for the only son who has tried to please her.

Inheritance Versus Love

The vexed relation between inheritance and individual tastes and preferences is apparent even in Corneille's own evaluation of this play. Corneille's claim that this is his favorite among all his tragedies may be related to his realization that, unlike *Le Cid*, *Horace*, or *Cinna*, *Rodogune* has little chance of representing his literary legacy for future generations. It is certainly significant that in his 1660 "Examen," Corneille compares *Rodogune* to a child favored by his father:

I have often been asked at court which of my works I most valued, and I found those asking the question so prejudiced [prévenus] in favor of *Cinna* or *Le Cid* that I have never dared reveal all the love I have always felt for this play [*Rodogune*], which I would gladly have voted for. . . . Perhaps this preference of mine can be likened to the kind of blind fondness [inclinations aveugles] many fathers have for certain of their children at the expense of the others; perhaps there is an element of narcissism [amour-propre] in all this, in that this tragedy seems to me more my own than those that came before it, because of the surprising incidents that are purely my own invention and had never before been seen in the theater; perhaps, finally, the play has a small measure of real worth, in which case my fondness for it is not altogether misplaced. (*Oeuvres complètes*, 417)

Like Séleucus himself who repeatedly "prévient" his brother, the public that prefers Corneille's "elder" plays are prejudiced in their favor; only the author of *Rodogune* sheepishly admits a weakness for this "younger" drama. Corneille attributes this preference to his own individual taste, to what he implies is the greater originality of this play, a phenomenon that can be explained in light of the metaphor of the play as youngest child. In order to raise their oldest children as heirs carrying on a tradition, parents must rein in their impulses toward originality or individuality. The force of the family inheritance often keeps parents at a certain formal distance from their heirs, in contrast to the more individual fondness or "inclination" they might feel for younger children, on whom their name and reputation generally do not depend to the same extent.[12]

This is precisely what the undecidability of birth order in *Rodogune* is about: the movement from an ethic of continuity and repetition—the prioritization of a stable tradition linking the generations, if need be at the expense of individual happiness—and toward an ethic of discontinuity and renewal, one that values individual preferences more than the stable transmission of the heritage of the past.

Antiochus, the surviving son, ends up as the heir to both his parents, but in quite an unexpected way. As Mitchell Greenberg observes, Séleucus' mistrust of his mother paradoxically reflects his similarity to her.[13] Antiochus, by contrast, misunderstands his mother precisely because he is so unlike her, but that does not mean he is not his mother's heir. Rather, he is her heir by something other than resemblance: he makes up for his dissimilarity to her by serving her and pleasing her. Consequently the idea that Antiochus might one day produce a child who resembles his mother becomes not the kind of blessing that most grandparents view as the crowning achievement of their familial careers, but rather a threat and a curse: Cléopâtre's final malevolent wish for Antiochus is that he might one day produce "un fils qui me ressemble" [a son who resembles me] (1824). Cléopâtre's life and death give Antiochus an unhappiness "without precedent":

"des malheurs sans exemple" (1839). The latter phrase, echoing by its half-rhyme Cléopâtre's dying words, "un fils qui me ressemble," connotes not only an unparalleled misfortune, but also a life and death whose example Antiochus will not follow.[14]

As for Antiochus' relation to his father, nothing could be further from the legacy Don Diègue bestows upon his son in *Le Cid* than the one Nicanor leaves Antiochus. *Rodogune* undermines the notion, dear to the heart of the first generation of tragedies, that family inheritance is a source of continuity; here love replaces the legacy of honor and glory in establishing the link between father and son. Antiochus does, indeed, resemble his father, but the way we are informed of that fact is through the lover they share, Rodogune, who establishes this filial resemblance in her double apostrophe, first to the dead father, then to the living son whom she loves, but whose identity she has not yet revealed:

> Mais aujourd'hui qu'on voit cette [Cléopâtre's] main parricide
> Des restes de ta vie insolemment avide,
> Vouloir encor percer ce sein infortuné,
> Pour y chercher le coeur que tu m'avais donné,
> De la paix qu'elle rompt je ne suis plus le gage,
> Je brise avec honneur mon illustre esclavage,
> J'ose reprendre un coeur pour aimer et haïr,
> Et ce n'est plus qu'à toi que je veux obéir.
> Le consentiras-tu cet effort sur ma flamme,
> Toi, son vivant portrait, que j'adore dans l'âme,
> Cher Prince, dont je n'ose en mes plus doux souhaits
> Fier encor le nom aux murs de ce palais? (875–86)

> But today, with Cléopâtre's murderous, insolent hand
> Eager to snuff out what remains of your existence,
> And to plunge a dagger into my wretched breast
> In search of the heart you once gave to me,
> I will not be the victim of this broken peace of hers,
> To save my honor I must end my fabled enslavement,
> And dare revive a heart that again will love and loathe,
> From this day on, I listen only to you.
> And you, his living portrait, you whom my soul adores,
> Will you consent to my heart's new enterprise,
> Dear Prince, whose name my gentle wishes cannot force
> My tongue to entrust to these palace walls?

The precious image of Cléopâtre trying to stab the heart that Nicanor gave Rodogune and that beats within his lover's breast illustrates that the real source of intergenerational continuity in this play is not the inheritance of a code of family honor, as it was in *Le Cid*, but rather the inheritance of a love.[15]

Indeed, just as Nicanor "passes on" his heart to Rodogune, his dying words to her, "Vengeance! Adieu: je meurs pour vous!" (862) [Revenge! Farewell! It is for you that I die!], remind us that vengeance, a key feature in upholding family honor in plays like *Le Cid*, *Horace*, and *Cinna*, here no longer remains within the confines of the family. It is Rodogune — whose name may well be reminiscent of "Rodrigue" — who is charged with the task of avenging Nicanor's death, even if she is never ultimately able to incite his sons into fulfilling their duty.[16]

> Si c'est son [Nicanor's] coeur en vous [Antiochus] qui revit et qui
>   m'aime,
> Faites ce qu'il ferait s'il vivait en lui-même.
> A ce coeur qu'il vous laisse osez prêter un bras;
> Pouvez-vous le porter et ne l'écouter pas?
> S'il vous explique mal ce qu'il en doit attendre,
> Il emprunte ma voix pour se mieux faire entendre.
> Une seconde fois il vous le dit par moi:
> Prince, il faut le venger. (1167–74)

> If Nicanor's heart, beating in your breast, loves me,
> Do as he would do if it were still beating in his.
> Dare let your arm take action for this heart he has left to you;
> How can you ignore his heart when it is something you possess?
> If what it expects from you is not quite clear,
> It is borrowing my voice to speak more plainly.
> For a second time, it has me tell you this:
> Prince, avenge his death.

Here conjugal love is not opposed to familial revenge, but is the potential agent of familial revenge, just as it is the potential agent of continuity between the generations. In *Le Cid*, Rodrigue is the eager arm that carries out the will of the father as head of the lineage. In *Rodogune*, Antiochus is the reticent arm that is meant to take its orders not from the father's head but from his heart, the very heart the father has given to Rodogune to transmit to his son as his only legacy ("ce coeur qu'il vous laisse").

Thus in the transitional play *Rodogune*, Séleucus loses out because he is caught between two ethics. He refuses to give satisfaction when satisfaction is the necessary and sufficient condition imposed upon him, but while he shrinks from what will come to be commonplace in the second generation of tragedies, that is, the favoring of love even at the expense of duty and honor, he stops short of behaving like a first-generation hero, which would entail acting as his father's agent of revenge by killing his mother, whatever the consequences. Nevertheless, the play leaves little doubt that Séleucus' loss is greater than Antiochus' gain. When all is said and done, the most innovative aspect of *Rodogune* is the opening up of primogeniture to competition and individual satisfaction. Its most conservative aspect is the closing off of competition and individual satisfaction from the realm of heroism: the brother who will not stoop to compete may well be excluded from inheriting power, but he is still more heroic than his brother. The description of Séleucus' demise, particularly his touching delusion that the man he sees with his dying eyes is not his tutor, Timagène, but his brother (1637– 48), stirs up all our sympathy for him, and certainly a good deal more admiration than Antiochus' feckless behavior when he is nearly tricked into drinking his mother's poison. If Séleucus cannot be said to be defending an ethic of the past, at least he is defending against an unheroic ethic of the present. However much Pierre Corneille appears to have complicated the game of sibling rivalry so that each side has its own trump cards, dramatically he is still stacking the deck in favor of the older-brother figure — even if he cannot quite bring himself to reveal that an older brother is what he is.

The Younger Brother Speaks Out: Thomas Corneille's *Persée et Démétrius*

Thomas Corneille, in his *Persée et Démétrius*, not only undermines the stability of primogeniture — which Pierre already does in *Rodogune* — he also makes the younger brother into the worthier, more heroic of the two. Thomas' play is about a clearly defined older and younger brother; if one accepts the terms of primogeniture, there is no question of legitimacy here. But *Persée et Démétrius* is far more radical than *Rodogune* precisely in that it does not accept the terms of primogeniture. Rather than simply questioning the worth of a particular heir, Thomas Corneille portrays the corruption of the system of entitlement that automatically makes Persée an heir. Implicit in the depiction of the two brothers is the very real possibility that the older-brother heir is flawed not in spite of his position as heir, but rather because of it.

Let us summarize the events of the play. Persée and Démétrius, respectively the older and the younger son of Philippe, the king of Macedonia, are both in love with the Thracian princess, Erixène. The action is set off by Persée's claim that Démétrius, jealous of his position as heir apparent and fiancé of Erixène, tried to kill him the previous day by poisoning him at the banquet following the annual wargames. Unlike *Rodogune*, which underplays the question of sibling rivalry, *Persée et Démétrius* foregrounds the competitiveness between the brothers from the moment of Persée's opening speech to his father's friend, Didas, whom he would like to make an ally in his struggle against his brother:

En vain jusques ici, résolu de me taire,
Je me suis déguisé les attentats d'un Frère,
En vain, quoique ma mort fût l'objet de ses voeux,
Du sang qui nous unit j'ai respecté les noeuds,
Sa haine chaque jour en devient plus ardente,
Plus je la dissimule, et plus elle s'augmente.
. . . .
Démétrius jaloux du Trône de mon père
Ne peut voir sans fureur que l'âge m'y préfère;
Et le titre d'Aîné qui m'acquiert ses Etats,
Est un crime trop grand pour ne m'en punir pas.
                        (1:1; *Poëmes dramatiques*, 3:319–20)[17]

Up to now, I have vowed to say nothing,
In vain I have closed my eyes to my Brother's attacks,
In vain I have honored the ties of blood we share,
Even though my death was his dearest wish,
His hatred stronger every day:
The more I cover it up, the stronger it grows.
. . . .
Démétrius is jealous of my father's Throne
And enraged that it's mine because of my age;
And my title as Elder, which gives me my father's Lands,
Is too great a crime not to be punished.

Persée claims that his "aînesse" is a privilege his younger brother cannot forgive him for, but in fact it will turn out to be inseparable from Persée's unscrupulousness. For it gradually emerges that Persée's dire portrait of his younger brother is false, Persée's goal simply to convince his father that

Démétrius is a threat to royal authority. In addition to the false accusation of attempted murder, Persée also reveals his brother's alliance with Rome, the usurper of what Persée sees as legitimate, inherited power (1:1; 3:321), and has spurious reports of Démétrius' treachery planted among Philippe's spies in Rome.

The final ploy Persée hits upon is to convince his father to order Démétrius to marry Didas' daughter so as to incite Démétrius, in love with Erixène and loved by her, to balk at the request and rebel against the king. When Démétrius decides instead to bide his time, and Erixène discovers that his "lâche obéissance" (3:1; 3:349) [cowardly obedience] has made him the fiancé of another, she agrees out of spite to marry Persée. Fooled by Erixène's feigned indifference, Démétrius believes she never really loved him: "Mais l'air indifférent dont ma perte est conclue / Marque une âme à l'oubli dès longtemps résolue" (3:6; 3:359) [But the indifference with which she heard that I was lost to her / Is the sign of a soul long intent on forgetting me]. After a final attempt to wrest Erixène away from his brother (4:3), Démétrius puts an end to any pretense of obeying his father. In his final words onstage, he tells his father that unless he is put to death, he will kill Persée if his brother marries Erixène (4:5; 3:371).

Démétrius is given *le beau rôle* in the dénouement of the tragedy as well. He is vindicated by a report that the Roman spies' tales of treason were lies. To Persée's chagrin, Philippe then gives Erixène the freedom to marry Démétrius, and just as she is about to accept, the report of Démétrius' suicide arrives. The play ends with the narration of Démétrius' death: we discover, with ample quotations of the dying prince's last words to pull at our heartstrings, that he killed himself for love of Erixène.

Brothers Trading Places:
The Younger as Hero, the Elder as Victim

It would be hard to think up a plot that gives more advantages to the younger brother. For someone who inherits nothing, Démétrius seems to have a great deal, not the least of his attributes being, paradoxically, that he has had to strive for whatever he has attained. As is typical of younger siblings, Démétrius has had to learn to form alliances and to make himself popular. His alliance with Rome is, not surprisingly, much resented by his father and his older brother, both of whom expect their authority to come to them automatically, by inheritance, rather than from a consolidation of power. Indeed, this easy alliance of the younger sibling with Rome makes perfect sense in terms of the stress laid in French Classical tragedy on Rome's rejection of hereditary monarchy.[18] The fact that Démétrius is loved by his own people is much emphasized and seems to give him the same kind of stamp of popular approval that is not uncommonly bestowed upon underdog figures: perhaps it is easy to be fond of someone you do not expect ever to have authority over you.

One of Thomas Corneille's cleverest devices in this play is the initial false portrait given of the younger brother, who before he arrives onstage is said to be a scheming, underhanded malcontent. While this masquerade, which may be related to Thomas' weakness for *coups de théâtre*, is not long maintained, it is a shrewd manipulation of audience expectation. By creating a false but plausible negative image of the younger brother in the minds of the spectators, is the playwright not replicating the disadvantages that younger brothers in general must overcome? For this reason, it is essential that the audience figure out the truth about Démétrius for themselves even before he appears onstage (1:5). We soon discover that Démétrius has the backing not only of the Romans but also of the common people, which makes Didas hesitate to side with the older brother: "Avec l'appui du Peuple à ses voeux favorable, / Démétrius, Seigneur, lui [to Didas] paraît redoutable" (1:2; 3:322–23) [With the support of the People, who side with him, / Didas finds Démétrius quite daunting, Sire].[19] And Persée's credibility is further damaged when he admits Démétrius is also preferred by Erixène (1:2).

Just in case there is any doubt as to the brothers' relative worth, Erixène welcomes Démétrius onstage by swiftly summarizing their various advantages:

> Persée au désespoir de cette préférence,
> Qu'emportent vos vertus sur l'heur de sa naissance
> Blessé de leur éclat, s'en forme contre vous
> Tout ce qui peut aigrir l'esprit le plus jaloux. (1:5; 3:329)

> Persée is in despair over my preference for you,
> For your virtues far outweigh the advantage of his birth,
> They wound him by their brilliance, and cause him to fall prey
> To all that can embitter the most jealous of minds.

"Your virtues" versus "the advantage of his birth": these are the clear battle lines drawn between the worthy younger brother and the unfairly favored older one. The only character to hold out against the increasingly obvious falseness of Persée's accusations against his brother is Philippe, who demonstrates a father's natural tendency to trust and believe his heir.

Although Démétrius' true worth dawns upon the audience only gradually, once he arrives, all doubt is erased: here again, Thomas' play is quite the opposite of Pierre's in that Thomas' brothers could not be easier to distinguish. Démétrius' strength of character is manifest in his willingness to compete against his brother and also to rebel against his father. In Pierre Corneille's play, direct sibling rivalry remains in the shadow, the twins' differences brought out mainly by their dissimilar relation to their mother. Conversely, in Thomas' play the father's role is subordinated to the brothers' relation to each other; Philippe seems to be onstage as an extension of their rivalry.

As for Persée, this is an heir who sees himself as a persecuted victim: while his position crumbles before his very eyes, he remains incapable of adapting to changing values. The fact that the older brother has no redeeming features is especially harsh, since he feels he is supposed to have been born with everything. Persée is a weakling whose most characteristic action is whining to his father about his brother:

> Détestez maintenant l'ardeur insatiable
> Où la soif de régner plonge une âme coupable;
> Mais en la détestant daignez vous souvenir
> Que vous avez à plaindre aussi bien qu'à punir.
> Que celui dont la rage aspire à perdre un Frère
> Sente à jamais des Dieux l'implacable colère,
> Mais qu'au moins l'opprimé pour s'en mettre à couvert,
> Dans l'appui de son Roi trouve un asile ouvert.
> Contre la trahison c'est le seul que j'espère,
> Je n'ai pour m'en sauver que les Dieux et mon Père,
> S'il me faut fuir ici de secrets attentats,
> Je n'ai point de Romains qui me tendent les bras.
>   .   .   .   .
> Et, tandis qu'en vous seul je fonde mon appui,
> Vos Peuples, les Romains, tout enfin est pour lui. (2:3; 3:338)

> I ask you now to loathe the unslakable passion
> That parches his guilty soul with a thirst to reign;
> But while you are hating it, pray do not forget
> That your role is to pity me as well as to punish him.

May he whose fury seeks to destroy his Brother
Be made to feel the eternal wrath of the Gods;
But may he who is oppressed at least find shelter,
May his King's support grant him the asylum he needs.
Against this betrayal, where else can I turn?
I have only the Gods and my Father to save me.
If I must seek refuge here from these secret plots,
It is because I have no Romans waiting to help me out.

. . . .

So while you are my lone and sole support,
Your People and the Romans: he's got everyone on his side.

There are few sights more pitiful than a person born to privilege set adrift
on the dangerous seas of a merit system. The threat posed by his valorous
younger brother forces Persée to do something to solidify his position, but
all he can do is appeal to his father for assistance. Persée sees his father's
function as not only punishing his brother, but also feeling sorry for Persée
himself. He has apparently been raised to make this assumption, since
Philippe, even before confronting his two sons about their squabble, has
made up his mind about who is in the right: "Je connais que Persée a raison
de se plaindre" (2:1; 3:333) [I know Persée is right to complain]. Persée's
whole speech, including his claim to be free of any power base in Rome or
among the people of Macedonia, comes off sounding less like a pledge of
fidelity to the king than an older brother's fit of jealous rage that everyone
likes his baby brother better than him: "tout enfin est pour lui."

Persée continues his complaining until the end of the play. When his
true colors have been revealed and caused his father to retract his permission to marry Erixène, Persée wallows in his misfortune, completely unaware that his "bad luck" might actually be a result of his bad behavior:
"De quelque dur revers que le sort me menace; / Je ne demande point d'où
me vient ma disgrâce" (5:4; 3:385) [Whatever setback fate threatens me
with, / I will not ask to know the source of my disgrace]. The most chilling
aspect of the heir's attitude is his passive paranoia. No longer being automatically favored by his father by virtue of his position makes him feel he
has been persecuted his whole life: "Cédez à ce penchant dont l'indigne
imposture / Toujours en sa [Démétrius'] faveur suborna la Nature" (5:4;
3:385) [Give in to your weakness and its worthless posing / That always
swayed Nature in Démétrius' favor].

The clearest manifestation of Persée's weakness is his inability to com-

pete directly. Even when he addresses his brother, he hides behind the
authority of his father and of the gods:

> Mais, si ce que je suis tient le vôtre [destiny] borné,
> Prenez-vous-en aux Dieux qui m'ont fait votre Aîné.
> L'usage ici reçu, le jugement d'un Père
> Pour régner après lui veulent qu'on me préfère,
> Et votre bras armé pour répandre mon sang
> Vous peut seul donner droit de monter à son rang. (2:3; 3:337)

> But if your destiny is held in check by who I am,
> Blame it on the Gods who have made me your Elder.
> The custom of this place and the judgment of our Father
> Mean that I have preference to reign after him,
> And only by taking up arms to spill my blood
> Might you gain the right to assume his rank.

Although Persée imagines his brother mounting a direct attack upon him,
his speech betrays his own inability to compete. He is unembarrassed at
telling his brother not to blame him for his problems but rather the gods
who made him the elder brother. And when he finally gets around to
alluding to a possible direct attack, he says Démétrius will have to kill him
to be named as successor, thus placing his brother in an active position. He
does not even suggest that in such circumstances he would fight back, but
rather depicts himself as a future martyr to younger-brother aggression.

A dramatic example of the brothers' opposite ways comes in their final
confrontation (4:3). Démétrius opens the scene with a frontal assault on
his brother's position: "Ah, ne l'acceptez point cette foi [Erixène's hand]
qui m'est due, / Elle est encore à moi, je ne l'ai point rendue" (4:3; 3:366)
[Oh, don't accept her promise, she owes it to me, / Her promise is still
mine, I have not given it back]. In the face of this open hostility, the only
counterattack Persée can muster is an arch, supercilious scorn:

> Si sa foi, ce haut prix où le vôtre [love] s'oppose,
> Est tellement à vous qu'en vain elle en dispose,
> Comme c'est le seul bien où je veuille aspirer,
> Du moins jusqu'à demain laissez-moi l'espérer.
> Le terme est assez court, et sûr, quoi que je tente,
> De voir mes voeux trompés confondre mon attente,

Par pitié jusque-là vous pouvez me souffrir
La douceur d'un espoir qu'ils aiment à nourrir. (4:3; 3:366)

If her promise, the high reward your love defends,
Is so much yours she's not free to give it out,
At least until tomorrow let me hope to get it,
Since it is the only thing of value to which I aspire.
It is not much to ask for, and since you are sure to find
My expectations foiled, whatever I do, by my deluded desires,
Humor me until then, out of pity you can grant
The sweetness of a hope that's taken root in my desires.

Irony is frequently the last resort of those who lack a more obvious source of power; a character like Racine's Andromaque, whose irony has sometimes been overlooked, is an example of this same phenomenon.[20] Rather than taking up the gauntlet and repaying Démétrius' blusterous attack in kind, Persée falls back on irony, pointing out that Démétrius surely cannot object to a twenty-four-hour delay in the certain realization of his desires. Even in his ironic pose, the only role Persée is capable of playing is that of a disfavored son, a deluded, ineffectual object of pity.

When Démétrius loses his temper and threatens violence, the king, as if magically whisked in by the danger to his heir, arrives in the nick of time; in effect, the father's arrival safeguards the position that his heir could not long hold onto alone.[21] Persée, content to let his father fight his battles, takes his leave, first of his brother — "Voici le Roi, vous lui direz le reste" (4:3; 3:368) [Here's the King, tell it to him] — then of his father — "Seigneur, je me retire. / Contre Démétrius je n'ai rien à vous dire" (4:4; 3:368) [Sire, I shall withdraw. / I have nothing to say to you against Démétrius]. Rather than repenting for past lies told, Persée simply finds it wiser to tell lies about his brother in his absence.

Even the king himself, the repository of power, is ultimately cowed by Démétrius. When Philippe makes up his mind to rid himself of his younger son, he exhorts himself to rise up against Démétrius, as if the father were the renegade and underdog rather than the son:

Veux-tu rougir toujours des fers que tu te donnes,
Et pour un peu de sang qu'il t'en pourra coûter,
As-tu le coeur si bas qu'il tremble à les quitter?
Non, non, c'est trop gémir, bravons la tyrannie. (4:7; 3:375)

Will you spend your whole life ashamed, willingly shackled,
And for fear of a few drops of blood that might have to be shed,
Are you so fainthearted that you tremble to break free?
No, no, enough of moaning! It is time to confront tyranny.

It is true that Démétrius has the force of Rome behind him, but these words of a reigning king who feels the "tyranny" of his younger son are still a reversal of what one might expect. As in the case of Persée's attitude toward Démétrius, it is less Philippe's hostility or fear that are surprising — the history of monarchy, in France as elsewhere, provides ample instances of family members, including younger sons, challenging royal authority — than the terms in which they are expressed. Just as the heir presents himself as oppressed and victimized by his less favored brother, the ruling monarch describes his struggle against his younger son's rising power not as the quelling of a rebellion but as a rebellion against tyranny. Even the father seems to be taking the younger son as the point of reference.

The Heroism of Love

Démétrius resembles Antiochus in *Rodogune* in that both younger-brother figures are portrayed as more lovable than their counterparts, but while the endearing but ineffectual Antiochus is upstaged by his twin's heroic demise, Démétrius' success in love is just one more advantage he has over his brother. Antiochus' extreme love for both Cléopâtre and Rodogune compromises him; Séleucus' noble stance comes from his refusal to pay the price demanded by the two women. By contrast, Démétrius' valorization of love does not compromise his heroism but helps to constitute it.

Démétrius makes his priorities clear in his first appearance onstage, when he refuses to yield to Erixène's demands that he flee to safety in Rome:

Hélas! Madame, hélas! quand le sort nous accable,
Est-ce aimer comme il faut qu'être si raisonnable?
Pour moi, dans les revers dont je suis combattu,
Je ne me pique point d'avoir tant de vertu;
Vous voir est le seul bien qui peut flatter ma flamme. (1:5; 3:331)

Alas, Madam, alas! With destiny at our throats
Is being so rational the right way to love?

With all these problems hard upon me
I must say high virtue seems not to matter much.
The only good that calms my passion is being with you.

Démétrius declares his allegiance to love as his highest value: "être si raisonnable," a succinct description of the maddening, logical poses struck by lovers like Chimène and Rodrigue in Pierre Corneille's early plays, is not compatible with true love, presented here as Démétrius' "only good," an absolute next to which "virtue" counts for nothing. Démétrius closes the scene without having resolved the political question—we don't know if he will agree to leave for Rome—because once Erixène's sigh tells him she loves him, nothing else matters: "Et comme pour ma flamme il n'est point d'autre bien, / Après ce doux aveu, je n'écoute plus rien" (1:5; 3:332) [Since there's nothing else of value for my passion, / After this sweet admission, I've nothing left to hear].

Persée on the other hand spends much of his time playing at being an early Corneille hero for whom love is to be subordinated to the political domain, but the role is utterly incoherent and unconvincing. He counters Erixène's proto-Racinian plea to be allowed to follow her heart and marry Démétrius with lines that make him sound like a latter-day version of l'Infante in *Le Cid*:

Un coeur qui pour le Trône a mérité de naître,
Quand il prend de l'amour, s'en rend toujours le maître.
De ses vastes désirs l'insatiable ardeur
L'asservit en esclave au soin de sa grandeur.
Sa flamme s'accommode aux desseins qu'il achève,
Il ne la laisse agir qu'autant qu'elle l'élève,
Et ne cède aux transports qui forment de doux noeuds
Que quand l'ambition a rempli tous ses voeux. (1:3; 3:327)

When a deserving heart that is born to take the Throne
Possesses love, it must always be its master,
For the sake of its grandeur it puts love in chains,
Using the unslakable energy of its vast desires.
Passion must give way to the will of the heart
Which fans its flames only if they rise toward the heavens,
The heart yields to the transports of sweet affection
Only when ambition has carried out its commands.

Persée's claim that those of high birth are able to control their feelings sounds impressive. The only problem is that it is contradicted by the fact that he fell in love with Erixène in spite of himself:

> D'abord je n'eus dessein que de nuire à ce Frère,
> Ayant su son amour par un décret fatal,
> Sans me sentir Amant je me fis son Rival,
> Mais las! Je n'appris pas longtemps à la connaître,
> Qu'en secret je devins ce que je feignis d'être. (1:2; 3:324)

> At first my plan was just to harm my Brother,
> So when by a fatal decree I learned of his love,
> I made myself his Rival without feeling like a Lover,
> But alas! I had no sooner begun to know her,
> Than I secretly became what I was pretending to be.

In spite of his rhetoric of mastery, Persée is a man out of control; everything happens to him in spite of himself and his honor. For him love is not even a clear countervalue to duty, but rather a by-product of his obsessive jealousy of his brother.

Unlike Antiochus, who muddles through *Rodogune* alive, Démétrius is given a noble death to enhance his heroic identity even further. His death scene seals his identification with love to the exclusion of all other values, as his dying words indicate:

> Mais j'aurais de mon feu cru trahir la tendresse
> Si j'eusse refusé ma vie à ma Princesse.
> Comme pour elle seule on m'a vu la chérir,
> Quand elle veut ma mort il m'est doux de mourir. (5:6; 3:386)

> But had I refused to give my life for my Princess,
> I would have thought my love for her betrayed,
> Since I loved life itself for her and her alone,
> How sweet it is to die if my death is her desire.

What kills Démétrius is his innocence: he dies taken in by Erixène's feigned indifference to his forced engagement to another, believing it proves that she never loved him. And his gullibility only adds to the final image of the prince as one who loved not wisely but too well. By comparison, Philippe, the grieving father, disdainfully dubs himself "malheureux politique" (5:6; 3:386) [wretched schemer].

Persée et Démétrius is a far cry from *Rodogune*, in which the equally unjust death of one of the two brothers appears to "solve" the problem of inheritance. In Thomas' play, by contrast, the death of the noble younger son leaves no possibility for inheritance whatsoever, as the play's final words suggest the death of both Philippe's surviving son — "Qu'il périsse, aussi bien de sa jalouse haine / Il faut que tôt ou tard il ressente la peine" (5:7; 3:391)[22] [May he perish, for one day or another / He must suffer the pain of his jealous hatred] — and the king himself: "Et qu'on me mène ailleurs, après un tel malheur, / Sous mes tristes remords expirer de douleur" (5:7; 3:391) [And after such great misfortune, take me to some place / Where under my guilt's sorry weight I may die from grief].

If Pierre Corneille's most complex treatment of sibling rivalry destabilizes primogeniture by making the younger-brother figure inherit the throne and yet still giving a moral victory to the heroic, martyred older-brother figure, Thomas Corneille's treatment of the same issue completely undermines the justice of a predetermined inheritance based on birth order. In *Rodogune*, the inapplicability of primogeniture extends beyond the confusion over the brothers' birth order; it becomes a sign that neither brother is his father's heir as Rodrigue was his father's heir, and that inheritance no longer follows along the same paths that it once did. But Séleucus, by ultimately refusing to play by the new rules, seems to conjure up a kind of nostalgia for the old rules even if he cannot really play by them, either.[23] In *Persée et Démétrius*, it is not only the older brother's failure to inherit that is at issue, but the breakdown of an entire ethic underlying the privileges of primogeniture. A radical reading of *Persée et Démétrius* might speculate that Persée is a greater victim of primogeniture than Démétrius, for his expectations of heirship leave him unequipped to deal with the evolution of values and mores. In spite of the play's gloomy outcome, we witness the consecration of a younger-brother hero who earns the privilege of being his father's heir but dies before he can benefit from that privilege. If Démétrius is taken in by the falseness of those around him, that is to his credit: this is a play in which the younger brother's naïveté leads not to his punishment but to his sacrifice. The focus of *Persée et Démétrius* is not merely the difference between two siblings, but rather the decadence and corruption of a system of inheritance that makes the older brother into a scheming, resentful weakling, and that cannot save the virtuous younger brother from his martyrdom.

7

The Brother as Father, the Father as Brother

Pierre Corneille's *Nicomède* and Thomas Corneille's *La Mort d'Annibal*

It is a case of literary fratomania perhaps unparalleled in the history of Western drama. In 1650, at the age of forty-four, Pierre Corneille composes *Nicomède*, a tragedy about two competing half-brothers, Nicomède and Attale. In 1669, at the age of forty-four, Pierre's younger brother Thomas uses the same historical material to stage *La Mort d'Annibal*, a play about two characters who are still named Nicomède and Attale but who are no longer brothers. And yet in obscuring the sibling relation that originally linked these two characters inherited in some sense from his own brother, Thomas does not so much leave the problem of siblinghood behind as he carries the conflict inherent in Pierre's drama to its logical conclusion.

In *Nicomède* the older brother, the play's titular hero, regains the kind of clear-cut advantage that was not apparent in the relation between the twin brothers of *Rodogune*,[1] but *Nicomède* is not simply a movement backward toward primogeniture.[2] Although Nicomède, the older brother, is portrayed as a natural leader, the question of moral inheritance is complicated by the fact that the older generation, represented by Nicomède's and Attale's father, the weak, corrupt Prusias, presents no moral model at all. Quite the opposite of first-generation plays such as *Cinna*, *Nicomède* sees the apotheosis not of the father figure but of the older brother as a spiritual legator and ethical model: it is Nicomède, not Prusias, who establishes the play's moral heritage and who, in the end, gives his younger brother his identity.

The older generation's moral abdication in *Nicomède* is carried further in Thomas Corneille's *La Mort d'Annibal*. Thomas reformulates the entire family constellation in such a way as to undermine the very structure of inheritance. While Thomas' Nicomède and Attale are not literal brothers, here as in *Persée et Démétrius* the younger-brother figure has a certain number of advantages. The figure of Prusias is debased to such an extent that he is merely a third rival to Nicomède and Attale, who vie for the hand of Elise, Annibal's daughter, but adoption plays an important function as an alternative to inheritance along bloodlines: Thomas refocuses his drama ethically on the older generation by making of Annibal, who in Pierre's play is already dead, an alternate ethical model, a good father who makes up for the bad father, Prusias. Like several of Racine's plays, the conclusion of *La Mort d'Annibal* is played out in terms of an adoption: at the moment of his death, Annibal names Nicomède his spiritual heir.[3] But the play's vision of inheritance is in fact more radical than this would suggest, for in the end the drama undermines any notion of a positive inheritance passed on by imitation or resemblance between the generations and leaves us rather with an image of inheritance defined purely by resistance, that is to say, by difference.

Nicomède: Older and Bolder

With *Nicomède*, one of the few tragedies put on during the Fronde, Pierre Corneille returns to the theme of sibling rivalry, but he treats it in quite a different way than he did in *Rodogune*. Let us briefly summarize the action of the play. Nicomède, the son and principal military support of the king of Bithynia, Prusias, rebels against the king's decision to marry off Laodice, the queen of Armenia, not to Nicomède, who loves her, but rather to his younger half-brother, Attale. Attale, the son of Prusias and his second wife, Arsinoé, was raised in Rome; he has just been escorted home by the Roman ambassador, Flaminius, to carry out the agreement that Attale would be returned to his parents in exchange for Annibal (Hannibal), Rome's most famous enemy, who had sought sanctuary in Prusias' kingdom. If all went as Prusias and Arsinoé intended, Nicomède would end up "a victim of the plotting of his stepmother, who does her best to prevent him from succeeding his father, the king, according to the normal order of primogeniture."[4] Naturally things do not go as planned: Annibal, refusing to be delivered into the hands of the Romans, commits suicide before the action of the play begins, and Flaminius is left with no booty to bring back to Rome other than Nicomède, Annibal's disciple and spiritual heir. Flaminius thus orders Prusias to hand over Nicomède as a hostage and to name Attale, who is entirely under Rome's sway, as his heir. While Nicomède is being sent from the city in exile, the population, which prefers him to his brother, rebels; in the confusion Nicomède is saved by a mysterious stranger who in the play's final scene is revealed to be Attale. Nicomède offers to yield the throne to his younger brother on the condition that he can continue to be his military strongman, the role he played for his father. A general reconciliation of all parties takes place, with Arsinoé agreeing to end her feud with Nicomède after his generous offer, Attale in complete admiration of his brother, and the Roman ambassador prepared to try to smooth things over between the Roman Senate and Nicomède.

Among the various ways *Nicomède* differs from *Rodogune*, none is more important than the fact that in the later drama there is no doubt as to the relative age of the two half-brothers and the differences between them. Nicomède and Attale start out with little resemblance, as Nicomède points out in an irate speech to his father: "Seigneur, nous n'avons pas si grande ressemblance / Qu'il faille de bons yeux pour y voir différence" (1355–56) [Sire, we are not so much alike / That one needs good eyesight to see that we are different]. The two half-brothers do not share the same mother: Nicomède's mother, who is presumably dead, is never mentioned, while Attale's mother, Arsinoé, is a major player in the dynastic squabbling that constitutes the play's action. This active intervention of Attale's mother on his behalf does not, however, give him an advantage over Nicomède; rather, Attale is constrained by having a mother who exercises a good deal of control over him, while the motherless Nicomède is freer to act as he sees fit. Attale also has a powerful figurative mother, Rome, but once again any potential advantages he might draw from this second mother figure come at the expense of his greatly limited independence.

When the curtain rises Nicomède and Attale do not know each other, and even once they are introduced they seem to come from two different worlds. In their first scene, a confrontation over Laodice, whom both brothers love, Attale, who was raised in Rome, has no idea of his rival's identity. To Attale's claim that Rome will help him win Laodice's hand (154), Nicomède, who has the double advantage of being the older brother and of knowing he is the older brother, responds in this way:

> Et ne savez-vous plus qu'il n'est princes ni rois
> Qu'elle [Rome] daigne égaler à ses moindres bourgeois?
>
> . . . .
>
> Songez qu'il faut du moins, pour toucher votre coeur,
> La fille d'un tribun ou celle d'un préteur,
> Que Rome vous permet cette haute alliance,

Dont vous aurait exclu le défaut de naissance,
Si l'honneur souverain de son adoption
Ne vous autorisait à tant d'ambition. (165–78)

Have you forgotten so soon that in Rome's proud eyes
No prince or king is a match for her humblest citizen?
. . . .
Remember, you must not lose your heart
To less than the daughter of a Roman magistrate;
Rome is your ticket to an ambitious marriage
Which otherwise your inferior birth would have ruled out
If the sovereign honor of being an adoptive Roman
Had not allowed you to set your sights so high.

Nicomède makes plain his disdain for his brother as Rome's protégé. True, Attale's poor reasoning—regiphobic Rome would certainly not support the marriage of one of its citizens to a foreign queen—compels Nicomède to bring up Rome's dislike of hereditary monarchs, but only an older brother's instinctual superiority allows him to be so dismissive of his younger brother's claims. In stating that without Rome's support Attale, a nonheir, would be unworthy of any ambitious match, Nicomède manages to allude quite witheringly to his brother's "inferior birth."

Attale, the younger brother, has two identities, but neither one is advantageous. By birth, he owes Nicomède fidelity and subservience. By alliance, he has quite a distinct identity as an adoptive Roman,[5] but given the heir's scorn for Rome's toadies, that identity does not provide Attale much of an edge, either, as is apparent in Laodice's rebuke to him:

Puisqu'il [Nicomède] vous a déplu vous traitant de Romain,
Je veux bien vous traiter de fils de souverain.
En cette qualité vous devez reconnaître
Qu'un prince votre aîné doit être votre maître. (205–8)

Since Nicomède made you cross by calling you a Roman,
I'll gladly call you a king's son.
In that capacity you must concede
That the prince, as your elder, must be your master.

Attale cannot win. If he is a Roman, his brother can lord it over him by rubbing in his dependence on Rome and his worthlessness without his connection to Roman power. If he is not a Roman, he is merely Nicomède's younger brother.

It is thus only to be expected that neither Laodice nor Nicomède takes Attale seriously. In his commentary on an interchange between Nicomède and Laodice (4:3), Serge Doubrovsky writes: "In a universe in which primogeniture is enough to substantiate the claims of an absent monarch . . . , everyone receives an essence, and a fixed position in the hierarchy of essences. . . . Nicomède has a certain *weight of being*, to which no act of Attale or support for him can provide a *counterweight*."[6] Nicomède and Attale meet onstage three times before the climactic scene of revelation that ends the play,[7] and if we examine their interactions, we discover that neither brother ever acts as if the younger poses a challenge to the elder.

In the first of these meetings, as Nicomède and Attale bicker in Laodice's presence over which brother will marry her, Attale, unaware of Nicomède's identity, cannot bring himself to address his mysterious rival directly, but channels his rebukes to him through Laodice: "Si cet homme est à vous, imposez-lui silence, / Madame, et retenez une telle insolence" (183–84) [If this man is in your entourage, Madam, / Make him be still and rein in his insolence]. In *Persée et Démétrius* it was the older brother who was unable to compete directly; here the younger brother, Attale, is incapable of facing up to Nicomède. Even when Attale is about to explode at the end of the scene, he addresses Laodice rather than Nicomède — "Ah! Madame, souffrez que ma juste colère . . ." (239) [Ah! Madam, allow my righteous anger . . .] — his frustration having the impact of a temper tantrum rather than a serious threat.

When the two men finally exchange words directly, their concluding speeches in this scene punctuate the inequality of the entire interaction:

ATTALE:
Ah! Seigneur, excusez si vous connaissant mal . . .
NICOMÈDE:
Prince, faites-moi voir un plus digne rival.
Si vous aviez dessein d'attaquer cette place,
Ne vous départez point d'une si noble audace,
Mais comme à son secours je n'amène que moi,
Ne la menacez plus de Rome ni du Roi.
Je la défendrai seul, attaquez-la de même,
Avec tous les respects qu'on doit au diadème.
Je veux bien mettre à part, avec le nom d'aîné,

Le rang de votre maître où je suis destiné,
Et nous verrons ainsi qui fait mieux un brave homme. (265–75)

ATTALE:
Ah! Sire, forgive me, not knowing who you were . . .
NICOMÈDE:
Prince, show yourself to be a rival worthy of me.
If your intention was to attack this place,
Do not give up on your noble, bold scheme,
But as I've brought only myself to protect this place,
Put an end to your threats about Rome and the King.
I shall defend this place alone; attack it that way, too,
Maintaining all due respect for royal power.
I am willing to put aside my title as elder,
And my rank, which is destined to make me your master,
And then we shall see who looks the better man.

Whereas Attale's bravado quickly turns to obsequiousness when he realizes who his mysterious adversary is, Nicomède sets the tone for the subsequent rivalry between the brothers. In claiming to set aside the superiority that accompanies his title as elder, he may level the playing field, but he also demonstrates that he establishes the rules.[8]

The second scene between the two brothers offers another example of the haughtiness belying Nicomède's pretense of egalitarianism. Nico-mède's reproach to Attale shows that generosity can have a hidden agenda of imperiousness:

J'avais mis bas, avec le nom d'aîné,
L'avantage du trône où je suis destiné;
Et voulant seul ici défendre ce que j'aime,
Je vous avais prié de l'attaquer de même,
Et de ne mêler point surtout dans vos desseins
Ni le secours du Roi, ni celui des Romains.
Mais ou vous n'avez pas la mémoire fort bonne,
Ou vous n'y mettez rien de ce qu'on vous ordonne. (1005–12)

I had dropped, along with my title as elder,
The advantage of the crown I am destined to wear;
I wished to defend what I love here alone,

And I asked that you attack in a similar spirit,
And that, above all, your plan not be spoiled
By assistance from the king, or help from the Romans.
But either your memory is not very keen,
Or you never remember what you're told to do.

"Mettre bas" the name of older brother: the irrevocable nature of the elder's advantage is encapsulated in this single juxtaposition. In this context "mettre bas" means "drop," but the verb also retains its association with childbirth: "mettre bas le nom d'aîné" suggests giving birth to the title of elder brother. Even as he is purportedly disavowing the advantages of primogeniture, Nicomède retains the privilege of alone being able to choose to do so. How ironic is Nicomède's rebuke to Attale that he has forgotten that they are to fight it out as equals ("you never remember what you're told to do").

Attale's response only underscores Nicomède's superiority:

Seigneur, vous me forcez à m'en souvenir mal,
Quand vous n'achevez pas de rendre tout égal:
Vous vous défaites bien de quelques droits d'aînesse,
Mais vous défaites-vous du coeur de la Princesse,
De toutes les vertus qui vous en font aimer,
Des hautes qualités qui savent tout charmer? (1013–18)

Sire, you have forced me to forget what I've been told,
For you haven't finished evening things out:
You have given up some of your rights as elder,
But have you given up the Princess' heart,
Or your virtues, which are the reason for her love,
Or your noble qualities that charm all those around you?

Attale's entire speech, which continues for another dozen lines, is a paean to the older brother he has begun to worship. And Nicomède's response is no less condescending for being conciliatory: "C'est n'avoir pas perdu tout votre temps à Rome, / Que vous savoir ainsi défendre en galant homme: / Vous avez de l'esprit, si vous n'avez du coeur" (1031–33) [You didn't waste all your time in Rome, / Since you learned to defend yourself well with words: / If your courage is lacking, your wits are sharp]. This backhanded compliment is surprisingly recognizable as a typical older-sibling retort: "At least you're clever — luckily, because you have no other redeeming features."

The third meeting of the brothers (4:4) occurs when Prusias reverses their roles by naming Attale his heir and sending Nicomède as a hostage to Rome in his place (1375–82). How do the two brothers react to the news they've been switched, the younger son now the king's "sole heir" ("mon seul héritier" [1377]), the former heir punished, like Séleucus in *Rodogune*, by the loss of his *droit d'aînesse?* Nicomède's sharp words are to be expected: "Vous m'enverrez à Rome!" (1383) [You're sending me to Rome!]. As for Attale, he does not open his mouth once during the entire scene.

The Older Brother as Kingmaker: Subverting the Father

In the end Nicomède is given a power greater than that of an oldest son: the power of replacing his father not as heir, but as legator. Nicomède, not Prusias, is in charge of the family inheritance at the end of the play. In the final scene, Nicomède reappears to announce that the rebellious crowds have been assuaged and to make peace with all parties present: his father, his stepmother, and the Roman ambassador. But the most important business of the final scene is to identify Nicomède's savior, the anonymous stranger who helped him escape the captor who was to deliver him into the hands of the Romans. This man, his face hidden, refused to reveal himself—until now.

NICOMÈDE:
L'auteur d'un si grand coup m'a caché son visage,
Mais il m'a demandé mon diamant pour gage,
Et me le doit ici rapporter dès demain.
ATTALE:
Le voulez-vous, Seigneur, reprendre de ma main?
NICOMÈDE:
Ah! laissez-moi toujours à cette digne marque
Reconnaître en mon sang un vrai sang de monarque.
Ce n'est plus des Romains l'esclave ambitieux,
C'est le libérateur d'un sang si précieux. (1819–26)

NICOMÈDE:
The author of this great action hid his face from me,
But took my diamond as proof of his identity,
And said he'd bring it back to me tomorrow.

ATTALE:

If you wish, Sire, you may take it from my hand.

NICOMÈDE:

Ah! allow me to recognize, thanks to this noble mark,
In you, my blood, the true blood of a monarch.
You are no longer the Romans' ambitious slave,
You are the liberator of this precious blood.

It is Attale's brother, not his father, who recognizes in the young prince the blood of a king. Taken in isolation, Nicomède's lines sound more like the words of a father recognizing his paternity than those of a brother conceding a spiritual kinship between himself and his younger brother. It may be questionable by the end of the play if Nicomède is still his family's heir, but he is certainly in charge of its heritage.[9]

Corneille does not actually elaborate on the political outcome of the drama; if, as is likely, Attale becomes king, he will be a monarch of doubtful power.[10] The drama's lack of closure may be Corneille's way of saying that the question of who will inherit the throne is less important than the play's commentary on the evolving nature of inheritance. In his final conciliatory speech to Arsinoé, Nicomède concedes any right to the throne so long as he can be the power behind it ("Si vous pouvez souffrir qu'il soit Roi de ma main" [1802] [If you can bear your son's being crowned by my hand]). Starting out as a brother figure vying for the throne, Nicomède ends up as a father figure naming the successor to the throne, the one true judge of his brother's worth. Rather than a king, Nicomède is a kingmaker.

This final metamorphosis is prepared for by Nicomède's entire relation with his father, the unimpressive Prusias. While Corneille has modified his historical sources to present Prusias in a less villainous light — the historical Prusias attempted to kill his son, who in turn had his father put to death[11] — he still characterizes Nicomède's father as a political toady to Rome, a thrall to his second wife, and a weak, capricious father and king.[12] The historical Nicomède merely killed his father. Corneille's Nicomède goes a step further. By appropriating his father's function as legator, he bypasses him.[13] "Fraternity at the end of *Nicomède* manages against all odds to impose its terms on patriarchal and Roman authority alike without seeking to abolish the one or needing to vanquish the other. . . . This is the true accomplishment of the playwright and his hero here: to vitiate the figures of legitimate authority without actually deposing them."[14] The true rivalry in the drama is not between the two brothers over the right to be the heir, but between the elder brother and the father over the right to name the heir:[15] "In the critical reversal of perspectives between the generations, it is Nicomède, not Prusias, who constitutes the true *mirror* of the realm, whence a crucial displacement of the center of gravity that the seeming equilibrium of the dénouement does not completely manage to cover up."[16]

Even were Nicomède to be his father's heir, he would not be his heir by imitation.[17] Because he has extended the king's land and influence, because he is a stronger figure than his father, and because his moral model is Annibal rather than Prusias, Nicomède is portrayed as something much greater — and hence more threatening to the king — than a passive heir to power. As Nicomède himself points out later on, his expansionism is a more serious threat to Rome than his status as a representative of hereditary monarchy:

Si j'avais donc vécu dans ce même repos
Qu'il [Attale] a vécu dans Rome auprès de ses héros,
Elle [Rome] me laisserait la Bithynie entière,
Telle que de tout temps l'aîné la tient d'un père. (645–48)

So if I had spent my life standing idly by
Just as Attale spent his life in Rome with his heroes,
My legacy from Rome would be all of Bithynia,
Just as it has always been passed on from father to eldest son.

Nicomède is both more and less than a traditional *aîné*: more because he is instrumental in naming the heir, and less because he does not name himself as the heir. Both of these aspects of his role call into question the rules and function of inheritance.

At the end of the day, the drama's attitude toward primogeniture is quite difficult to define.[18] The finest example of the complexity of attitudes towards inheritance comes in Nicomède's address to his father about what might happen after the king's death:

Et vos peuples alors, ayant besoin d'un Roi,
Voudront choisir peut-être entre ce Prince [Attale] et moi.
Seigneur, nous n'avons pas si grande ressemblance
Qu'il faille de bons yeux pour y voir différence,
Et ce vieux droit d'aînesse est souvent si puissant
Que pour remplir un trône il rappelle un absent.

Que si leurs sentiments se règlent sur les vôtres,
Sous le joug de vos lois j'en ai bien rangé d'autres,
Et dussent vos Romains en être encor jaloux,
Je ferai bien pour moi ce que j'ai fait pour vous. (1353–62)

And your people, in need of a King at that time,
Perhaps will wish to choose between Attale and me.
Sire, we are not so much alike
That one needs good eyesight to see that we are different,
And the ancient birthright of the elder is often so strong
That it beckons to a man far away to fill an empty throne.
But if they tailor their wishes to yours [and choose Attale],
I've had practice enough conquering people for you,
And even if the Romans look on with spite,
I shall do for myself what I did for you.

The events Nicomède imagines following Prusias' death are jumbled, to say the least. He first implies that whomever Prusias names as his heir, the people will have to choose whom they wish as a ruler; of course they will select him. The idea that it is the people who choose a successor contradicts many other stated assumptions in the drama. Nicomède next imagines the people will call him out of exile not because he is more deserving but because he is the elder: "ce vieux droit d'aînesse" dies hard. Here he is evoking a different path to power altogether, even if the path leads to the same man, himself. Finally, if Attale is named as the heir and the people are foolish enough to agree, Nicomède has no doubt that he will easily be able to take control of lands he has already been instrumental in conquering: "I shall do for myself what I did for you"; translation: I will wrest the throne away from my brother. Rather than examining the question from a single coherent perspective, it is as if Nicomède were rehearsing various possible means of deciding between himself and Attale as successor to Prusias.

Prusias himself does not have a cohesive attitude toward primogeniture. When the Roman ambassador orders Prusias to name Attale as his heir instead of Nicomède, Prusias responds in this way:

Je crois que pour régner il [Attale] en a les mérites,
Et n'en veux point douter après ce que vous dites.
Mais vous voyez, Seigneur, le Prince son aîné,
Dont le bras généreux trois fois m'a couronné,

Il ne fait que sortir encore d'une victoire,
Et pour tant de hauts faits je lui dois quelque gloire. (547–52)

I believe that Attale is deserving of the throne,
And what you have just said erases all doubts.
But Sire, the Prince, the elder, stands here before you,
His valorous arm has won me three kingdoms,
Why, his latest victory has just taken place,
And for all his noble actions I owe him some mark of glory.

Here as well we are given a sense of overdetermination. Is Prusias hesitant to name Attale as his heir because of birth order, that is, because of "le Prince son aîné"? Or is it because of Nicomède's achievements? Since Nicomède is both the older brother and the greater hero, we would not necessarily have to choose between these reasons if Prusias himself did not offer this double explanation.

What the overdetermination of Nicomède's superiority suggests is that being the elder makes him naturally a better fighter and leader than Attale. Corneille could have chosen a single criterion to justify Nicomède's worthiness: he could be simply the better man, or the older brother with a right to rule. But this is not the case. Once again, as in *Rodogune*, Corneille presents a kind of hybrid situation in which both the advantages of birth and differences in character count in the establishment of an heir.

This straddling effect places both *Rodogune* and *Nicomède* halfway between the first generation of tragedy and the second, between Pierre Corneille's first, most famous tragedies and the tragedies of Racine. In these two plays Corneille focuses attention on the sibling relation, the family tie that will dominate Racine's theater, but Corneille's two pairs of brothers in these plays are not *frères ennemis* in the same way the identical twins in Racine's first play are. Etéocle and Polynice kill each other in an attempt to differentiate themselves from each other; they can't bear their utter equality. By contrast, what causes a conflict between Antiochus and Séleucus is neither their similarity nor their difference, but rather their relation to their mother, whereas the clear differences between Nicomède and his brother are ultimately eclipsed by the vexed relation between Nicomède and his father. And although Attale is first presented as Nicomède's opponent and rival, he comes to resemble the brother from whom, as we have seen, he receives his ethical heritage. Attale's seamless admiration for his brother's ethical model is so exaggerated in the play's final scene that one might call the end of *Nicomède* one of Corneille's most extraordinary whitewashes, a peerless scene of general reconciliation that has the exact opposite effect of one of Shakespeare's pandemic endings, à la *Hamlet*. Here we are privy to an erasure not of all hope, but of all difference. Everyone agrees to agree.[19]

"King for Two Days": Thomas Corneille's *La Mort d'Annibal*

As was the case in his treatment of the theme of sibling rivalry in *Persée et Démétrius*, Thomas Corneille takes his brother's destabilization of primogeniture a step further. In Thomas' *La Mort d'Annibal*, the relation between the two brother figures is once again reversed: Attale, who is not Nicomède's brother in Thomas' play but remains a younger-brother figure, is presented as more powerful and independent than Nicomède, whose role and stature are reduced considerably. In addition, Thomas paints a chilling portrait of the degraded, corrupt Prusias which precludes any possibility that the father figure might provide a viable ethical model, but at the same time offers an alternative moral model from the older generation in the form of Annibal. Thus the failed transmission of a moral heritage between Nicomède's biological father and himself is compensated for by Nicomède's successful inheritance of his adoptive father's legacy.[20] And the tragedy's final paradox is that this adoptive inheritance, which already presupposes a breakdown of the kind of continuity by blood that is the very premise of the tragic conflict in a play like *Le Cid*, is also a very different type of inheritance, a legacy of resistance, negation, and death.

The plot of *La Mort d'Annibal* is somewhat more complex than that of *Nicomède*. As the title suggests, the action begins earlier than *Nicomède*, before the death of Annibal, who, along with his daughter, has been given asylum by Prusias. The curtain rises a short time after the announcement of the death of Attale's older brother, Eumène, which places Attale on the throne of Pergamum. In his first meeting with Prusias as king, Attale reveals his desire to marry Annibal's daughter, Elise. Prusias, who is also secretly in love with Elise, tells Attale he cannot support his marriage to her because his own son, Nicomède, may wish to marry her also. But when Nicomède asks permission of his father to wed Elise, Prusias again demurs, this time claiming that as Annibal's son-in-law, Nicomède would draw Rome's enmity. The love-stricken Prusias desperately vows to have his son and rival sent to Rome as a hostage, even though he knows Elise will marry no one who will not agree to join her father's fight against Rome, which he is incapable of doing.

Meanwhile, Nicomède asks Annibal for Elise's hand, and in spite of the Carthaginian's affection for him — he considers him his adoptive son — he feels that Attale, who is already a king in his own right, would be a more useful political ally in the fight against Rome than Nicomède, a mere heir to the throne. Prusias gets the Roman ambassador, Flaminius, to favor Prusias' own marriage with Elise on the condition that Prusias turn Annibal over to him. While Prusias, in an ironic echo of *Le Cid*, is debating the viability of this course of action — will Elise agree to marry the man who betrayed her father? — Flaminius is informed that Attale's older brother, Eumène, is in fact still alive, so that in marrying Attale, Annibal's daughter would unknowingly be marrying someone without any power, precisely what Rome desires. Flaminius thus supports the marriage of Elise and Attale, and to counter Attale's advantage, Prusias plots to have Annibal abducted and turned over to the Romans and to spread the rumor that he has been abducted by Attale. Nicomède saves his mentor and future father-in-law from his abductors, but not in time to prevent him from taking poison to ward off captivity in Rome. At the end of the play Prusias is killed by an unknown hand, while Attale's fate is unclear. The curtain falls as the dying Annibal enjoins his daughter and Nicomède to keep his spirit of resistance alive by carrying on the fight against Rome.

The most important transformation Thomas brings to this material is that the quarreling siblings of Pierre's play are not even related by blood in this one, and we may wonder why a younger brother would take up the challenge of reworking a story about sibling rivalry already treated by his older brother — a gesture that is surely an example of literary sibling rivalry — and make it into a story that is not explicitly about sibling rivalry. Is it not paradoxical that Thomas would compete with his older brother by eliminating a story of sibling rivalry? But as my analysis of the play will demonstrate, the theme of sibling rivalry has not in fact disappeared from Thomas' play, but he has treated it indirectly, which allows him to give precedence to the younger-brother figure in an unexpected way.

By making Attale into the younger brother of a man who is presumed dead but returns to life halfway through the drama, Thomas allows Attale to play at being king. Eumène might just as well have been Attale's father as his brother, but in that case Attale would have been the heir to the throne. As it is, the Roman ambassador, on hearing the news of Eumène's return, can dismissively characterize the younger brother as "un Roi de deux jours" (5:3; *Poëmes dramatiques*, 4:239) [King for two days].

Corneille draws attention to Attale's status as Eumène's younger brother by making us wonder initially about Attale's precise relation to Eumène: Attale is listed in the cast of characters as "successeur d'Eumène" and describes himself as "Le sang infortuné de ce malheureux Roi" (1:1, 4:173) [The unfortunate blood of that wretched King]; neither phrase tells us whether he is the deceased king's son or his brother. Only when Prusias refers to the late king as a brother and a king is the relation clarified: "Il [Eumène] eût nourri pour nous une éternelle haine, / Et malgré vous, l'honneur vous eût fait une loi / De suivre le Destin et d'un Frère et d'un Roi" (1:1; 4:174) [Eumène would have kept alive an eternal hatred for us, / And in spite of your wishes, your honor would have forced you / To follow the Fate of your Brother and your King].

As this quotation suggests, Attale, unlike his supposedly deceased older brother, about whom Prusias observes, "Son orgueil ne lui put enlever d'autre accord / Que de promettre aux Dieux ma défaite ou sa mort" (1:1; 4:174) [His pridefulness would not let him agree to anything / Except a promise to the Gods to defeat me or die], is immediately presented as a conciliatory force. He is a man whose wish to make peace with his brother's enemies emanates from a position of strength, not of weakness. Thomas' Attale is much more like his own Démétrius than he is like Pierre's Attale; Thomas' character has the advantages of being both a younger sibling and a brother who is dominant in spite of his birth order. A person of self-assurance who as a younger-brother figure must also learn to make alliances, he is both powerful and diplomatic, conciliatory when possible and confrontational when necessary. Attale refuses to kowtow to Flaminius' demands that he not consider marriage with Elise; when Annibal warns him of the risk he is running by asking for Elise's hand, he replies "Pour disposer de moi, prends-je loi de personne? / Seigneur, j'en crois ma flamme, et ne consulte plus" (3:2; 4:206) [In making my own decisions, am I ruled by anyone else? / Sire, I listen to my passion, there's nothing else to consult]. And yet he is also loath to alienate Rome unnecessarily and does his best to win the Roman ambassador over to his side:

Flaminius d'abord m'a traité de rebelle;
Mais enfin le voulant convaincre de mon zèle,
J'ai su si bien entrer dans tous ses intérêts,
Que par l'hymen d'Elise il comble mes souhaits. (4:3; 4:222)

At first Flaminius considered me a rebel;
But as I wished to persuade him of my support,
I figured out a way to uphold his interests so well
That he ended up approving of my marriage to Elise.

Attale is capable of modesty; when he learns that Nicomède might be interested in Elise, he tactfully backs off: "Ah, Seigneur, je lui cède, / Quoi qu'Elise à mes yeux fasse briller d'appas, / Si le Prince y prétend . . ." (1:1; 4:176) [Ah, Sire, I yield to him, / However much Elise's charms dazzle me, / If the Prince is courting her . . .]. Yet in his attempts to woo Elise later on, he insists on the status bestowed upon him by his high birth, "les droits de ma naissance" (3:1; 4:205). The latter phrase is rather startling in the mouth of a younger son; it is only through a fluke, the dramatic device of the false death of Eumène, that Attale has the short-lived luxury of a birthright to bandy about.

A startling reversal is effected by Thomas' modifications: his Nicomède is unceremoniously told by Annibal he is a less advantageous match for Elise than Attale:

Et quand je vous compare avec nos plus grands Rois,
Dans le faible honteux qu'ils laissent tous paraître,
Je ne vois que vous seul qui méritez de l'être.
Mais pour moi ce mérite est un bien imparfait,
C'est peu qu'en être digne, il faut l'être en effet. (2:4; 4:196–97)

And when I compare you to our greatest Kings,
With the shameful weakness that all of them reveal,
I see that you alone deserve to be a King.
But to me your merit is an imperfect advantage,
It's not enough to be deserving, you must actually be King.

The irony of this speech delivered to an older son and heir is that taken out of context, it has all the trappings of an impassioned condemnation of primogeniture: it sounds as if it were being addressed to a deserving younger son who must inevitably be passed over because of the disadvantages of his position.

All in all Thomas' Nicomède is a far cry from the exemplary figure of Pierre's drama. Thomas' character is a fairly minor figure until the very end of the play: as David A. Collins points out, he appears in only eight scenes —

by contrast, Prusias and Elise are each present in eighteen scenes[21] — and he remains offstage for a very long stretch (2:5–4:4).[22] Collins also observes that while Pierre's Nicomède is "a free agent able to act energetically on his own behalf," Thomas' character is "the spiritual child of Annibal and acts always as his dutiful subordinate."[23] Pierre's Attale had a father, a mother, and Rome on his back, while his Nicomède had no mother and a weak father. Thomas' Attale has no living parents, as opposed to Nicomède, who has two fathers, one weak but tyrannical, the other strong but intimidating.

One factor in the smaller role played by Nicomède in Thomas' play is Prusias' expanded role uneasily straddling the generations, collapsing any sense of direct inheritance: if Nicomède in Pierre's play ends up a father figure, Prusias in Thomas' is a brother figure. By making Prusias a rival for Elise's hand, Thomas escalates intergenerational confusion. The conflict no longer hinges on a parent who has the power to withhold or bestow his legacy, but rather on which of three rivals — belonging to two generations but equalized by their competition — is preferred by Elise. Prusias' non-paternal role is summarized by Flaminius' response to Prusias' willingness to send Nicomède to Rome as a hostage.

PRUSIAS:
N'aurez-vous pas mon Fils qui répondra de moi?
Vous en puis-je donner un gage plus sincère?
FLAMINIUS:
Non, si c'était un Fils que vous vissiez en Père;
Mais ce Fils aime Elise, et vos transports jaloux
Le livrent aux Romains moins pour eux que pour vous. (3:6; 4:216)

PRUSIAS:
Won't you have my Son to answer for me?
I could not give you a safeguard closer to my heart.
FLAMINIUS:
That would be true, if you looked at your Son through a Father's eyes.
But your Son loves Elise, and in your jealous rage
You have your reasons for handing him over to the Romans.

Prusias' ethical abdication creates a distrust of models, a concept central to Classical ethics and esthetics. Nicomède implicitly criticizes his father through his dissatisfaction with examples: "Les exemples, Seigneur

[Prusias], n'ont rien qui m'embarrasse. / Chacun a sa conduite, et tel peut succomber / Où tout autre, après lui, craindra peu de tomber" (1:3; 4:181) [Examples are something I don't put much stock in, Sire. / Each one of us acts differently, and one person might give in / Where those that follow have no fear of failure]. That Nicomède keeps his comments general — "Chacun," "tel" — only strengthens his tacit condemnation. And when Prusias' role in the plot against Annibal is revealed, Nicomède reiterates his support for his adoptive father using the semantically charged word "sang" in a way that again demonstrates how far we have come from the world of *Le Cid*: "tant que j'aurai du sang, / J'appuierai votre haine, et soutiendrai mon rang" (5:8; 4:244) [while blood flows through my veins, / I will support your hatred, and uphold my rank]. When Nicomède says he will defend his nobility as long as he has a drop of blood in his body, the word "sang" is evacuated of its usual metaphorical meaning in Classical tragedy, "lineage." "Sang," reduced to connoting individual survival, is no longer a sign of intergenerational continuity, for Prusias has just been proven to be a completely unworthy model to follow.

Adopting Difference

But where genetic inheritance flags, adoptive inheritance takes up the slack. In *La Mort d'Annibal*, Thomas Corneille refocuses on the paternal relation by expanding the role of Prusias and introducing the character of Annibal, but this does not mean his play represents a return to the direct, imitative heritage of Pierre's early tragedies. For one of Thomas' most important innovations is incorporating the character of Annibal as a figure embodying a counterethic that paradoxically opposes both Rome and the kind of direct inheritance that Rome itself opposes. Rome, with its mistrust of hereditary monarchy and its perennial wish to play kingmaker so as to retain control of its allies and conquests, is often portrayed as an underminer of predetermined inheritance; but that does not mean Annibal, the main resister to Rome, is himself a defender of positive, imitative inheritance. Rather, he is a figure embodying a kind of antilegacy of pure resistance and pure difference.

From the outset Nicomède is the Carthaginian's adoptive offspring, as Prusias implies: "Vous savez près de lui [Annibal] quel rang ce Fils [Nicomède] possède" (1:1; 4:176) [You know how Annibal feels about this Son]. The usual Classical substitution whereby Prusias refers to his son as "ce Fils" as opposed to "mon Fils" helps to suggest that Nicomède is Annibal's son as well. Annibal plainly expresses his paternal feelings for Nico-mède: "J'eus toujours pour vous, Prince, une tendresse extrême, / Et vous considérant comme un autre moi-même . . ." (2:4; 4:195) [I have always felt extreme tenderness for you, Prince, / And considering you as another form of myself . . .].

Annibal's first entrance onstage is cleverly timed to suggest that the adoptive heritage he offers picks up where genetic heritage—the continuity of the blood—breaks down. In this scene, Nicomède has just discovered that he is preferred by Elise, and he has insisted that he will go as a hostage to Rome to save her and her father, all the while retaining "the full liberty / Required by the pride of the blood whence I spring" ("l'entière liberté / Que du sang dont je sors exige la fierté" [2:2; 4:193]). These words iron-ically conjure up the perverse Prusias, the only carrier of Nicomède's blood we are privileged to meet. Annibal's first entrance at this very moment thus seems a kind of correction: it is as if the adoptive father were called forth by the noble son's naïve desire to follow a paternal model.

The ethical model Annibal provides for Nicomède is different in kind from the paternal model offered by someone like Don Diègue in *Le Cid*, for example. While Don Diègue's paternal role consisted of inculcating a cer-tain moral code in his son, Annibal's pose of tireless resistance requires a rel-egation of the very things Don Diègue passes on to his son. Annibal implies as much when he tells Nicomède of his lifelong oath to fight the Romans:

A peine au jour encor j'avais ouvert les yeux,
Que j'en [the Romans'] jurai le perte en présence des Dieux.
A ces nobles serments j'ai sans réserve aucune
Immolé biens, honneurs, repos, gloire, fortune. (2:4; 4:197)

Hardly had I opened my eyes on my first day of life
When I swore in the name of the Gods to bring the Romans down.
Without the least regret I have sacrificed to this noble oath
Possessions, honors, peace, glory, fortune.

This last line is a succinct inventory of what family heritage represents for Don Diègue: wealth, honors, stability, glory, and good fortune. And these are the very things that according to Annibal must be given up.

The value of this purely negative legacy should be seen not as a cohe-sive counterethic that might provide an alternative to primogeniture, but simply as a challenge to a system of inheritance perceived as stifling and unfair.[24] But Annibal's legacy is paradoxical by any measure, for it is a legacy of nonconformity and difference. This is apparent in both of Annibal's last scenes, in his parting words to Elise and in his dying words in the play's final scene. When he tells his daughter "C'est du sang qu'il nous faut en de pareils malheurs" (4:8; 4:232) [What we need in such misfortune is blood], once again blood does not connote lineage, but rather a willingness to give up one's own life. A dying father who says that what he needs in his misfortune is blood might be thought to be reaffirming the value of blood ties, but Annibal is referring to a legacy of self-sacrifice rather than the soothing belief that after one's death one's blood is continued through one's children. Unlike Nicomède and his father, Elise receives her own father's example: "L'exemple sera grand, je vais le recevoir" (4:8; 4:232) [Your example will remain great, I shall receive it]. But Annibal leaves a legacy not of continuity but of rupture, as he indicates in his death scene: "le Ciel [me] ramène, / Pour vous faire encor mieux hériter de ma haine" (5:8; 4:243) [I've been brought back by the Heavens, / To make sure you inherit my hatred].

It is for this reason that the union between Nicomède and Elise is presented in terms of a common hatred as much as a shared love. Nicomède's love for Elise is essentially a function of his devotion to Annibal: as Nicomède says, "la Fille sur moi peut autant que le Père" (1:3; 4:180) [the Daughter has as much power over me as the Father]. And the fact that the heritage passed along by Annibal to both his daughter and his son-in-law is a negative heritage explains the suggestion of sterility in Elise's description of the folly of loving someone as unfortunate as her: "Et me vouloir aimer, serait sans aucun fruit / Livrer sa destinée au malheur qui me suit" (1:5; 4:184) [Trying to love me is fruitless, it would mean / Handing over your fate to the misfortune that follows me]. Marriage with Elise is "fruitless," for what "follows" her is not a progeny, but unremitting misfortune. In reality the implication of nonheritage in these words is not a result of bad fortune, but rather a willful decision on the part of Elise: if she is to receive her father's paradoxical legacy, her *raison d'être* must be simply to resist Rome's oppression. Hatred of the Romans, then, is her only dowry: "De ma haine pour eux mon amour prend la loi, / Et c'est la seule dot que j'apporte avec moi" (1:5; 4:186) [My love takes its cues from my hatred for them, / And that's the only dowry that I have to offer]. Hatred of the Romans is also the only path to Elise's heart: "L'art de toucher mon coeur, c'est de servir ma haine" (4:7; 4:231) [The way to touch my heart is to be useful to my hatred].

The ultimate enigma of *La Mort d'Annibal* is that the drama concludes with Nicomède's and Elise's "inheritance" of a legacy that attacks the very conception of inheritance. Thomas Corneille's introduction of adoption as the central motif of his reworking of the material used by his brother in *Nicomède* should be read not as the solution to a problem — the breakdown of the direct transmission of an unchanging family inheritance, both material and ethical — but as an expression of a problem. The power of Annibal's legacy of resistance and death ultimately lies not in correcting the moral turpitude of Nicomède's biological father, nor in reestablishing the continuity between the generations, but in recognizing that society's traditional means of providing that continuity are no longer viable.

8

Degenerating Inheritance

Timocrate, *Oedipe*, and *La Thébaïde*

When Racine presents his first tragedy, *La Thébaïde*, in 1664, a scant five years after Pierre Corneille's *Oedipe*, it might appear that like Thomas Corneille, he is following in the formidable footsteps of the greatest tragedian of the previous generation. *La Thébaïde* is, after all, the story of what goes on in the house of Laius in the generation following the death of Oedipus. How appropriate, we might believe, that Racine would help to initiate a new generation of tragedies by dramatizing the conflicts experienced by the next generation in the very same story that has just been treated by his most illustrious predecessor.[1] And yet things are not so simple. *Oedipe* should be read not only as a forerunner of Racine's *Thébaïde*, but also as a response to one of the great theatrical sensations of the seventeenth century: Thomas Corneille's *Timocrate*, which held the stage for an unparalleled six months in 1656, three years before Pierre broke a theatrical silence of eight years with his *Oedipe*.

Before discussing the thematically linked *Oedipe* and *La Thébaïde*, let us speculate about the impact that *Timocrate* might have had on Pierre Corneille's play in particular.[2] From the time of the presentation (and failure) of his *Pertharite* (1651) to that of *Oedipe* eight years later, Pierre Corneille gives up the theater, a silence that André Stegmann attributes partially to Thomas' rising star: "Thomas has obviously taken up the torch with promising successes. . . . In 1656, Thomas' *Timocrate* is the greatest hit of the century" (*Oeuvres complètes*, 542). *Timocrate* is the story of a king who poses as a commoner in order to win the hand of a princess, rather than, as we might expect, the reverse: a commoner who pretends to be a nobleman. The play probably owes its great success in part to the clever masking of the suitor's true royal identity until near the end of the play—Thomas may have gotten the basic idea from Pierre's *Don Sanche d'Aragon* of a few years earlier, which also features a king parading as a commoner, but Pierre rather spoils it all in that play by revealing Carlos' true identity to the audience early on, in act 2.

Timocrate well exemplifies the conflicting value-systems we have been discussing throughout this work. The play seems to suggest that its title character must have two identities and that each contributes something to his heroic status. He must be a man of high birth, but he cannot take the privileges of royalty for granted; rather, he must embody several quite distinct types of virtue — including a certain degree of humility — in order to earn the right to wed the princess. And while it is difficult to know exactly why the public thronged to *Timocrate* in such unprecedented numbers, it is certainly possible that the prospect of a king acting like a commoner pleasantly scandalized mid-seventeenth-century audiences in the same way that late-twentieth-century filmgoers have been titillated by role-switching confections such as *Trading Places*, *Tootsie*, and *Mrs. Doubtfire*.

Double Identity: Thomas Corneille's *Timocrate*

The plot of *Timocrate* simply literalizes the problem of conflicting identity that underlies much of Pierre Corneille's early theater. Upon the death of the king of Crete, the king's son, Timocrate, takes the throne. The problem is that Timocrate is in love with Eriphile, the daughter of the queen of Argos and of the late king, who was killed in a war with Crete that is still being waged. Timocrate's love for Eriphile is thus doubly impossible, for not only is Eriphile the princess of a country with which Timocrate's own land is still at war, but she is also the daughter of a man killed by Timocrate's father. When Timocrate besieges Argos and offers to make peace at the price of marriage with Eriphile, the queen instead promises her daughter's hand to anyone who defeats and kills Timocrate, thus saving her country and avenging her husband's death. In the double whammy of obstacles it places in the path of love, the demands of patriotism paired with those of familial honor, *Timocrate* is like a combination of *Le Cid* and *Horace*.

This plot appears destined to generate the same sort of grave pronouncements about divided allegiances as Pierre Corneille's early tragedies, but Timocrate's double role gives Thomas' play a subtly comic twist well suited to its less deterministic view of inherited identity. Faced with the impossibility of wooing Eriphile in any direct way, Timocrate takes on the identity of a soldier in the Argive army and wins her over in the guise of one of her own fighting men. By the time the curtain rises Timocrate, parading under the name of Cléomène, has had such success at this ploy that Eriphile much prefers him to her aristocratic suitors, Cresphonte and Léontidas — neighboring kings eliminated without further ado in act 3 in an offstage battle against Timocrate — and Nicandre, an Argive prince who laments the difficulty of competing with two kings and by the same token foolishly refuses to take the lowly Cléomène seriously. The contrived and contorted action of *Timocrate* is such that no one — neither the other characters nor the audience — is informed that Cléomène is actually Timocrate until near the end of the drama. While various plot twists might have led an unusually alert viewer to harbor suspicions about the double identity — Timocrate as Timocrate is never seen onstage; he is described as lowering his visor in battle (so as not to be recognized); and his exact whereabouts are suitably unclear at crucial moments — the public was certainly intended to remain in the dark until the grand revelation scene.

Even after Cléomène has at last revealed who he really is, his double identity is maintained. The queen insists on honoring her promise to give her daughter to the man who "defeats" Timocrate; that man, ironically, is Cléomène. But she also refuses to take back her vow to exact revenge for her husband's death by demanding the death of Timocrate. The solution proposed by Cléomène / Timocrate and accepted by the queen with reluctance — for she, too, like everyone else, has been won over by Cléomène — is for her to allow Cléomène to marry her daughter, thereby fulfilling her first obligation, and then to put Timocrate — the same man, but with a different identity — to death. This is not destined to be, of course, as we might suspect, given the playful overtones lent to the drama by Timocrate's double identity. The Cretan army enters the city and forces the queen to abdicate, thus leaving Timocrate in complete control. The queen willingly relinquishes her oath of revenge, since it is no longer in her power to carry it out.

Whether *Timocrate* is read as a tragedy with a happy ending, like *Cinna* or *Nicomède*, or as a tragedy with comic elements, it is about the interplay between opposing identities.[3] Since the audience does not know the title character as anything but a humble soldier until late in the play, the problem of identity most strongly emphasized during most of the drama is the contradiction entailed by a commoner loving and being loved by a princess. *Timocrate* takes the love conflict in *Le Cid* a step further; what was difficult in that play becomes impossible in this one. Chimène wonders how she can love her father's killer, but Rodrigue in avenging the insult to his family is acting according to the conventions of his society — if not according to the king's wishes. Once Chimène has been ordered by the king to marry Rodrigue and has even admitted that she does indeed still love him, her continued opposition to the marriage is made to appear fastidious, the drama's unresolved conclusion a way of insinuating that with time Chimène will drop all her nonsense about her father's honor. The conflict in *Timocrate* would be analogous were it not for the intercession of Timocrate's false identity: Eriphile lamenting the madness of loving the son of her father's killer, or of wanting to marry her city's greatest enemy would indeed be similar to Chimène. But as it is, her situation is played out in quite a different manner.

Eriphile, a princess in love with a commoner, finds herself in even narrower straits than if she were in love with an enemy king. It is made perfectly clear that as a commoner Cléomène cannot hope to marry the princess, and yet he is also portrayed as the worthiest of her suitors. The final revelation of Cléomène's identity does not fully resolve the real uncertainty in this drama about that most Classical of concepts, rank. What is so fascinating about *Timocrate* is that there does turn out to be a remedy to Eriphile's problem, and that it comes *before* Cléomène reveals that he is Timocrate: when he claims to have captured Timocrate, thus saving the city of Argos, Cléomène suggests, and the queen ultimately concedes, that this grand action proves he must be of noble birth. In this play, the revelation of Cléomène's identity may be a *coup de théâtre*, but it is not an example of *rex ex machina*, because Cléomène's worth is manifest before the truth of his noble birth comes out. This paradox — the fact that the identity of the worthy, enterprising soldier and that of the enemy king are not only opposed, but are also made to blend into each other — is apparent in Cléomène's knotty aphorism, "La naissance est l'appui des courages mal nés" (4:3; *Poëmes dramatiques*, 2:221) [Birth is the stronghold of hearts of lowly birth], which suggests that if the value of well-born people comes only from their birth, they are not truly well born.

Is this not tantamount to saying that in order to be truly well born you must not rely completely on your birth? The playfulness of identity that gives the drama its impact is not simply based upon a mystery leading up to a revelation; rather, there is truth to both aspects of Timocrate's identity. Even after he has removed his mask, Eriphile compartmentalizes her feelings about him under his two different names, the man she loves being Cléomène, while the enemy king is Timocrate:

> Ah! si de cet hymen [with Cléomène] dépend le sacrifice [of
>   Timocrate],

Où d'un serment fatal l'expose l'injustice,
Ne crois pas que jamais ni le fer ni le feu
M'en puissent arracher le sacrilège aveu.
Ce coeur dont on l'attend doit trop à Cléomène,
Pour rendre mon amour ministre de la haine,
Et des Dieux indignés l'implacable courroux
Peut perdre Timocrate, et non pas mon Epoux. (5:1; 2:232–33)

Ah! if my marriage with Cléomène depends on Timocrate's sacrifice,
Which an unfair, deadly oath exposes him to,
You are wrong to assume that sword or fire
Could ever drive me to wish for that sacrilege.
The heart expected to wish such a thing owes so much
To Cléomène that it could not force my love to obey hatred,
And the unshakable wrath of the indignant Gods
Can destroy Timocrate, but not my Husband.

After our initial shock at the revelation of Timocrate's identity, the hind-sight peculiar to literary texts makes it seem inevitable that the admirable Cléomène has been Timocrate all along. In the end, what is most disorient-ing about this drama is not the fact that the two men are one and the same, but rather that Cléomène's identity and value are never fully subsumed by Timocrate's. The man who is in charge at the end of the drama may well be Timocrate. But the man Eriphile loves continues to be Cléomène.

Tragedy of an Older Brother: Pierre Corneille's *Oedipe*

This lesson of double identity will help us to make sense of Pierre Cor-neille's eccentric version of the Oedipus story, a complex and highly original treatment of the most famous of all Greek myths that is a fine barometer by which to measure the considerable changes in the nature and valence of familial inheritance that take place between the first and second generations of tragedy.[4] Pierre makes this forbidding tale of intergenerational conflict into a dynastic sparring match between a brother and a sister: he gives Oedipe a younger sister, Dircé, who spends most of the play expressing her dissatisfaction at having been passed over for the succession when Oedipe, believed at the time to be a foreigner, was given the throne for saving the city from the Sphinx. Here again, as in *Nicomède*, the older sibling and heir wins out, but in a most unconventional way: Oedipe discovers in the end that he is not a usurper but rather the rightful heir to the throne of Thebes. There is little doubt that it is a discovery he would just as soon have not made.

The example of *Timocrate* is important here in several ways. In Pierre's play as in Thomas', the discovery of "legitimacy" — Oedipe, like Cléomène, is revealed to be a king by blood — does not resolve the issues raised by the drama. Describing *Oedipe* as a play about a man who finds out he is the rightful king of Thebes would be oversimplifying matters, to say the least, and in the most famous versions of the story, particularly Sophocles' *Oedipus the King*, the revelation of Oedipus' origins, which coincides with his understanding the full extent of his misfortune, is a moment of such power and intensity that the political component of the drama fades into the background. Not so in Corneille's extraordinary, idiosyncratically politicized version of this material, in which the final revelation, coming on the heels of a great deal of bickering about succession and power distribution, is very much downplayed, indeed, almost anticlimactic. Even if the discovery of the title character's legitimacy is more acutely ironic in *Oedipe* than in *Timocrate*, the unsettling feeling that the discovery is somehow overshadowed by what has preceded, and in a sense does not fully mesh with the events of the play, persists in both dramas.

Moreover, the playfulness of double identity that is so central to *Timocrate* quite likely influenced Pierre Corneille's strange confection of the role of Thésée, who is in love with Dircé but poses as her brother throughout much of the play. Thésée knows perfectly well he is not Laïus' son, but his idea is to save the woman he loves from the oracular demand, pronounced by Laïus' ghost, that Laïus' blood be spilled in order to end the plague that has been decimating the city. It is probably inevitable that any version of the Oedipus story will deal with questions of identity, but as is the case with *Timocrate*, Corneille's *Oedipe* is a drama about how little is really determined or solved by the discovery of identity. Perhaps Pierre Corneille's greatest innovation is that his play is not only about the overdetermination of identity — you can never escape who you are — but also about its underdetermination in a world that has fewer and fewer stable notions about identity and the transmission of values between generations.

Pierre Corneille recognizes that his whole approach to this material differs from what it might have been a generation earlier:

I will not deny that after deciding to write about this subject, confident that I would have the support of all learned people, who consider it to be the masterpiece of antiquity, . . . I did have a moment of hesitation when I studied it more closely and at my leisure than I had when I first made my choice. I recognized that what seemed miraculous in those distant centuries might seem horrible in ours; that the strange and eloquent description of the way that unfortunate king puts out his own eyes . . . would disturb our sensitive ladies, who form the better part of the audience and whose companions naturally condemn anything the ladies find distasteful; and finally that because love did not enter into this subject and women played no important role, it was lacking the main ornaments that ordinarily gain us the public's favor. I have tried to remedy these ills as best I could . . . , which has made me lose the advantage I promised myself, that is, to be in many cases merely the translator of those great men who have preceded me. As I have followed a different road from theirs, I have been unable to meet up with them. (*Oeuvres complètes*, 566–67)

This passage indicates several important changes over time. The observation that contemporary audiences see things differently than those of antiquity is actually less important than the unstated implication that the influence of women among the viewing public is greater in 1659 than it was a generation earlier. It could be argued that in this second generation of tragedies, contemporary literary models, which have never been without importance for Corneille, eclipse the models of antiquity. In approaching this material Corneille is as different from his own earlier example as he is from his ancient literary models.[5] His description of his relation to his ancient predecessors — "As I have followed a different road from theirs, I have been unable to meet up with them" — makes it difficult not to think of Oedipus and Laius, whose confrontation at the triple crossroads has become emblematic of the impossibility for the chosen representatives of one generation simply to succeed their parents as the representatives of the previous generation: either to coexist harmoniously with them or to stay out of their murderous way. It is as if Corneille were attempting to avoid this kind of confrontation with the fathers by taking "a different road"; a road which places him face to face not with fathers, but with brothers. Pierre Corneille is now interacting as much with sibling figures — including his own younger brother — as with "the fathers" of ancient times.

A writer's way of treating an inherited myth never has a simple causality; still, it is difficult to see Corneille's transformation of the Oedipus myth into a drama of sibling rivalry as unrelated to his status as the older brother of an up-and-coming literary figure. It takes some doing to make the story of Oedipus into the tale of a royal succession disputed by a younger sibling who has now come to maturity, but that is exactly what Corneille has done.[6] Corneille's reframing of the story in terms of the sibling relation must have been intentional; nothing in the myth encouraged him to give Oedipe a sibling. He makes Oedipe's sibling a sister not only because of the importance of a female protagonist to hold the interest of the women in the audience, but also because Laius' oracle stating that he is destined to be killed by his own son means that any male child born to Jocaste would have been left out on a mountainside to die.

One of the most intriguing aspects of this play is that much of it must have appeared to the viewing public as a simple distraction from the brutal truth of Oedipe's identity.[7] Oedipe differs from Timocrate in that the audience at least knows the truth of his double identity from the very start, and since the public is aware that Oedipe is Dircé's older brother, this is a drama whose central point — Dircé's protests about Oedipe's usurpation of power — seems a moot point. As we might suspect, when Oedipe's identity is revealed, the question of Dircé's birthright is summarily dropped.

Oedipe is a play in which the questions of royal succession in general and primogeniture in particular remain extraordinarily vexed and yet are never allowed to drop out of sight. The tandem issues of the unwitting older brother's legitimacy and the unyielding younger sister's attempt at being her father's heir transform the stark lines of the dreadful family tragedy into an ill-defined mass of sibling discontent. A number of ultimately inapplicable complications are raised before Oedipe's true identity is revealed. Was Laïus' rightful successor the presumed outsider, Oedipe, or Laïus' daughter, Dircé? Even if it was Oedipe, is the king's rightful successor one of his two sons (343–46) or Dircé, to make up for Oedipe's assumption of a throne to which he apparently had no right by blood? The main reason Oedipe insists that Dircé must marry her cousin, Aemon, is that the latter is less of a threat to his own power and authority than Thésée, a king in his own right: "Aemon serait pour moi digne de la princesse: / S'il a de la naissance, il a quelque faiblesse" (265–66) [In my view Aemon would be worthy of the princess, / He is well born, but has a certain weakness]. And yet in his negotations with Dircé, Oedipe hints that she and Aemon might one day rule: "Son hymen toutefois ne vous fait point descendre; / S'il n'est pas dans le trône, il a droit d'y prétendre" (405–6) [But marriage to him won't be a step down for you; / Though he's not on the throne, he has a rightful claim to it]. Even at the end of the play, after the revelation of Oedipe's identity, the question of succession does not disappear. In Oedipe's final speech he asks Dircé and Thésée, whose marriage he no longer opposes, to make peace between his two sons, whose claim to the throne has just been distressingly reaffirmed: "Prenez soin d'apaiser les discords de mes fils" (1875) [Take care to appease my sons' disputes]. It is as if Corneille ended his play with a proleptic invitation to Racine to take up the story where he left off.

Another factor complicating the question of succession is the portrayal of Oedipe's younger sister, Dircé, as the psychological heir of her father, a would-be heroine whose old-style valor remains one of the main thrusts of the drama. Dircé, whom Corneille in his preface calls "the only heir to [Laïus'] crown" (*Oeuvres complètes*, 567) and who repeatedly asserts her birthright and Oedipe's lack of legitimacy (421–24, 468–74, 510–12, 533–36), is willing to sacrifice herself to save her city and her family in spite of their poor treatment of her. When the ghost of Laïus appears and demands that his own blood be spilled to put an end to the plague, Dircé volunteers with a heroic zeal that surpasses even that of Iphigénie in Racine's play: "Admire, peuple ingrat, qui m'as déshéritée, / Quelle vengeance en prend ta princesse irritée" (627–28) [Admire, ungrateful people that disowned me, / What sort of revenge your wronged princess takes]. The point is, of course, that she does not take revenge on the city that disinherited her, but gladly accepts the sacrifice of her life, her enthusiasm for the idea of giving up her life out of a sense of obligation to her father's memory putting her at the antipodes of earlier would-be heroines like Chimène, whose attempts to fulfill her duty toward her own father are forced, at times even resentful.[8] If Dircé is added to the story largely to satisfy what Corneille correctly perceived as a new generation of theatergoers more strongly influenced by women, perhaps it is not surprising that he portrays Dircé as if she were simply an early Cornelian hero in skirts, a woman as inflexible as Don Diègue in her valuing of glory over love.

In her quest to be perceived as her father's rightful heir, Dircé strongly rejects any identification with her mother, from whom she strives to maintain a disdainful distance, as she tells Jocaste:

Votre second hymen [to Oedipe] put avoir d'autres causes [besides love];
Mais j'oserai vous dire, à bien juger des choses,
Que pour avoir reçu la vie en votre flanc,
J'y dois avoir sucé fort peu de votre sang.
Celui du grand Laïus, dont je m'y suis formée,
Trouve bien qu'il est doux d'aimer et d'être aimée:
Mais il ne peut trouver qu'on soit digne du jour
Quand aux soins de sa gloire on préfère l'amour. (873–80)

You may have married Oedipe for reasons other than love;
But I daresay, having given the matter much thought,
That although I was given life in your womb,

I cannot have received very much of your blood.
The blood of the great Laïus from which I was formed
Knows well how sweet it is to love and to be loved:
But his blood does not feel one is worthy of living
When one puts love before the concerns of glory.

Dircé implies that she is of her father's blood but not of her mother's, thus reflecting an Aristotelian, patrocentric view of genetics according to which the father is the true parent, the mother merely a medium by which the paternal essence is transmitted to the child:[9] "[Je] sentais dans mon coeur le sang de mes aïeux. / C'était ce même sang dont vous m'avez fait naître" (896–97) [I felt my ancestors' blood in my heart, / It was the same blood of which you made me a descendant].

This Athena-like espousal of the masculine contributes to the portrait of Dircé as her father's would-be heir, but her attempt to become Laïus' successor is presented with a certain degree of irony. The daughter's idealization of her father is in keeping with her status as heir, but its obvious oversimplification of Laïus' motivations gives the lie to the entire notion of normative inheritance. She is surely mistaken in believing her father was killed in the course of a trip undertaken to consult the oracle out of loving concern for his daughter's future ("L'amour qu'il me portait eut sur lui tel pouvoir / Qu'il voulut sur mon sort faire parler l'oracle" [646–47]). That Jocaste attempts to veto the trip out of fear Laïus will do away with Dircé just as he did away with his firstborn son ("à ce dessein la Reine mit obstacle, / De peur que cette voix des destins ennemis / Ne fût aussi funeste à la fille qu'au fils" [648–50]) makes it likely that Laïus was on his way to Delphi to make sure his daughter would not grow up to kill him as he had already been told a son would. If Dircé's misguided idealization of her father potentially bolsters her position as his heir, he has no heritage to bestow other than an ironic legacy of intergenerational violence.[10]

A Sister, a Sister, My Kingdom for a Sister

If Dircé ultimately fails to become her father's heir, it is not because she is a woman and a younger sibling, or even because of the demands of the myth — having invented Dircé, Corneille could have left her on the throne at the end of the play and kept the rest of the story intact. Rather Corneille, even though he takes pains to incorporate the theme of sibling rivalry into his play, systematically treats the sibling bond, the *raison d'être* of the character of Dircé, as a mere distraction from the more serious business of the play. The ironic benefit to Dircé that results from Oedipe's catastrophic replacement of his father — by murdering Laïus, Oedipe probably saved his sister from being killed — epitomizes the function of the sibling bond as a kind of buffer against the dire nature of the parent-child relation.[11] The play features two sets of siblings, one actual but hidden, Dircé and Oedipe, the other open but fictional, Dircé and Thésée. The second pair in particular plays a crucial role in Corneille's undermining of inheritance.

Thésée's role as Dircé's would-be brother, a pure invention, does nothing to lend an air of gravitas to the proceedings. It is difficult to escape the impression that certain lines uttered by this phantom brother and his putative mother and sister have a faintly tongue-in-cheek air about them. Thésée: "Je l'aimais en amant, je l'aime encore en frère. / C'est sous un autre nom le même empressement; / Je ne l'aime pas moins, mais je l'aime autrement" (1118–20) [I loved her as a suitor, I still love her as a brother. / It's merely another name for the same affection; / I love her no less, just not in the same way]; Jocaste: "Eh bien! soyez mon fils, puisque vous voulez l'être" (1125) [All right, then! Be my son, since that's what you want to be]; Thésée (to Dircé): "Je ne puis en amant ce que je puis en frère / J'en garderai le nom tant qu'il [vous] faudra mourir" (1222–23) [There are things I cannot do as a lover that I can as a brother, / I'll continue to call myself your brother as long as you have to die]; Dircé: "Ah! Prince, s'il se peut, ne soyez point mon frère" (1262) [Oh! Prince, if it is possible, do not be my brother]; Thésée (to Oedipe): "Seigneur, je suis le frère ou l'amant de Dircé" (1487) [Sire, I am the brother or the lover of Dircé]. This catalogue of peculiar pronouncements raises a whole host of questions. Could these lines truly be uttered with tragic decorum?[12] Why would Corneille repeatedly draw attention to the falseness of Thésée's identity as Dircé's brother, especially when the situation is fairly simple and the audience unlikely to be confused? And can one escape the impression that the entire incest motif raised by this surprising turn of events is treated, if at all, with a jeer, or even a leer — "I love her no less, just not in the same way" — rather than with the fear and trembling appropriate to tragedy?

Maybe that is precisely the point: Corneille deflects the horror of the actual mother-son incest, which he does not dwell upon, via the potential brother-sister incest, which he invents. What's more, brother-sister incest certainly did not conjure up the same level of repulsion as mother-son incest in a seventeenth-century French audience, and the audience knows that Thésée and Dircé are not brother and sister. The sibling relation merely defuses the explosive charge of intergenerational disturbance.

The openendedness implied by Thésée's playful double identity may be the single element of *Oedipe* that most clearly marks its debt to *Timocrate*. The story of Oedipus is always a tale of double identity: a drama about a chosen leader (*tyrannos*) who is a hereditary king (*basileus*), a Corinthian who is a Theban, the savior of his city who is the destroyer of his family, and the investigator of a crime who is the criminal. All of this is true in Corneille's version, too; what is different is that the revelation of the double identity does not have the same devastating impact as in other dramatizations of the myth, a change made possible largely by the character of Oedipe's sister.

Corneille's version of the story is surprising up to the very end: the narration of the dramatic suicide of Jocaste after her discovery of what she has done is postponed until after Oedipe's exit from the stage, so that his final scenes, which also precede his self-blinding, are with Dircé. And rather than scenes of recrimination and remorse, they are scenes of sisterly commiseration. When at last Oedipe has full understanding of his situation, he does go through the usual inventory of skewed familial relations it creates, calling himself "l'assassin de mon père" (1765) [my father's murderer], "le mari de ma mère" (1766) [my mother's husband], and "Le frère de mes fils et le fils de ma femme" (1770) [My sons' brother and my wife's son], but this de rigueur lamentation, recited to two minor characters, has surprisingly little impact. The first words Oedipe addresses to a member of his family after the revelation are about his identity as Dircé's brother, the one familial relation not rendered abnormal by the dire events of the play, for Oedipe has neither killed nor slept with his newly discovered sister, but has merely spent a lot of time arguing with her about her choice of a mate.

OEDIPE:
Votre frère est connu, le savez-vous, Madame?
DIRCÉ:
Oui, Seigneur, et Phorbas m'a tout dit en deux mots.
OEDIPE:
Votre amour pour Thésée est dans un plein repos.
Vous n'apprehendez plus que le titre de frère
S'oppose à cette ardeur qui vous était si chère. (1790–94)

OEDIPE:
Your brother has been revealed, have you heard, Madam?
DIRCÉ:
Yes, Sire, Phorbas told me the gist of it.

OEDIPE:
You can put you fears to rest about your love for Thésée.
You no longer have to fear that the name of brother
Is an obstacle to the passion so dear to your heart.

"The name of brother" superficially refers to Thésée's identity as a brother Dircé could not have married, but it also evokes Oedipe's identity as a brother who will not oppose the union. But why at this cataclysmic moment would Oedipe point out that he, who turns out to be Dircé's brother, now gives her his blessing to wed Thésée, who turns out not to be her brother? On the one hand, the audience never had any doubt that the danger of incest between Dircé and Thésée was spurious; on the other hand, focusing on Oedipe's normal relation with his sister rather than his sociopathic relation to his parents distracts from the high drama of the situation. It is as if the central function of the sibling drama were to mute the horror of a parental tragedy that is not given full voice.

If there is a dénouement in the history of Western drama tailor-made to create a sense of all-encompassing desolation, it is the end of the story of Oedipus and Jocasta. But such is not the case in Corneille's version. When Dircé finds out who Oedipe is, she suddenly becomes the model sister, as if that single kernel of a positive relation made up for the familial devastation. Dircé insists that her brother has done nothing wrong: "Quel crime avez-vous fait que d'être malheureux?" (1819) [What is your crime, besides being unlucky?]. Even more surprisingly, she persists in her willingness to sacrifice herself to save the city on the theory that even at this late date, the shade of Laïus might been asking for her blood rather than Oedipe's:

> Ainsi j'espère encor que demain, par son choix,
> Le ciel épargnera le plus grand de nos rois.
> L'intérêt des Thébains et de votre famille
> Tournera son courroux sur l'orgueil d'une fille
> Qui n'a rien que l'Etat doive considérer,
> Et qui contre son Roi n'a fait que murmurer. (1851–56)

> So it is still my hope that tomorrow the heavens
> Will choose to spare the greatest of our kings.
> The interests of the Thebans and of your family
> Will divert the heavens' wrath onto a prideful daughter
> Who has no status the State must keep in mind,
> And has done nothing for her King except to grumble.

Dircé, dropping her claim to the throne, offers to sacrifice herself less to save the city than to make up for her earlier insubordination. One might foresee that the uncovering of Oedipe's identity would lead to expressions of remorse, but who would have thought it would be the remorse of a younger sister making amends for her earlier disrespect toward an older brother whom she now tries to pass off as her father's rightful heir?

Blood Double: Racine's *La Thébaïde, ou Les Frères ennemis*

In its shifting of dramatic focus away from the parent-child axis and toward the sibling axis, Pierre Corneille's version of the Oedipus myth certainly paves the way for Racine's first tragedy, *La Thébaïde* — more commonly known in the seventeenth century as *Les Frères ennemis* — just as Thomas Corneille's *Timocrate* with its permeable view of identity undoubtedly contributed to *Oedipe*. But neither *Timocrate* nor *Oedipe* fully prepares us for the upending of family structure that takes place in *La Thébaïde*. It is not simply the fact that Racine's drama is almost exclusively focused on the sibling bond that marks it as a play ushering in a new generation, whereas earlier sibling dramas like *Horace*, *Rodogune,* and *Nicomède* featured influential parental figures as well.[13] It is the very nature of inheritance and of family hierarchy that undergoes a radical transformation in Racine's dramatic début.

In *La Thébaïde*, a tragedy about Oedipus' and Jocasta's feuding twin sons, the sibling bond no longer involves inheritance or legitimacy, that is to say, the advantage of being chosen by the previous generation, or a relation of imitation establishing continuity with that older generation. Rather, the sibling bond is about the desire for differentiation *purely within the present generation*. Racine makes Oedipus' sons into twins, which they are not in the ancient versions he consulted,[14] and unlike *Rodogune*, which is fueled by the question of which twin was born before the other,[15] *La Thébaïde* never once brings that question up. In the light of plays like *Rodogune*, *Nicomède*, and Thomas Corneille's very recent *Persée et Démétrius* — not to mention the social realities of the day — Racine could hardly have been unaware of the issue of birth order and its potential importance in the identification of an heir. But he places the battle between Etéocle and Polynice on a level playing field.[16] The character whose name is mentioned in conjunction with the phrase "droits de la naissance" (227)[17] [birthrights] is not Etéocle or Polynice, but rather the vilainous Créon, Jocaste's brother, who plays the twins off each other with the idea of "inheriting" the throne from his late nephew, Oedipe, and marrying his niece, Antigone, who is in love with his son, Hémon. And while Créon is the only surviving character at the end of the drama—a highly doubtful benefit—his unfulfilled wish to join the others in death suggests that rather than surviving to enjoy inheriting the throne (by default), he is denied the right to die.

The central conflict of the play arises from Etéocle's obstinate refusal to share power with Polynice, who overreacts, in typical tragic fashion, by besieging the city; predictably, the brothers duel to their mutual destruction. The war between the brothers results from Oedipe's earlier refusal to name an heir and his deathbed wish that power be shared by his two sons in alternating year-long reigns. Etéocle took power first not because he is the older brother—although he may coincidentally be the firstborn—but only by chance, as his mother reminds him: "Le sort vous appela le premier à l'empire" (88) [Your lot was to come to power first]. If it were ever stated that Etéocle is the older brother, this might conceivably be construed to mean that destiny, one of the meanings of the word "sort," gave Etéocle the age advantage and thus brought him to power first— although in that case a term like "naissance" would have conveyed the meaning more clearly. And given that the relative age of the brothers is never brought up, we may assume that what Jocaste is alluding to is the fact that they drew lots—what the French call "tirer au sort"—to see who would assume the throne first.

When Etéocle refuses to follow his father's instructions and step down after his first year on the throne, he is not acting as an imperious older sibling, but rather as a man who will not give up the power to which he has grown accustomed. He does it not because he has a right to do it, but because he thinks he can get away with it. When Polynice calls Etéocle a usurper (460, 521, 1152), the term does not have the same impact as Dircé's claims in *Oedipe*, for Oedipe gains legitimacy, for what it is worth, when he is revealed to be Dircé's older brother. By contrast, *La Thébaïde* implies age has nothing to do with it: if Polynice had come to power first, he probably would have done the same thing as Etéocle has done, and Etéocle would be calling him a usurper.

Oedipe's dying wish and its disastrous results set the stage for Racine's more general destabilization of inheritance throughout his tragedies. By refusing to select a single heir, Oedipe may be trying to avoid either being unjust or setting off a dynastic civil war, but his attempt ironically illustrates one of the advantages of primogeniture, which favors stability across time, even if that comes at the expense of fairness. Moreover, as in many of

Racine's tragedies, there is no positive legacy in this drama but only a negative one, a family curse,[18] as is clear in Jocaste's address to the sun:

> Mais ces monstres [Etéocle and Polynice], hélas! ne t'épouvantent
> 		guères:
> La race de Laïus les a rendus vulgaires;
> Tu peux voir sans frayeur les crimes de mes fils,
> Après ceux que le père et la mère ont commis.
> Tu ne t'étonnes pas si mes fils sont perfides,
> S'ils sont tous deux méchants, et s'ils sont parricides;
> Tu sais qu'ils sont sortis d'un sang incestueux,
> Et tu t'étonnerais s'ils étaient vertueux. (27–34)

> But these monsters, alas! don't frighten you at all:
> Laïus' lineage has made them quite ordinary;
> You can gaze without horror upon my sons' crimes,
> After those that their father and mother have committed.
> You are not amazed if my sons are perverse,
> If they are both evil, if they are kin-murderers;
> You know they are the products of an incestuous blood,
> And you would be amazed if they were virtuous.

This is a parody of familial continuity, of truisms like "Tel père, tel fils" or "chip off the old block." Of course those bits of folk wisdom do not always refer to positive traits, but in the first generation of Classical tragedy, the family inheritance is nearly always a thing of great value that brings with it prestige and glory. In *La Thébaïde* and in much of Racine's theater, inheritance is a burden one cannot avoid or escape.[19]

Oedipe in Corneille's play also has a dire familial heritage, but the demands made by Laïus' ghost are quite different from those of the oracle requiring the spilling of blood in *La Thébaïde*. A comparison of the two pronouncements is instructive.

> Un grand crime impuni cause votre misère,
> Par le sang de ma race il se doit effacer,
> 	Mais à moins que de le verser,
> 	Le ciel ne se peut satisfaire,
> Et la fin de vos maux ne se fera point voir
> 	Que mon sang n'ait fait son devoir. (*Oedipe*, 605–610)

A great unpunished crime is causing your suffering,
It must be washed clean in the blood of my lineage,
   But unless it is shed,
   The heavens will not be satisfied,
And the end of your troubles will not be seen
   Until my blood has done its duty.

Thébains, pour n'avoir plus de guerres,
Il faut, par un ordre fatal,
Que le dernier du sang royal
Par son trépas ensanglante vos terres. (*La Thébaïde*, 393–96)

Thebans, for there to be no more wars,
It is essential, by a fatal order,
That the last of the royal blood
Bloody your lands with its death.

It is true that in many ways *Oedipe* is a far cry from *Le Cid*, but Laïus' shade demanding that his heir pay the debt owed him is not unlike the spilled blood of Chimène's father calling out to her for revenge. Dircé and Thésée, and later Oedipe, duke it out over exactly whose blood Laïus' dire pronouncement is calling for, but the burden ends up falling, predictably, on the shoulders of his oldest son and heir.

By contrast, the oracle in Racine's play completely subverts the notion of a duty that might be part of a legacy passed on by order of primogeniture: the blood to be shed is identified as "le dernier du sang royal," a phrase that could mean either the youngest (lastborn) member of the royal family, or the latest or last shedding of royal blood. The first of these definitions is the most interesting for our purposes: the fact that the oracle is asking for the blood of the youngest rather than the oldest representative of Oedipus in the next generation demonstrates yet again that Racine's world of siblings is not the same as the world of the first generation of tragedy. The youngest scion of the doomed Oedipus clan is neither Polynice nor Etéocle, but Créon's younger son, Ménécée, described as "le dernier de nos princes" (631) [the youngest of our princes], who commits suicide in an attempt to end the conflict. In his heroic, dying speech, Ménécée emphasizes his status as the youngest: "Je suis le dernier sang de vos rois descendu, / Qui par l'ordre des dieux doit être répandu" (645–46) [Of your kings I am the latest blood descended, / Which by the gods' order must be shed]. "The gods' order" echoes the term "fatal order" in the oracle; both phrases seem to denote a predetermined order of birth, the death of the youngest, as a possible solution to the impasse.

But Racine carries his relative disregard for birth order even further. The concatenation of events shows that although Ménécée's spectacular suicide between the opposing armies causes a momentary truce, it does not fulfill the oracle's demands, since it does not bring the war to an end. Clearly Ménécée's blood is just the latest blood shed ("dernier sang") in a long history of bloodshed. The oracular phrase "par un ordre fatal" (394) turns out not to mean "by a predestined order" (of birth), but rather something vague like "what fate demands." Here again, even though we are told Ménécée is younger than his own brother and his warring cousins, birth order has no effective role in the drama; it neither causes the conflict nor can solve it.

What we are left with, then, is a pure desire for differentiation in the present. Neither Etéocle nor Polynice seeks to be an heir; both men simply want power, their struggle more openended than in a situation governed by primogeniture. Créon aggravates the brothers' mutual hatred, but they need no help from him. The fight for the throne is played out within the younger generation, which no longer aims to imitate the previous generation but rather seeks to establish difference within the present one.

The play repeatedly undermines imitation, a seminal concept for the Classical period, as a source of legitimacy. The twins' mutual repugnance is, ironically, the only thing they agree on and are willing to imitate in each other: it is a paradoxical attraction that brings them together and then repels them. Whereas an heir is produced by the union of two sexually and genetically differentiated partners, the reciprocal hatred of Etéocle and Polynice is portrayed as a parodic life force. The brothers' exultation in their misadelphia is so strong that it has the impact of a kind of eroticism. Etéocle, for example, fairly revels in his execration of Polynice:

> Je ne veux point, Créon, le haïr à moitié,
> Et je crains son courroux moins que son amitié.
> Je veux, pour donner cours à mon ardente haine,
> Que sa fureur au moins autorise la mienne;
> Et puisqu'enfin mon coeur ne saurait se trahir,
> Je veux qu'il me déteste afin de le haïr. (937–42)

I do not want to hate him halfheartedly, Créon,
And I fear his wrath less than his friendship.
To give free rein to my passionate hatred,
I wish his rage would at least legitimate mine;
And since my heart cannot be untrue to itself,
I want him to hate me so that I may hate him.

When characters speak of being true to their heart, that usually means not betraying their love; here it refers to hatred. By a perverted notion of imitation, Etéocle wishes that his brother might detest him so that he could imitate that hatred, which would thus be legitimized ("autorise"). This entire speech, which deals with family hatred rather than love and remains within a single generation, deforms the very notion of inheritance.

The converse of this mimetic hatred is the refusal on both brothers' part to take the initiative in compromising or making peace. In their only onstage meeting (4:3, 973–1202, one of the longest scenes in all of Racine's theater), Etéocle and Polynice stare at each other in silence, completely immobilized by their fear of being the first to make a concession. Jocaste, at first a hopeful and then a horrified witness to the scene, is forced by her sons' silence and inaction to provide a running commentary:

Commencez donc, mes fils, cette union si chère,
Et que chacun de vous reconnaisse son frère:
Tous deux dans votre frère envisagez vos traits:
Mais pour en mieux juger, voyez-les de plus près,
Surtout que le sang parle et fasse son office.
Approchez, Etéocle; avancez, Polynice . . .
Hé quoi? loin d'approcher, vous reculez tous deux?
D'où vient ce sombre accueil et ces regards fâcheux?
N'est-ce point que chacun, d'une âme irrésolue,
Pour saluer son frère attend qu'il le salue,
Et qu'affectant l'honneur de céder le dernier,
L'un ni l'autre ne veut s'embrasser le premier? (979–90)

So begin this dear union, my sons,
And let each of you recognize his brother:
Both of you, see your own features in your brother's face:
But to see how much alike you look, come closer,

Yes, let your blood speak and do its job.
Approach, Etéocle; come forward, Polynice . . .
What's this? you won't come closer, but back away?
Why this somber welcome, these spiteful looks?
Is it not that each of you with an undecided soul
Awaits a brother's greeting before greeting him,
And that as a point of honor not wanting to give in first,
Neither of you wishes to be the first to embrace?

While the producing of an heir starts with a premise of difference (male/female, the commingling of exogamous groups) that is overcome through compromise (genetic combination of the parents) and imitation (inculcation of an ethical heritage in the younger generation), the "union" of Etéocle and Polynice, to borrow Jocaste's term, starts with sameness and moves toward irreconcilable difference.[20] This scene gives the most convincing evidence in the play that the brothers are identical rather than fraternal twins[21] — "see your own features in your brother's face" — but as each man sees himself in his brother, the result is not the unison of like quantities but rather the magnetic repulsion of two identical charges, neither brother willing to be the first to extend his hand in friendship. The brother that broke the mirror image with a gesture of reconciliation — "Qui voudra le premier triompher de sa rage" (996) [The one who is the first to get the better of his rage] — would succeed in being different, since the other brother would not imitate him, but the one thing to which neither Etéocle nor Polynice will resort to break the involuntary mimetic bond is being the first to make peace.

The ironic use of the motif of imitation as a means of undercutting traditional notions of inheritance continues in Jocaste's anticlimactic suicide before the brothers' eyes at the end of this scene. Etéocle and Polynice are so mesmerized by the erotics of their hatred that they pay no heed to their mother's escalating distress. Just before she gives up her own blood in an attempt to assuage the oracle and put an end to her sons' fighting, Jocaste makes a final ironic speech praising them as role models:

Surpassez, s'il se peut, les crimes de vos pères;
Montrez, en vous tuant, comme vous êtes frères:
Le plus grand des forfaits vous a donné le jour,
Il faut qu'un crime égal vous l'arrache à son tour.
Je ne condamne plus la fureur qui vous presse;

Je n'ai plus pour mon sang ni pitié ni tendresse:
Votre exemple m'apprend à ne le plus chérir
Et moi je vais, cruels, vous apprendre à mourir. (1183–90)

Outdo, if you can, your forefathers' crimes;
Kill each other to show that you are brothers:
The greatest of crimes was what caused your birth,
And an equal crime must in turn cause your death.
I no longer condemn the rage that's hard upon you;
I no longer feel pity or love for my blood:
Your example teaches me not to hold it dear
And I will teach you, heartless ones, how to die.

This mordant maternal death cry is a parody of a dying parent's legacy to her surviving children. Jocaste's whole speech hinges on the idea of imitation and repetition between the generations, but once again in the domain of crime rather than in the realm of honor and glory: in demanding that her sons live down to their familial heritage, in effect she is recognizing that they are about to commit "an equal crime" to her own and Oedipe's crime in conceiving them. The dying parent's poignant wish that her children might one day go beyond the best their ancestors had to offer is also reversed into an acerbic taunt: "Outdo, if you can, your forefathers' crimes." Finally, Jocaste's last words concede the older generation no longer provides an example for the younger, but vice versa: "Your example teaches me not to hold it [my blood] dear." The only way she can become a model for her sons is in her suicide: "And I will teach you, heartless ones, how to die." The irony of this statement doubles back onto Jocaste: she means to say that given the breakdown of the parent's traditional role as ethical model, the only way she can get her sons' attention is by dying. But a second layer of irony makes her statement literally true: she is teaching her sons how to shed their own blood.

The irony of reversed mimesis is also applicable to the deaths of Etéocle and Polynice and to the death of Antigone. Polynice is first announced as the victor over his brother, since he strikes what appears to be a fatal blow, but as he reaches to take Etéocle's sword from his hand, the dying king musters his last ounce of strength to push it into Polynice's heart. Even in death the brothers cannot be distinguished, the death of one leading to the death of the other. All the way up to the end of this fraternal *folie à deux*, there is no advantage in being the first: Polynice cannot hold onto his

victory any more than Etéocle could hold onto the throne. Polynice is the
first to strike a deathblow, but with his final gasp of life Etéocle gets the
last laugh:

> Il [Etéocle] lui perce le coeur; et son âme ravie,
> En achevant ce coup abandonne la vie.
> Polynice frappé pousse un cri dans les airs,
> Et son âme en courroux s'enfuit dans les enfers.
> Tout mort qu'il est, Madame, il garde sa colère,
> Et l'on dirait qu'encore il menace son frère:
> Son visage, où la mort a répandu ses traits,
> Demeure plus terrible et plus fier que jamais. (1377–84)

> Etéocle stabs his brother's heart; and his delighted soul
> Breathes its last as it carries off this feat.
> Polynice, struck down, shrieks aloud, and his soul
> Full of wrath takes its flight to the underworld.
> Although he is dead, Madam, he has kept his anger,
> And he looks as if he were still threatening his brother:
> His face, over which death has spread its [or his brother's] features,
> Remains more terrifying and prouder than ever.

He who kills last, laughs last. For Polynice, the main pleasure in killing
Etéocle had been that at last he thought he would be different from his
brother; the subsequent victory of Etéocle over Polynice is not so much in
taking away his life — neither brother appears to value that very highly —
but in taking away his difference. The word "trait" or feature, echoing the
scene in which Jocaste asks the brothers to observe how similar their facial
features are, here implies that only as death gradually erases all trace of
individual expression from the brothers' faces will they finally relax into the
complete sameness they both abhorred and resisted in life.

The parody of inheritance continues to the very end of the tragedy.
Antigone, just before committing suicide in order to escape the advances of
her debauched uncle, tells Créon that what he can do to win her love is to
imitate her ("M'imiter") (1416), but he is not allowed to do so, prevented
by the guards from taking his own life when he discovers she has put an end
to hers. The young Antigone rather than the ancient Créon is the last
member of the royal family to be allowed to die, and as such is apparently
the fulfiller of the oracle asking for the shedding of the "dernier sang." When

Créon says, "Je suis le dernier sang du malheureux Laïus" (1499) [I am the last blood of the unfortunate Laïus], he is right only in the sense that he is the last member of the family left alive, not the youngest. Perhaps this is the final ironic reversal of *La Thébaïde* in terms of its peculiar depiction of inheritance: Antigone, the last person who dies, may well be the youngest character in the entire cast of characters, perhaps even younger than Ménécée. By contrast, Créon, the only representative of the family left alive, is not only a member of the older generation, but also probably the oldest character in the drama. If there is an inheritance here, it appears to be going in the wrong direction.

PART IV

THE SECOND GENERATION

9

The Younger Brother
Comes into His Own

Britannicus, *Bajazet*, and *Mithridate*

La Thébaïde is a harbinger of the second generation of Classical tragedies in that the play upends a number of the first generation's assumptions about primogeniture. In Racine's first tragedy, as we have seen, birth order is never once brought up in the very situation in which it might have been the most useful, that is, in the potential establishment of some sort of legitimated differentiation, however arbitrary, between Etéocle and Polynice. When birth order is alluded to in *La Thébaïde*, in the self-sacrifice of Ménécée and Antigone in response to the demands of the oracle, the youngest, not the eldest, is the spiritual heir of the bloodline, a position of questionable benefit, since it instantly leads to death. And while Racine's subsequent tragedies do not have a monolithic perspective on primogeniture—for example, some plays, like *Bajazet*, make birth order operative in the establishment of an heir, while others, like *Mithridate*, do not—there is no doubt that they present a very different vision of inheritance than the early plays of Pierre Corneille.

Among the complications that abound whenever the question of royal succession is raised in Racine's theater, one of the most important stems from the fact that Racine tends to portray younger siblings in a more sympathetic light than firstborns. The younger sibling's appeal is not something Racine invents; this very ancient literary topos is put to good use by Thomas Corneille in *Persée et Démétrius*, and Pierre Corneille flirts with it in *Rodogune*, although not without a great deal of ambiguity. Nevertheless, Racine's favoring of younger siblings is more extensive and more systematic than anything to be found in Pierre Corneille's early theater. As we shall see, in spite of the considerable differences in setting, theme, and treatment that distinguish *Britannicus*, *Bajazet*, and *Mithridate*, all three of these dramas concerning "murderous rivalries between brothers"[1] portray younger brothers who are worthier to inherit power than their older counterparts. Moreover, these three plays demonstrate that the younger sibling's position evolves over the course of Racine's theater. Starting with the doomed, noble younger stepbrother who is the titular hero of *Britannicus*, Racine goes on to present a more convincingly heroic (if equally doomed) younger brother in *Bajazet*, only to give the younger brother his crowning reward in *Mithridate*.

Britannicus: Inheritance and Adoption

The story of a son disinherited by his father in favor of a usurper who proves to be unworthy, *Britannicus*, Racine's first and most famous Roman play, suggests that there are two quite distinct considerations in the transmission of the title of emperor: biological heredity and adoption. Britannicus, the son of the emperor Claudius, is thrust far from power when his father divorces his mother, Messalina, and marries his own niece, the ambitious, corrupt Agrippina. After much plotting, Agrippina gets Claudius to adopt her son, Domitius, who under the name of Nero becomes emperor after Agrippina does away with Claudius before he can change his mind about the succession. The drama stages the distressing victory of the adopted older stepbrother, the emperor Néron, over the slighted Britannicus, the noble, wronged youth who, according to Racine's play, grew up assuming he would follow in his father's footsteps. The conflict between the two stepbrothers culminates in Néron's poisoning of Britannicus in a *crise de jalousie* over Junie, whose status as a direct descendant of Augustus would apparently have given her the potential of solidifying and legitimating the political position of either of the stepbrothers, both of whom had wished to marry her.

A number of critics have observed the apparent inconsistency in Racine's representation of the transmission of power in the Roman Empire, but they are divided about how to interpret it. Georges May opines that "Racine misleadingly attributes to the Roman Empire the hereditary principle of the crown that actually belongs to the French monarchy,"[2] while in his notes to *Britannicus* Alain Viala writes, "Racine projects seventeenth-century conceptions onto the world of Rome. In Rome adoption was a legitimate mode of succession."[3] By contrast Volker Schröder takes the position that Racine's play reveals an inherent weakness in the Roman political system, which apparently never completely shed the dynastic mentality of a monarchy even though it professed to reject the concept of purely hereditary succession. Thus, according to Schröder, Racine's play reflects the fact that heredity and choice both remain important factors in the transmission of power for the Romans: "Rome is the one hesitating; *Britannicus* reveals this hesitation, and its disastrous consequences for the State. Racine quite faithfully reconstitutes the various factors that determine imperial succession so as to reveal the weaknesses of the Roman system, which thus simply underscore the virtues of French-style hereditary monarchy."[4]

To the debate over whether Racine's hesitation over the transmission of power in *Britannicus* is anachronistic or is intended to reflect a corresponding inconsistency in the Roman political system, I would like to add a third possibility: that the ambiguity about how power is transmitted in *Britannicus* reflects the changing nature of French society that we have observed throughout this study. While the Salic laws are quite securely in place when Racine writes *Britannicus*, the hereditary principle, as we have seen, is being called into question and undermined by many different interests, including the king himself. I submit that the vexed representation of power transmission in *Britannicus* may be read as an expression of this complex sociohistorical evolution.

Racine does not in fact completely invent the notion that Britannicus' exclusion from power is unjust, but if he is actually basing the fundamental outline of his story on his main historical source, the Latin historian Tacitus' *Annales*, he certainly overstates his case. While Tacitus gives some evidence for this sense of injustice — he mentions a faction of Romans who find the treatment of Britannicus unfair, and says that Claudius' will was not read aloud at his funeral for fear of stirring up the crowd's indignation at hearing that a father preferred his stepson to his son[5] — the belief that Britannicus as the emperor's son had an ironclad right to succeed him is largely Racine's invention. While blood ties indisputably played a part in the choice of successors at least until Nero's death put an end to the first imperial dynasty, the idea that they might bestow an automatic right of succession on a given individual corresponds not to Roman practice, but to the Salic laws of royal inheritance which governed the transmission of power in France until the Revolution.

If *Britannicus*, like a number of Racine's other plays, is the story of a failed adoption, adoption is a defining feature of the Roman political system. From the time of Julius Caesar until the reign of Nero, not a single emperor was the son of the preceding emperor. Generally the new emperor was adopted by the old one before the latter's death; Claudius himself was an exception to this pattern. In the years following Nero's death, the emperor Vespasian did transmit power to his sons, first Titus and then Domitian — this is the single incident from Roman history that was treated by both Racine and Corneille, in *Bérénice* and *Tite et Bérénice*, respectively.[6] But after the death of Domitian in 96 A.D. and for approximately one hundred years corresponding more or less to the Golden Age of the Roman Empire, the model of adoption became the official means of transmitting power from one emperor to the next.[7]

How does the conflict between inheritance and adoption play out in *Britannicus*? First of all, inheritance by blood is presented as a source of legitimacy. Agrippine in particular prides herself on her blood ties with emperors past and present. In speaking with Burrhus, whom she herself chose as Néron's tutor, she flaunts the superiority of her inherited power over Burrhus' delegated power:

> Certes, plus je médite, et moins je me figure
> Que vous m'osiez compter pour votre créature,
> Vous, dont j'ai pu laisser vieillir l'ambition
> Dans les honneurs obscurs de quelque légion,
> Et moi qui sur le Trône ai suivi mes ancêtres,
> Moi, fille, femme, soeur et mère de vos maîtres. (151–56)

> Certainly, the more I reflect, the less I comprehend
> How you dare consider me one of your creations,
> You, whose ambition I could have left to rot
> Amidst the obscure honors of some legion or other,
> While I, on the throne, was a follower of my ancestors,
> The daughter, the wife, the sister and the mother of your masters.

What Agrippine is saying is that Burrhus is her "créature," not the other way around. He may have merit, which is why she chose him, but she has the legitimacy of blood, which is why she had the power to choose him, and still has the power to get rid of him. Similarly, in her dastardly disinheriting of Britannicus,[8] Agrippine recognizes that she has transgressed the hereditary right to succession: "Je sais que j'ai moi seule avancé leur [Junie's and Britannicus'] ruine; / Que du trône, où le sang l'a dû faire monter, / Britannicus par moi s'est vu précipiter" (60–62) [I know that I alone precipitated their doom; / I know Britannicus saw me push him off the throne / Which his blood gave him the right to call his own]. Although

Agrippine hopes to get her son back in line and keep him in power, she is clear eyed about the overlooked blood rights of Britannicus. She imagines a dispute between Britannicus and Néron precisely in those terms, describing Britannicus as "le fils d'un empereur / Redemandant la foi jurée à sa famille" (842–43) [an emperor's son / Demanding the return of the fidelity sworn to his family].

As for Junie, Agrippine knows Néron's abduction of her may be a covert attack on the blood ties the two women share: "Ne tient-il qu'à marquer de cette ignominie / Le sang de mes aïeux qui brille dans Junie?" (227–28) [Is his goal not to cover with shame / My ancestors' bright blood flowing through Junie's veins?]. Junie's direct hereditary link to Augustus is presented as a source of power so great that it is seen as threatening, as Burrhus tells Agrippine: "Elle est dans un palais tout plein de ses aïeux. / Vous savez que les droits qu'elle porte avec elle / Peuvent de son époux faire un prince rebelle" (238–40) [She is in a palace filled with her ancestors. / You know that the rights she carries along with her / Can turn whomever she marries into a rebel prince]. The notion that Junie as a direct descendant of Augustus possesses a dangerous kernel of legitimacy may well, as Volker Schröder claims, correspond to some extent to the complexities of the Roman political system,[9] but there is little doubt that Racine's audience looked at the character of Junie through eyes accustomed to the practices of the French court, not the Roman Empire. In this perspective Junie's inalienable connection to a form of legitimacy, and thus the potential threat she might pose, would be instantly recognizable.

Nevertheless, in *Britannicus* this concept of legitimacy by heredity has its limits. First of all, given the complexity of the blood ties linking the four players in this dynastic soap opera, establishing legitimacy by blood is not an easy task. For example, even though Britannicus is presented as having a claim to power by virtue of being Claudius' biological son while Néron is the emperor's adoptive son, Britannicus is also the only one of the four main characters who is not a direct descendant of Augustus but rather a collateral descendant: his ancestor is Augustus' sister, Octavia.[10]

A more important limiting factor of genetic legitimacy in *Britannicus*, as in much of Racine's theater, is that here, as in *La Thébaïde*, blood ties with one's ancestors are presented as a burdensome, constraining force as much as a legitimizing one. As Georges May observes, "The unfortunate heroes' belief in a fatality that is all the less avoidable for being in their blood . . . justifies most dramatically the rightness of Racine's instincts in staging the stories of latter-day descendants of unfortunate lineages rather than their more famous ancestors themselves."[11] Néron's story, like Phèdre's, is one of a deferred but inevitable heeding of the unvirtuous cry of the ancestors' blood. Harriet Stone writes, "Like Phèdre, Néron must recognize that his freedom to act is limited, that his efforts to realize his desire are (pre)destined to fail."[12] Racine alludes to the notion, possibly drawn from Suetonius, that Néron's father, Domitius Ahenobarbus — whose name, meaning "a beard the color of henna," makes him a spiritual ancestor of Barbarossa — came from a family with a mournful, savage bent: "Des fiers Domitius l'humeur triste et sauvage" (36). Thus Néron, unlike Phèdre, has a deranged father as well as an unscrupulous, power-hungry mother. Perhaps that is why Néron's period of virtue lasts a shorter time than Phèdre's struggle against her fatal love for Hippolyte. Similarly, Britannicus is presented as being his father's son, for worse rather than for better: Claudius, a gullible, manipulable man around whom Agrippine dances treacherous circles, produces an equally naïve son. As will be the case for the virtuous Xipharès in *Mithridate*, the memory of Britannicus' traitorous mother apparently serves only to reinforce his identification with his father.

Given this ambivalent view of blood ties, now a source of genetic legitimacy, now a source of intergenerational genetic recidivism, it is no wonder that *Britannicus* generates a similarly ambivalent view of adoption. On the one hand, Racine takes a certain amount of liberty with his historical sources in order to present Néron's adoption by Claudius as indisputably giving him a less legitimate claim to power and inheritance than Britannicus' direct blood ties to the late emperor. Britannicus himself, speaking to Narcisse, laments the loss of a position to which he was "destined": "Tu sais si pour jamais, de ma chute étonné, / Je renonce à l'Empire où j'étais destiné" (321–22) [Remember how, stunned by my downfall, I gave up / Forever the Empire I was destined for]. Junie echoes this sentiment in speaking to Néron: "J'aime Britannicus. Je lui fus destinée / Quand l'Empire devait suivre son hyménée" (643–44) [I love Britannicus. I was promised to him / When the Empire was supposed to follow his marriage]. On the other hand, Néron's adoption by Claudius is seen as a potential source of virtue for Néron, a metaphor for his possible escape from his dreadful family inheritance. Let us not forget that in first-century Rome adoption is quite an ordinary path to empire, and even Tacitus does not dispute that the people of Rome favor Nero's adoption by Claudius, and indeed take in stride the young emperor's murder of Britannicus to consolidate his position of power.[13] In his discussion of the role of adoption in Racine's theater Philip Lewis writes, "Adoption reveals individuals' ability to escape their origins and to constitute relations anchored in human invention and personal engagement."[14]

The strongest proponent of the view of virtuous adoption in *Britannicus* is Néron's tutor, Burrhus, as is indicated in a speech to Agrippine:

> Madame, c'est un fils qui succède à son père.
> En adoptant Néron, Claudius par son choix
> De son fils et du vôtre a confondu les droits.
> Rome l'a pu choisir. Ainsi, sans être injuste,
> Elle choisit Tibère adopté par Auguste;
> Et le jeune Agrippa, de son sang descendu,
> Se vit exclu du rang vainement prétendu. (860–66)

> Madam, Néron is a son succeeding his father.
> By adopting him, Claudius made the choice
> Of exchanging the rights of his son and yours.
> Rome has that right. After all, she justly chose
> Tiberius, who had been adopted by Augustus;
> And young Agrippa, descended from Augustus' blood,
> Saw himself excluded from the position he vainly claimed.

Burrhus sees adoption as an alternate, if not a superior form of succession ("c'est un fils qui succède à son père"); no wonder he is also a great believer in Néron's freedom to "adopt" virtue over crime. But Burrhus himself is forced to witness the shattering of his illusions about adoption: when Néron observes Britannicus' death with the dispassionate demeanor of a hardened criminal, "heredity and nature prove stronger than the education and moral guidance of a Stoic."[15]

The conflict between adoption and inheritance by blood makes the relation between Néron and Britannicus difficult to define in terms of birth order. Because Néron's legitimacy depends upon his adoption, he finds himself in the paradoxical situation of being an older brother and an heir to the throne who is nonetheless obliged to be pleasing to others, for his power is not simply inborn. This is the very conflict that sets off the action of the play: Néron, tired of having to behave himself to earn his position, wants to start acting like an imperious hereditary ruler: "L'impatient Néron cesse de se contraindre; / Las de se faire aimer, il veut se faire craindre" (11–12) [Impatient Néron is dropping his self-restraint; / Tired of trying to be loved, he wants to be feared]. That Agrippine has no compunctions about calling her son to task for his ingratitude toward her underscores the fact that he would not be in power had it not been for her machinations, and that consequently his position is not that of a typical firstborn heir.

Néron's ambiguous status as simultaneously an heir and a nonheir is analogous to his ambiguous status as an older-brother figure. While he and Britannicus are not blood brothers, the text repeatedly draws our attention to their sibling-like rivalry, as Jacques Scherer observes: "*Britannicus* demonstrates that, if the fraternal relation is associated with murder, inversely, murder engenders a . . . fraternal relation in the poetic imagination. History teaches us that Nero had Britannicus put to death. It does not teach us that the two men were brothers, or even half-brothers. . . . Sexual rivalry triggers [Néron's] unjust action, which is enough to bring forth the fraternal relation, which, once mentioned, will then be alluded to eight more times in the play."[16] The fact that Britannicus is younger than Néron—Tacitus mentions Britannicus' youth as one of the reasons for Nero's popular support— is alluded to by Britannicus: "Et ma jeunesse même écarte loin de moi / Tous ceux qui dans le coeur me réservent leur foi" (325–26) [And my very youth keeps far away from me / All those who in their hearts hold their allegiance in reserve]. Britannicus is certainly presented as naïve by comparison to Néron, but here again, Racine seems to be hedging his bets. The allusions to Britannicus' natural right to inherit the throne seem to justify Britannicus' portrayal as direct and confrontational, whereas Néron, the older of the two men and the one who is presently in power, is crafty and ironic, characteristics more often associated with laterborns with their need to resort to indirect paths to power.

Britannicus can be read, then, as a story in which adoption and genetic inheritance go head to head, and this is in fact the case in much of Racine's theater. If *Britannicus* is the story of a less-than-satisfactory adoption, one might describe a number of Racine's other plays in the same terms. At the end of *Andromaque*, Pyrrhus' adoption of Astyanax instantly leads to the former's assassination. *Iphigénie* reaches its violent climax when the adopted Trojan woman, Eriphile, discovers who her birth parents are and commits suicide. *Phèdre*, as we shall see, ends with what is surely one of the most convoluted adoptions in the history of literature, and *Athalie*, Racine's last play, carries a final lesson about the limits of adoption: as Racine himself indicates in his preface to the play, the supposedly virtuous Joas, the grandson of the monstrous Athalie but the adoptive son of the virtuous Joad and Josabet, eventually heeds the cry of the blood and kills his adoptive brother, an act worthy of his grisly grandmother and one that Racine sees as leading directly to the Hebrews' subsequent misfortunes.[17] Racine's last play, like his theater as a whole, might thus be taken to say that adoption as a means of limiting the power of blood ties is worth a try, but that it never quite works out.

Bajazet: Splendor and Misery of the Younger Brother

Bajazet is the first — but not the last — of Racine's tragedies in which an older sibling plays a crucial role without actually being present onstage.[18] The play tells the story of Amurat, an Ottoman sultan, and his younger brother, Bajazet, a potentially dangerous political rival, whom he has left behind a virtual prisoner in the seraglio while he goes off to battle the Babylonians. In Amurat's absence, his chosen proxy is Roxane, the woman whom he loves and has named as the sultaness — "il a voulu / Qu'elle eût dans son absence un pouvoir absolu" (103–4) [he wanted / Her to have absolute power in his absence] — and to whom he has given the power of life and death over Bajazet. The situation is complicated by the grand vizir, Acomat, who wishes to wrest power away from Amurat by allying himself with Bajazet and overthrowing the sultan. Acomat's strategy is to lure Roxane into falling in love with her captive and shifting her allegiance from the older brother to the younger, who has popular support. As is often the case in Racine's drama, love is not far removed from cruelty and subjugation: Bajazet's transformation from prisoner to love object is not difficult to effect, especially since Bajazet's true (but secret) mistress, Atalide, is a skillful go-between who, fearful for her lover's life, repeatedly reassures Roxane of Bajazet's love.

Up to the time the curtain rises, Acomat's strategy of using Roxane's love for Bajazet to keep the prince safe from his older brother's hostility has been successful: Roxane has already ignored one message from Amurat demanding that she put Bajazet to death: "Grâces à mon amour, je me suis bien servie / Du pouvoir qu'Amurat me donna sur sa [Bajazet's] vie" (313–14) [Because of my love, I have made good use / Of the power Amurat gave me over his life]. But Roxane's demands for affection increase in direct proportion to the risks she runs in keeping Bajazet alive, and he cannot ultimately convince her of his love. Bajazet is put to death, and as the curtain falls and Amurat approaches Constantinople with his army of janizaries, Roxane is executed for her treachery, and Atalide, in despair over her lover's death, commits suicide, one of the only examples of onstage violence in all of Racine's theater.

Amurat never appears onstage, but the characterization of the older brother as a hateful figure of tremendous power resonates throughout the drama. Amurat is inaccessible, menacing, and fearsome; not a single character expresses the slightest affection for him. Roxane naïvely (and erroneously) believes that Amurat loves her with utter devotion — "Souveraine d'un coeur [Amurat's] qui n'eût aimé que moi" (1533) [Queen of Amurat's heart, sole object of his love] — but at least she is honest enough to avoid posing as an admirer of his. Even before Acomat arranged for her to meet Bajazet, it is clear that Roxane was never in love with his older brother.

Amurat's hold over others, emanating from his inherited position of power,[19] is threatening and preemptive. He can never fully depend on anyone. If he must delegate power, he remains vigilant and suspicious — "Un vizir aux sultans fait toujours quelque ombrage: / A peine ils l'ont choisi, qu'ils craignent leur ouvrage" (185–86) [Sultans are always resentful of the vizir: / Hardly have they chosen him when they start to fear their decision] — and he makes sure that others have more to fear from him than he has to fear from them. His basic tool for keeping others in line is thus fear, and because he, too, is afraid of the power of others, his relations are characterized by the wariness of parties who refuse to show each other their backs. In speaking of Amurat's adversarial relation with the janizaries, Osmin says, "Comme il les craint sans cesse, ils le craignent toujours" (44) [Just as he always fears them, they always fear him]. Since Amurat has no fidelity to his troops, the janizaries have none to him. So long as he is victorious, the army will show him "a blind and lowly obedience" ("L'exemple d'une aveugle et basse obéissance" [62]). But at his first sign of weakness they will demonstrate that he, not the Babylonians, is their worst enemy: "S'il fuit, ne doutez point que fiers de sa disgrâce / A la haine bientôt ils ne joignent l'audace" (65–66) [If he flees, they'll surely be proud of his disgrace, / And soon bold enough to let their hatred show].

Amurat's archenemy is the man he fears the most not because of his actual power but because of his potential power: Bajazet. Amurat mistrusts and wishes to do away with his younger brother precisely because he is his equal in birth (if not birth order). Acomat describes the sultans' mistrust of their brothers: "Le frère rarement laisse jouir ses frères / De l'honneur dangereux d'être sortis d'un sang / Qui les a de trop près approchés de son rang" (106–8) [Brothers rarely let brothers enjoy / The dangerous honor of descending from a bloodline / That gives them a rank too close to theirs]. Thus, Acomat continues, Amurat's trigger-happy attitude toward Bajazet is typical:

Il [Amurat] partit, et voulut que fidèle à sa haine,
Et des jours de son frère arbitre souveraine,
Roxane, au moindre bruit, et sans autres raisons,
Le fît sacrifier à ses moindres soupçons. (129–32)

When Amurat left, he wanted Roxane to be faithful
To his hatred, to be sovereign judge of his brother's fate,
And at the slightest rumor, without further ado,
To sacrifice him to her slightest suspicions.

The only thing that has kept Amurat from killing his brother is concern for the lineage: "Mais malgré ses soupçons, le cruel Amurat, / Avant qu'un fils naissant eût rassuré l'Etat, / N'osait sacrifier ce frère à sa vengeance" (123–25) [But in spite of his suspicions, cruel Amurat, / Until the birth of a son secured the State, / Did not dare sacrifice his brother to revenge].

Despite Amurat's position as a hereditary ruler responsible for the continuation of his lineage, his concern for his bloodline cannot hold a candle to his lust for power. That he will finally order Bajazet put to death in spite of the lack of an heir[20] is prefigured by the fact that he earlier took the unprecedented step of giving the title of sultaness to his favorite before she had borne him a male child: "il a voulu que l'heureuse Roxane, / Avant qu'elle eût un fils, prît le nom de sultane" (101–2) [Roxane was fortunate: he wanted her / To take the title of sultaness before she gave him a son]. Roxane herself is aware that her fate differs greatly from that of most of the sultan's mistresses: "Il faut qu'un fils naissant la [the sultan's mistress] déclare sultane. / Amurat plus ardent, et seul jusqu'à ce jour, / A voulu que l'on dût ce titre à son amour" (298–300) [Only the birth of a son makes a mistress into a sultaness. / Amurat, more passionate, is the first up to this day, / Who has wished that title to be a result of his love]. Rather than respecting the customs of his forebears, Amurat has jumped the gun both in giving Roxane the title of sultaness and in ordering his brother, the heir to the throne, put to death. This double disrespect for the demands of the lineage is inconsistent with his identity as a hereditary ruler.

The older brother in *Bajazet* enjoys the same sort of inherited privilege we encountered in the first generation of tragedies, but here he is a totally corrupt figure. If inherited privilege is portrayed in this way, perhaps we are being invited to reflect on its potential for abuse rather than grandeur. *Bajazet* resembles *Britannicus* insofar as the older sibling, the ruler, is portrayed as a tyrant, a law unto himself.

Another indication of Amurat's disrespect for the demands of the lineage is his choice of a foreign woman of low birth as his sultaness. As Jacques Morel observes, "Racine makes Atalide (like Junie) a woman of princely birth. Roxane, by comparison, is no more than a commoner."[21] By selecting Roxane "Entre tant de beautés dont l'Europe et l'Asie / Dépeuplent leurs Etats et remplissent sa cour" (98–99) [Among the many beauties that Europe and Asia / Send forth from their Lands to fill his court], Amurat demonstrates the tyrant's favoring of his own whims and desires. Unlike the noble Atalide, a first cousin of Amurat's (169) who, had he chosen her as sultaness, would have reinforced his position by her birth,[22] Roxane is a woman that we — and Amurat — know very little about. We do not know where she comes from or why she left her country and her family behind. And even if Amurat presumably knows, which we do not, if she is European or Asian, her nationality and family background are clearly beside the point, her beauty a necessary and sufficient asset in Amurat's eyes.

In contrast to the portrait of the older-brother heir as a distant, unlovable autocrat, Bajazet is characterized as a man who has no power but is loved by everyone except, of course, Amurat himself; indeed, as a figure whose lack of power makes him lovable. The opposition between the two brothers could hardly be made more strongly: "Le superbe Amurat est toujours inquiet; / Et toujours tous les coeurs [of the soldiers] penchent vers Bajazet: / D'une commune voix ils l'appellent au trône" (215–17) [Haughty Amurat is always ill at ease; / And all the soldiers' hearts always lean toward Bajazet: / With a single voice they call him to the throne]. The older brother is arrogant and powerful but troubled. The younger brother, whose very survival is precarious, captures the hearts of one and all. If we are given no adjectives here to distinguish Bajazet from Amurat, who is described as "superbe" and "inquiet," this is perhaps because Bajazet remains an unknown quantity whose attraction — and hence power — are purely relative to others, contingent upon their devotion to him and his cause. The older brother, born to power, is preoccupied with conserving and consolidating his position. The younger brother, who may or may not be kept around once he has fulfilled his role as a "spare" to the royal heir, survives by being pleasing to others.

Nowhere in Racine's theater is the difficulty of the younger sibling's position made clearer than in the portrait of Bajazet as a nonheir who must ingratiate himself in order to avoid being put to death. Acomat opines that Bajazet purposefully set out to capture Roxane's heart: "Bajazet est aimable; il vit que son salut / Dépendait de lui plaire, et bientôt il lui plut" (155–56) [Bajazet is lovable; he saw that his salvation / Depended on pleasing her, and soon he pleased her]. Roxane, by contrast, refuses to attribute any such motivation to the object of her affections: "Malgré tous ses malheurs, plus heureux que son frère, / Il m'a plu, sans peut-être aspirer à me plaire" (309–10) [In spite of all his misfortunes, more fortunate than his brother, / Bajazet pleased me, perhaps without trying to please me]. These two interpretations disagree about the degree to which the prince is aware of his appeal and manipulates Roxane into loving him, but they fully concur about Bajazet's power — and need — to please. Roxane is quite blunt about this when she presents him with an ultimatum:

> Mais avez-vous prévu, si vous ne m'épousez,
> Les périls plus certains où vous vous exposez?
> Songez-vous que sans moi tout vous devient contraire,
> Que c'est à moi surtout qu'il importe de plaire?
> Songez-vous que je tiens les portes du palais,
> Que je puis vous l'ouvrir ou fermer pour jamais,
> Que j'ai sur votre vie un empire suprême,
> Que vous ne respirez qu'autant que je vous aime?
> Et sans ce même amour qu'offensent vos refus,
> Songez-vous, en un mot, que vous ne seriez plus? (503–12)

> But have you foreseen the sure dangers
> You expose yourself to if you don't marry me?
> Do you realize that without me everything is against you,
> That I am the one you must please above all?
> Do you realize that I'm the keeper of the gates,
> That I can let you out of the palace or keep you in forever,
> That I have supreme power over your survival,
> That you will keep breathing only as long as I love you?
> And without this very same love that is offended by your refusal,
> Do you realize, in a word, that you would no longer exist?

Roxane's most chillingly direct statement, that Bajazet continues to draw breath only if she loves him, makes her a figure of autocratic maternal power. Obviously Bajazet's position is quite extreme, but his plight resembles that of many younger siblings. All children would die without nurture, but these words are particularly poignant to the ears of a younger brother who instinctively understands from an early age that parents "need" only one heir, that he has no intrinsic value and must give remuneration for parental attention on a pay-as-you-go basis, unlike the heir, who is considered a good credit risk. Nonheirs must repay parental magnanimity with some kind of immediate gratification: devotion, thanks, and gratitude. No one would think of calling Amurat "ingrat" if he were to act according to his own desires, rather than comply with the demands of someone who had done him a favor.

Thus Bajazet's survival is tenuous throughout the play, the drama's imagery of womblike protection within the harem reinforcing his identity as a creature struggling to hold onto life: "Souffrez que Bajazet voie enfin la lumière: / Des murs de ce palais ouvrez-lui la barrière" (237–38) [Allow Bajazet to see the light of day at last: / Lift the barrier of the palace walls for him]. Raising the "barrier" of the seraglio would mean allowing Bajazet to "see the light of day," "voir le jour" being a Classical euphemism for "to be born." It would mean, in effect, giving him a chance to survive on his own, without any direct sustaining link to others. The liberation of Bajazet never takes place, and even when he has comprehended that he is likely to die because of his refusal to marry Roxane, he still continues to think in terms of all the debts of kindness to him that he will leave unpaid: "Pardonnez, Acomat; je plains avec sujet / Des coeurs dont les bontés trop mal récompensées / M'avaient pris pour objet de toutes leurs pensées" (616–18) [Pardon, Acomat; but I have reason to pity / Hearts whose indulgences, so poorly compensated, / Were kind enough to be concerned only with me]. Even in the face of death, the younger brother thinks of all the favors he owes to others.

The conventions of the period encourage Racine to provide a heroic past for Bajazet, but even in the descriptions of his military prowess, his name is inseparable from the domain of the sentiments. In his youthful military exploits, he is described as conquering the hearts of his fellow soldiers ("Emportant après lui tous les coeurs des soldats") (120). Amurat's mysterious message home sends a tremor through the hearts of his soldiers, who fear for Bajazet's life: "Tout le camp interdit tremblait pour Bajazet: / On craignait qu'Amurat par un ordre sévère / N'envoyât demander la tête de son frère" (72–74) [The whole camp trembled in silent fear for Bajazet: / They were afraid that Amurat had sent a harsh command / Demanding that his brother be beheaded]. While the janizaries wait to pounce on Amurat at the first glimpse of his jugular, they "tremble" for Bajazet, a word not obviously associated with Turkish soldiers: it is as if the mention of Bajazet softened the hearts they lost to him in battle.

Bajazet's need to be pleasing is so deeply ingrained that even when he thinks his reluctant promise to marry Roxane will give him a chance to escape from the harem and fight Amurat directly, he still thinks in terms of competing for people's affections, as he says to Atalide:

> Mais enfin je me vois les armes à la main;
> Je suis libre, et je puis contre un frère inhumain,
> Non plus par un silence aidé de votre adresse,
> Disputer en ces lieux le coeur de sa maîtresse,
> Mais par de vrais combats, par de nobles dangers,
> Moi-même le cherchant aux climats étrangers,
> Lui disputer les coeurs du peuple et de l'armée,
> Et pour juge entre nous prendre la Renommée. (947–54)

> But I finally see myself with weapons in hand;
> I am free, and my fight against my inhuman brother,
> Is no longer a silent struggle aided by your skill,
> A dispute over his mistress' heart in this place,
> But a real combat with admirable risks,
> That I myself can seek out in foreign climes,
> A dispute over the hearts of the people and the army,
> With noble Repute the only judge between him and me.

To the degrading act of consorting with his brother's mistress, Bajazet opposes military glory, but even here he thinks in terms of fighting for affection: "A dispute over the hearts of the people and the army." Bajazet will be fighting with different weapons — "les armes à la main" — but he will still be fighting the same fight: for others' hearts.

In the end, neither brother truly wins. Amurat will continue to rule, at least for the moment, but he is certainly not presented as heroic, nor is he faithful to the traditions by which he inherited power. Bajazet is appealing if nothing else, and we are led to believe that he could have been a great hero if only he had been the heir to power; as Atalide puts it in her apostrophe to the noble ancestors she and Bajazet share, "Héros, qui deviez tous revivre en ce héros" (1741) [Heroes, who should have lived again in this hero].

But Bajazet's association with the values of the second generation connects him not only to an ethic of love, but also to the market values of exchange and accommodation, and the combination of these two domains comes dangerously close to prostitution, as Roland Barthes writes: "His sexual ambiguity comes from his being a man who is prostituted: Bajazet is handsome, he gives himself to Roxane to garnish a benefit, he openly uses his beauty as an exchange value."[23] Bajazet hates his role and does ultimately reveal his disdain for Roxane's offer, but he is actually quite similar to Roxane. He knows his only source of power is being preferred to all others. Roxane is in a hinge position between the two brothers: chosen by the older brother for her beauty and subsequently made his political proxy, she then chooses the younger for his beauty and offers to give him a chance in the political domain. Her crude words about her power to make or break him could be spoken to her by Amurat: "Rentre dans le néant dont je t'ai fait sortir" (539) [Go back to the void I pulled you from]. The sultan's foreign lower-class mistress[24] and his superfluous younger brother are two of a kind.

Bajazet is thus the mirror image of a play like Pierre Corneille's Nicomède, in which the younger brother is allowed to become the heir to power, but the older brother wins a moral victory by providing the heroic model that the younger must follow in order to be his brother's "heir." In Bajazet, the older brother wins out completely in terms of power, which might seem to give the play an air of conservatism, but the younger brother is both lovable and potentially heroic. If he does not become the ruler of his country, that is his country's loss as much as his.

Mithridate: Choosing an Heir

As Alain Viala observes, Mithridate is Racine's last tragedy to feature sibling rivalry.[25] The play tells of the sons of the Oriental king, Mithridate, a vehement resister of Rome for forty years who shortly before the curtain rises spreads the rumor of his own demise to catch the Romans off guard. Mithridate's sons, Pharnace and Xipharès, mistakenly believing him to be dead, clash over politics and love: mainly they fight over the woman they both wish to marry, Monime. Monime happens to be the fiancée of their father, so that when Mithridate inconveniently turns up very much alive at the end of act 1, the two brothers scramble to cover their tracks.

During the course of the drama Mithridate discovers that both of his sons are in love with Monime, but rather than exacting the kind of bloody revenge which his fearsome reputation would have forecast, he yields Monime to the man she loves, Xipharès, who is also the king's greatly favored son. In the unusually uplifting dénouement of this Racinian tragedy, Mithridate meets a glorious, heroic, self-imposed death as a final gesture of resistance to Rome, and with his last breath, he passes on to Xipharès the only heritage remaining to him, the woman he loves — "Mais vous [Monime] me tenez lieu d'empire, de couronne; / Vous seule me restez: souffrez que je vous donne" (1671–72) [But you alone take the place of my empire and my crown; / You are all I have: let me give you to Xipharès] — and his soul — "Dans cet embrassement dont la douceur me flatte, / Venez, et recevez l'âme de Mithridate" (1695–96) [In this sweet, tender embrace, / Come receive the soul of Mithridate].

The theme of sibling rivalry evolves so dramatically over the course of Racine's career that one can hardly recognize the rivalry operative in *Mithridate* as the same phenomenon found in *La Thébaïde*. Unlike Polynice and Etéocle, who vainly try to differentiate themselves, the brothers in *Mithridate* are opposites. Pharnace and Xipharès are half-brothers: they do not share the same mother. And they are completely different in terms of character. Xipharès is the good brother, loved by Monime, much preferred by Mithridate, respectful of his father and disdainful of easy alliances with the Romans. Pharnace, his unscrupulous, unappealing rival, has nothing going for him.

The most important distinction between the brothers is that though they have each been given lands to govern after Mithridate's death,[26] Mithridate thinks of Xipharès as his heir:

Je le répète encor: c'est un autre moi-même,
Un fils victorieux, qui me chérit, que j'aime,
L'ennemi des Romains, l'héritier et l'appui
D'un empire et d'un nom qui va renaître en lui. (1067–70)

Let me say it once again: he's another form of myself,
A triumphant son who loves me, whom I love,
The enemy of the Romans, the heir and support
Of an empire and a name that will be reborn in him.

In speaking to Mithridate, Monime calls Xipharès "Ce fils victorieux que vous favorisez, / Cette vivante image en qui vous vous plaisez, / Cet ennemi de Rome, et cet autre vous-même" (1105–7) [This triumphant son that you favor, / This living image you like to see as your reflection, / This enemy of Rome, this other form of yourself]. Xipharès, Mithridate's heir and support, the repository of his name, the favorite son, the living image in which the father sees a source of immortality and the rebirth of another form of himself: if we accept the fact that Xipharès is Mithridate's heir, none of this is at all surprising. The only thing that is surprising is that Xipharès is Mithridate's younger son.

We are informed in the first scene of the play that Pharnace is the older brother, as Xipharès in his second speech claims to respect his brother's seniority: "Je sais en lui des ans respecter l'avantage" (19) [I know how to respect the advantage of his age]. This brief allusion to primogeniture is ironic not only because Xipharès is so obviously the actual heir, but also because Xipharès is the only character in the play to mention the older brother's supposed rights. *Mithridate* appears to tell a tale of ultimogeniture in which the younger-brother heir is alone in paying lip service to primogeniture.

In reality, *Mithridate* is neither about primogeniture nor about ultimogeniture, but rather about choice: the choice of an heir, the choice of a leader, and the choice of a spouse. Mithridate makes it perfectly clear that far from considering Xipharès his natural heir, he has chosen him as his heir:

Oui, mon fils, c'est vous seul sur qui je me repose,
Vous seul qu'aux grands desseins que mon coeur se propose
J'ai choisi dès longtemps pour digne compagnon,
L'héritier de mon sceptre, et surtout de mon nom. (615–18)

Yes, my son, you are the only one I can rely on, the only one
I chose so long ago as a worthy companion
To carry out my heart's ambitions,
The heir to my throne, and especially to my name.

Mithridate is not the only character to choose Xipharès over Pharnace. Arbate, Mithridate's confidant and the governor of the land of Nymphea where the play is set, is asked by Xipharès to choose between him and his brother: "C'est à toi de choisir quel parti tu dois prendre, / Qui des deux te paraît plus digne de ta foi" (108–9) [It's up to you to choose which side to be on, / Which of the two you deem worthier of your allegiance]. Arbate responds without hesitation: "Commandez-moi, Seigneur. Si j'ai quelque pouvoir / Mon choix est déjà fait, je ferai mon devoir" (117–18) [Give me orders, Sire. If I have any power / My choice is already made, and I'll do my duty]. But the fact that Xipharès even poses the question indicates not only his confidence in the outcome, but also his respect for choice.

Monime also chooses Xipharès, and one of the main reasons she chooses him is that she is free to select him or reject him; what legitimizes love in this play is not duty or obligation but rather freedom of choice. The tyrannical, one-sided love of Mithridate for Monime and of Pharnace for Monime is opposed to the free, reciprocal love of Monime and Xipharès. Monime's acceptance of her fate as Mithridate's future wife is a simple act of obedience: "J'obéis: n'est-ce pas assez me faire entendre?" (584) [I will obey: am I not making myself clear enough?]. Obedience is not enough, the king angrily responds — "Non, ce n'est pas assez" (585) — but it is the best Monime can muster. By contrast, Monime expresses her love for Xipharès in terms of reciprocity and exchange; she tells him that when he told her the story of his secret, unhappy love for her, he was also telling her story as well ("Vous n'en sauriez, Seigneur, retracer la mémoire, / Ni conter vos malheurs, sans conter mon histoire") (687–88).

That primogeniture is nevertheless a deeply ingrained phenomenon is apparent from the fact that the younger-brother heir not only claims to respect his older brother's age advantage but also applies the logic of primogeniture to the domain of the affections. To justify his love for Monime ("pour me justifier" [45]), Xipharès reminds his confidant "Que je vis, que j'aimai la reine le premier; / Que mon père ignorait jusqu'au nom de Monime / Quand je conçus pour elle un amour légitime" (46–48) [That I was the first to see and love the queen; / That my father had never even heard her name / When I conceived a legitimate love for Monime]. This is an example of what Volker Schröder has called the "primogeniture of the heart":[27] being the first to love Monime makes Xipharès' love for her "légitime." Xipharès reiterates the rights of amorous primogeniture when speaking to Monime: "Si le temps peut donner quelque droit légitime, / Faut-il vous dire ici que le premier de tous / Je vous vis, je formai le dessein d'être à vous?" (192–94) [If time can provide some legitimate right, / Must I tell you that I was the first / To see you and to hope one day to be yours?]. Xipharès' vocabulary of primogeniture merely underscores the fact that being first in time is not a real source of legitimacy in love, and certainly not the reason Monime loves Xipharès.

In *Mithridate* politics and love are less at odds than in many of Racine's tragedies: Xipharès is an easy choice over Pharnace both as an heir and as a lover. As if to reinforce the convergence between the two realms, the only clear legacy the besieged Mithridate can leave his chosen heir is Monime, who has herself chosen Xipharès. Thus the climactic transmission of Mithridate's legacy to Xipharès would appear to be an apotheosis of second-generation values, the victory of the younger brother over the elder and of choice over predetermination. To be sure, even though Xipharès is a more active, manifestly heroic figure than either Britannicus or Bajazet, *Mithridate* resembles those earlier dramas of sibling rivalry in its depiction of the younger-brother figure as more sympathetic than the elder.

And yet in spite of the play's affirmation of second-generation values, the final image of a heroic son who inherits his father's name and zealously accepts his duty to avenge his death — "Et par tout l'univers cherchons-lui des vengeurs" (1698) [And let us seek avengers for him throughout the universe] — reverberates with the glorious, feudal ethic of an earlier day. The peculiar aftertaste left by this conclusion invites us to question the precise value of Mithridate's final legacy to his younger son.

Mithridate is in the tradition of plays like *La Mort de Pompée* and *La Mort d'Annibal* in that the passing of the titular hero, who is idealized in death,[28] has the impact of the passing of an era. These dramas do not portray the transmission of values to the younger generation but question how to mourn the demise of values that cannot or should not be passed on. For if Mithridate is heroic in death — his obsession with meeting a noble end is one of his main motivations — this character based on a historical figure who was a cruel, vindictive despot may not appear quite so heroic in life. When Mithridate fumes against Monime and his sons and contemplates draconian measures against them all for displeasing him, he is made to sound like a first-generation patriarch who has wandered into a second-generation play. Given Mithridate's potential for making the lives of the younger generation nasty, short, and brutish, we might venture to say that Xipharès should thank his lucky stars that this drama is about Mithridate's death rather than his life, but not the least important way Xipharès acts as an heir throughout the drama is that in spite of his willingness to stand up to his pugnacious brother, he is by nature a respecter of paternal authority:

Autant que mon amour respecta la puissance
D'un père à qui je fus dévoué dès l'enfance,
Autant ce même amour, maintenant révolté,
De ce nouveau rival [Pharnace] brave l'autorité. (99–102)

As much as my love respected the power
Of a father to whom I was devoted from childhood on,
This same love is now in full revolt
And challenges the authority of this new rival.

Xipharès distinguishes between his father's legitimate authority and his brother's usurped authority. However feisty he may be in his dealings with Pharnace, he is incapable of rebelling against his father: "Quand mon père paraît, je ne sais qu'obéir" (366) [When my father appears, I can only obey].

The quandary left by Mithridate's death is, in effect, how to mourn him and receive his ambiguous legacy. Starting with his speech eulogizing the father he believes dead, Xipharès wonders how the younger generation should react to Mithridate's death:

Et j'ai su qu'un soldat dans les mains de Pompée
Avec son [Mithridate's] diadème a remis son épée.
Ainsi ce roi qui seul a durant quarante ans,
Lassé tout ce que Rome eut de chefs importants,
Et qui dans l'Orient balançant la fortune,
Vengeait de tous les rois la querelle commune,
Meurt, et laisse après lui, pour venger son trépas,
Deux fils infortunés qui ne s'accordent pas. (7–14)

I was told that some soldier handed over
Mithridate's sword to Pompey along with his crown.
So the king who spent forty years fighting alone
Against all of Rome's important commanders,
Who acted as a counterweight to Rome's power in the Orient,
Avenging the shared grievances of all the Orient's kings,
Has died, and leaves behind him to avenge his death
Two unfortunate sons who cannot see eye to eye.

Xipharès implies that the first point of contention between him and Pharnace that must be attended to is how to bury and avenge their father. A generalized uncertainty about how to deal with the demise of a king "que l'Orient, tout plein de ses exploits, / Peut nommer justement le dernier de ses rois" (301–2) [whom the Orient, bursting with his exploits, / Is right to call its last and final king] is precisely Mithridate's legacy, what he "leaves behind him." The allusion to Mithridate's forty years of struggle against Rome supposedly brought to an end by Pompey's receipt of the king's sword may also evoke the generation that has passed since Pierre Corneille's *La Mort de Pompée*, in which Pompey himself was a noble figure of old heroic values eliminated by the encroaching forces of the present.[29] Now, a generation later, Pompey is appropriately said to receive the sword of Mithridate, who is portrayed in a very similar light.[30]

Xipharès, the second-generation hero, cannot refrain from mourning the passing of the values of the first generation any more than first-generation figures like Jason and Curiace could ignore the onslaught of second-generation values. Like Racine himself, who comes into his own just as *Mithridate* is staged — the play probably premiered the day after he became a member of the Académie française and "corresponds to the precise moment Racine reaches the height of his glory"[31] — Xipharès embodies a transformation of the values of an earlier generation. And in the case of both the character and his creator, the transformation is perceptible as both a correction of earlier values and a falling away from them.

Monime, too, although she is a fierce defender of her right to choose and selects the younger brother over the older, also presents herself as a figure belonging to a very old tradition: "Ephèse est mon pays; mais je suis descendue / D'aïeux, ou rois, Seigneur, ou héros qu'autrefois / Leur vertu, chez les Grecs, mit au-dessus des rois" (248–50) [Ephesus is my homeland; but I am descended, Sire, / From ancestors, or kings, or heroes that the Greeks / In former times prized more highly than kings for their virtue]. If Mithridate is the "dernier roi" resisting Rome in this part of the world and is thus a figure of old heroism, Monime's ancestors must be lodged in the most privileged section of the Elysian Fields.

Monime's connection to an archaic ethic is reinforced by one of the liberties Racine takes with his historical sources: Monime is the daughter of Philopoemen (264), the reorganizer of the Achaean League, who died a half-century before the birth of Mithridates VI, the historical figure on whom Racine's character is based. The anachronism certainly suggests Monime is a character taken from the past.[32] Philopoemen is sometimes called the last of the Greeks, for he fought against Rome's inevitable encroachment. Monime thus becomes a figure who, like Aricie in *Phèdre*, is the last descendant of a very ancient family whose attachment to a lost tradition seems to contribute to the character's nobility.

Xipharès and Monime, representatives of a new ethic defined largely by opposition to Mithridate himself, still mourn the king's passing and vow to commemorate his values. Perhaps their paradoxical position can fairly be read as coinciding with Racine's recognition as the greatest figure of the second generation of tragedy, as a kind of authority or standard of the day, for if Racine has prevailed over the first generation of tragedians, the very nature of tragedy itself does not allow him ever to be fully free of the past.

An Older Brother's Loss

Pierre Corneille's *Tite et Bérénice* and Racine's *Bérénice*

That critics have called Racine's *Bérénice* (1670) his most "Cornelian" play is not surprising given the drama's lofty tone and the unwonted high-mindedness of its protagonists; it is all the more appropriate in that Corneille's *Tite et Bérénice* (1670) is one of his most "Racinian" plays. As we shall see, Corneille's play has a number of Racinian elements: the utter instability of love relations; the characters' endless shifting of allegiances and jockeying for position; the numerous permutations of pairings between lovers; in short, the geometry of power and love that we have come to associate with Racine more than with Corneille. Racine's highly successful *Andromaque*, which more or less launched the younger playwright's career, predates *Tite et Bérénice* by only about two years, and the convoluted love quartet that Corneille uses to structure his play — Domitian wants to marry Domitie, who wants to marry Tite, who wants to marry Bérénice — is undoubtedly influenced by Racine's famous four-linked "love chain" in *Andromaque* — Oreste wishes to marry Hermione, who wishes to marry Pyrrhus, who wishes to marry Andromaque. Moreover, Corneille's decision to feature sibling rivalry — he incorporates Tite's younger brother, Domitian, as a major character — may have been influenced by the prominence of the theme in Racine's early plays. To put it quite simply, one of Corneille's central strategies in competing with Racine seems to have been to write the kind of play he thought Racine would write.

To some extent, this also applies to Racine's own approach to the same historical material: he may be writing as much from what he imagines to be Corneille's point of view as Corneille is writing from what he imagines to be Racine's. Racine's *Bérénice* completely sidesteps the issue of sibling rivalry by omitting Titus' brother altogether.[1] Racine sets the events of his play earlier in Titus' reign than Corneille, just eight days after the death of Titus' father, the emperor Vespasian, so that the subject of Racine's tragedy is essentially Titus' coming to terms with and assumption of his father's legacy. Although Racine does incorporate one of his trademark love triangles into the story, the characters resolutely refuse to conduct themselves with the usual vengeful abandon of jealous Racinian lovers; in spite of a few outbursts of emotion, they remain quite civil in their dealings with rivals and rejecting lovers. Titus' final decision to follow his late father's dictates, as well as Bérénice's heroic espousal of duty at the expense of love, are reminiscent of the noble resignation-in-love of a Rodrigue or a Curiace.

The ongoing competition between Corneille and Racine has itself been seen as a relation between "frères ennemis," and if that is the case here, the younger brother's victory is quite clear: history has not been kinder to *Tite et Bérénice* than were Corneille's contemporaries, while the austere perfection of Racine's *Bérénice* continues to be admired to this day. But in fact both plays express the failure of the values of the first generation. Corneille's tragedy stages the sterility of the position of the older-brother heir — the play culminates in his decision not to produce an heir of his own — while Racine, even though he dramatizes the son's inheriting of his father's values, nonetheless emphasizes discontinuity, rupture, and conflict, concluding not with a reaffirmation of the values of the previous generation, but rather with one of his most lyrical expressions of loss.

Corneille's *Tite et Bérénice*: The Heir Without an Heir

Like *Nicomède*, *Tite et Bérénice* is a dynastic drama in which a younger brother is dominated by an older brother and in the end becomes his heir, but the differences between the two portrayals of the sibling relationship underscore the distance between the first and the second generations of tragedy. In *Nicomède* the younger brother, lacking a viable paternal model, imitates his older brother and paradoxically inherits from him a power the older brother himself never officially held. In *Tite et Bérénice*, the younger brother is once again depicted as subordinate, but the older-brother heir's inability to play his role convincingly and thus to provide a credible model to imitate leads to a skewed inheritance. When Tite announces that he will never marry and that Domitian, his younger brother, will consequently be his sole heir, he is not acting as a legator, like Nicomède, but rather as a figure of sterility and nongenerativity. Whether or not Tite is more heroic than Domitian, his willful nonproduction of an heir may be read as an abdication of the values of the first generation.

The conflict that opposes the late emperor Vespasian's two sons, Tite and Domitian, exemplifies more clearly than in any other play of Pierre Corneille's that we have examined the conflict between the values of the two generations of tragedy. Tite, the older son, does his best to embody feudal values: the trouble is that he is not very good at playing the role of an heir. In taking over his father's position, he claims to have internalized his father's point of view, as he tells his younger brother:

> Son [Vespasian's] trépas a changé toutes choses de face,
> J'ai pris ses sentiments lorsque j'ai pris sa place,
> Je m'impose à mon tour les lois qu'il m'imposait,
> Et me dis après lui tout ce qu'il me disait.
> J'ai des yeux d'Empereur, et n'ai plus ceux de Tite. (491–95)

> Vespasian's death changed the entire landscape,
> I assumed his heart when I assumed his position,
> In turn I force on myself the laws he forced on me,
> And recite to myself all the same lessons he used to recite to me.
> I have the eyes of an Emperor, not Tite's eyes.

After the father's death his heart ("sentiments"), his laws ("lois"), his lessons ("tout ce qu'il me disait"), and his vision ("des yeux d'Empereur") live on. Or so his heir would like to believe.

The test case of the father's ethical legacy is Tite's projected marriage to the daughter of Corbulon, a man chosen to be emperor before Vespasian but assassinated when his moral qualms kept him from assuming that title: "Son austère vertu rejeta ce grand nom" (90) [His austere virtue rejected that great name]. Corbulon's daughter, the haughty, ambitious Domitie, can be either a powerful political asset to Tite or a formidable threat: "Un vif ressentiment lui fera tout oser: / En un mot, il vous faut la perdre ou l'épouser" (425–26) [Her sharp resentment will make her try anything: / In a word, you must destroy her or marry her]. For this very reason, Domitie was chosen by Vespasian as a politically expedient wife for his heir; she is a woman who considers herself to the Empire born:

> Ce jeune esprit [Domitie], qu'entête et le sang de Néron
> Et le choix qu'en Syrie on fit de Corbulon,

S'attribue à l'Empire un droit imaginaire,
Et s'en fait, comme vous [Tite], un rang héréditaire. (417–20)

Her young spirit, made stubborn by Nero's blood
And the choice of Corbulon in Syria,
Fancies that she has a right to the Empire,
And like you considers it her legacy.

Tite states more than once that to marry Domitie would be to respect his father's wishes: "C'est le choix de mon père, et je connais trop bien / Qu'à choisir en César ce doit être le mien" (389–90) [She's my father's choice, and I know all too well / That she must be my choice if I choose as a Caesar]; "Domitie est le choix de Rome et de mon père" (983) [Domitie is Rome's choice and my father's choice].

The problem is that while Tite and Domitie are in love, they are not in love with each other. Tite loves Bérénice, the Queen of Judea, and Domitie loves Tite's younger brother, Domitian. Both of these relationships pose serious political problems. Although Bérénice is an ally of Rome and staunchly supported Tite in his recent conquest of her country, she is, nonetheless, a foreign monarch, and Rome mistrusts foreign monarchs. As for Domitian, as the late emperor's younger son he has no immediate prospects of assuming his father's title, so that Domitie's wish to become empress would have to be sacrificed were she to marry him instead of his brother.

Tite's choice between duty (Domitie) and love (Bérénice) is not qualitatively different from the tragic dilemma of other heroes of both the first and the second generation, but he does not manage to play his role with either the forbidding, unapproachable dignity of a first-generation duty-bound heir or the charismatic energy of a second-generation lover. Tite does his best to squelch his feelings and to do what he has to do — marry Domitie — at the expense of his happiness. But as Domitie drily observes, Tite "s'efforce à m'aimer, mais il ne m'aime pas" (38) [does his best to love me, but he does not love me].

Tite's reliance upon artifice, that is, the creation of a proper, external persona that contains and reins in feelings and desires rather than expressing them, accounts for his emotional distance. Domitie frets about her fiancé's fundamental absence — "Souvent même, au milieu des offres de sa foi, / Il semble tout à coup qu'il n'est pas avec moi" (33–34) [Often, in the midst of pledging to be mine, / It suddenly seems as if he is not even present] — while Tite berates himself for letting his love for Bérénice show in spite of himself: "J'en ai trop, et le mets peut-être trop au jour" (1354) [I have too much love for her, and perhaps let it show too much]. When the Judean queen unexpectedly returns to Rome, allegedly to pay homage to the new emperor but also, one suspects, to rekindle Tite's flame, the smitten emperor accurately portrays the split between his outer and inner being:

> Votre absence et le temps m'avaient fait quelque grâce;
> J'en craignais un peu moins les malheurs où je passe;
> Je souffrais Domitie, et d'assidus efforts
> M'avaient, malgré l'amour, fait maître du dehors.
> La contrainte semblait tourner en habitude;
> Le joug que je prenais m'en paraissait moins rude;
> Et j'allais être heureux, du moins aux yeux de tous,
> Autant qu'on le peut être en n'étant point à vous. (947–54)

> Your absence and the passage of time had given me some respite;
> They dulled my fear of the ordeal I must endure;
> I put up with Domitie, and in spite of my love for you
> I'd managed, by dint of will, to give an outward appearance of control.
> Constraint seemed to become second nature;
> The yoke I had assumed seemed easier to bear;
> And I was about to be happy, at least in the eyes of the others,
> As happy as one can be without belonging to you.

This speech has a broader impact than a lover's complaint; it is a poignant description of the plight of the heir, in control only superficially, "maître du dehors," so accustomed to not getting what he desires that self-denial becomes a natural turn of mind. Internal division, the silencing of a part of oneself, is already a familiar motif in the first generation of tragedies, but the elegiac mode of Tite's words makes one wonder if what is lost by the heir is not greater than what is gained. Being his father's heir entails the subordination of Tite's own individual perspective and happiness to the demands of the lineage to such an extent that he is no longer himself: he does indeed have "the eyes of an Emperor, not Tite's eyes."

While Rodrigue and Camille, faced with the terrible contradiction between their heads and their hearts, resort to dramatic action, Rodrigue risking his life in defense of his country and Camille losing hers in an attack upon her country, Tite is beset by inertia and indecision. What sets off the action of the play, ironically, is Tite's inaction: Domitie becomes concerned when he repeatedly postpones their wedding, which has already been in the works for more than six months (7), by endlessly adding to its pomp and grandeur: "Ce pompeux appareil, où sans cesse il ajoute, / Recule chaque jour un noeud qui le dégoûte" (27–28) [By constantly adding to this pomp and circumstance, / Every day he puts off a bond he finds distasteful]. Like Penelope secretly unraveling the shroud that she is making for Odysseus and that she says she must finish before she can decently take another husband, Tite uses the wedding arrangements to hide the fact that he cannot bring himself to give up someone he has loved and lost.[2] In the end Corneille's Tite plays a far lesser role in determining the outcome of the conflict than Racine's Titus, whom André Stegmann rightly labels "the more Cornelian of the two."[3]

Domitian: The Younger Brother as Huckster

By contrast to Tite, Domitian, ten years or "deux lustres" (810) his junior, is a representative of the values of the second generation: savvy, calculating, manipulative, and imbued with the unsettling spirit of a world in which there are few clear answers but nothing is out of the question. At the center of the younger brother's character is a sense of contradiction, opposition, and irony. He sees the potential weaknesses in his brother's posing and uses his perceptions to drive a wedge between the opposing parts of this would-be heroic character. For example, Domitian seeks to convince Bérénice that accepting his proposal would be an effective way of getting Tite to change his mind and come back to her:

En vain, par politique, il [Tite] fait ailleurs l'amant,
Il s'y réduit en vain par grandeur de courage:
A ces fausses clartés opposez quelque ombrage,
Et je renonce au jour, s'il ne revient à vous,
Pour peu que vous penchiez à le rendre jaloux. (746–50)

Tite's vain attempt to play the lover elsewhere is politic:
It's what his highmindedness reduces him to, but in vain.
Cast umbrage against these false lights,
And I'll give up the ghost if he does not come back to you,
Were you only inclined to make him jealous.

Domitian's irreverent attitude toward his brother's virtuous stance is apparent in the use of paradox and antithesis. Domitian says that Tite "is reduced" to loving Domitie out of "highmindedness" (literally, greatness of heart), a topological contradiction: does his love for Domitie diminish or increase his glory? Similarly, Tite's shining reputation becomes a false light that Bérénice can counter with the shadowy emotion of jealousy. Domitian's advice to Bérénice is to harness the power of irony, to accept his proposal in order to lead to precisely the opposite effect: to get Tite back. The logic he uses is that of supply and demand. Once Tite realizes Bérénice is no longer available, her value will rise so precipitously he will no longer be able to resist her.

Domitian's values are market values. He will do nothing for nothing and does his best to get the maximum return for the least expenditure. The best example of this comes in a scene between Domitian and Domitie (4:3) in which the latter, fearing Tite may break off the couple's engagement and marry Bérénice in spite of the political obstacles, asks Domitian to espouse her cause and prevent what would be a great humiliation to her. To Domitie's dismay, Domitian refuses to put himself on the line for her without a very clear idea of what benefits would be garnered from such an enterprise:

DOMITIAN:
Parlons à coeur ouvert, Madame, et dites-moi
Quel fruit je dois attendre enfin d'un tel emploi.
DOMITIE:
Voulez-vous pour servir être sûr du salaire,
Seigneur, et n'avez-vous qu'un amour mercenaire?
DOMITIAN:
Je n'en connais point d'autre, et ne conçois pas bien
Qu'un amant puisse plaire en ne prétendant rien.
DOMITIE:
Que ces précautions sentent les âmes basses! (1213–19)

DOMITIAN:
Let us speak openly, Madam. Tell me,
Can I expect such an action to bear fruit?
DOMITIE:
Are you checking on the salary you will get from helping me,
Sire, and is your love purely mercenary?

DOMITIAN:
I know of no other kind, and fail to understand
How a suitor can be of service and ask for no reward.
DOMITIE:
What a lowly soul these petty concerns portend!

Domitian sees his relation with Domitie in capitalistic terms. He will not work for free, nor will he lay out an investment without a guaranteed rate of return. In response to Domitie's characterization of his love as mercenary, he unflappably states that all love has an underlying motivation of self-interest.

Domitian does not come off particularly well in this scene, but his portrayal as a mercenary of the heart may be understandable given his disadvantageous position. True to his other depictions of older and younger brothers, Corneille has represented Domitian as inferior in a number of ways; Domitian's cry of frustration to Domitie, "Est-ce un crime pour moi que l'aînesse d'un frère?" (808) [Is my brother's seniority a crime I've committed?], requires no response. While the brothers' situations are analogous — each loves a woman he cannot easily marry — Tite manages for a time to keep his desires under wraps, whereas Domitian is not even up to trying. He begs his brother to change his mind and to marry Bérénice in spite of Rome's condemnation:

DOMITIAN:
Seigneur, à vos bontés laissez un libre cours.
Qui se vainc une fois peut se vaincre toujours:
Ce n'est pas un effort que votre âme redoute.
TITE:
Qui se vainc une fois sait bien ce qu'il en coûte:
L'effort est assez grand pour en craindre un second.
DOMITIAN:
Ah! si votre grande âme à peine s'en répond,
La mienne, qui n'est pas d'une trempe si belle,
Réduite au même effort, Seigneur, que fera-t-elle?
TITE:
Ce que je fais, mon frère: aimez ailleurs.
DOMITIAN:
                                        Hélas!
Ce qui vous fut aisé, Seigneur, ne me l'est pas. (513–22)

DOMITIAN:
Sire, give free rein to your indulgence.
He who masters himself once can always do so again:
It is not a task that your soul fears.
TITE:
He who masters himself once knows how difficult it is:
The task is hard enough to make one fear another.
DOMITIAN:
Ah! if your great soul can barely face it,
What will my soul, which is not of the same calibre,
Do when it is reduced to the same task, Sire?
TITE:
The same thing I have done, brother: love someone else.
DOMITIAN:
                              Alas!
What was easy for you is not easy for me.

Domitian's approach is typical of a younger sibling: his attempts to ingratiate himself and get his way are not constrained by dignity or pride. Uncon-
cerned with logic or coherence, he asks Tite to "give in" ("laissez un libre
cours") to his feelings of fraternal tenderness and simultaneously to resist his
love for Domitie, overlooking the fact that for Tite, abandoning Domitie
and allowing himself to love Bérénice would not be an act of self-control ("se
vaincre") but an abdication of self-control. Domitian believes his brother
can do anything ("It is not a task that your soul fears"), and when Tite
advises him to forget Domitie as he himself has "forgotten" Bérénice, Domitian is not above confessing his powerlessness compared to his brother,
musing that his soul is "not of the same calibre" as his brother's. The younger
brother's admiration for the older is epitomized by his delusional belief that
for Tite such things come easily.

    Still, the inequality between the two brothers is not so great as it was in
a play like *Nicomède*. Domitian may feel in his brother's shadow, and his
inability to control himself as Tite has learned to do may be a disadvantage
in terms of the heroic values of the first generation. But there is also something quite deliberate in Domitian's refusal to follow his brother's lead, and
a concomitant affirmation of the younger brother's difference. Domitian
does not simply imitate his older brother, as did Attale; he wins out in the
end without any fundamental change in his behavior. Choosing to integrate
Domitian into the story of Titus and Berenice — which Racine does not

do — allows Corneille to remind us at the conclusion of the drama that Domitian became emperor after Titus' death and reigned much longer than Titus (fifteen years as opposed to two).

Domitian's ambiguous status as an appealing underling and a tricky competitor is summarized by Domitie, who exclaims: "Je l'aime et le dédaigne" (157) [I love him and look down on him]. One could hardly imagine a more withering statement of the younger sibling's perennially endearing inferiority. Domitie puts a more positive spin on things when her paramour appears onstage:

> Daignez donc voir, Seigneur, quelle route il faut prendre,
> Pour ne point m'imposer la honte de descendre.
> Tout mon coeur vous préfère à cet heureux rival:
> Pour m'avoir toute à vous, devenez son égal.
> Vous dites qu'il vous aime, et je ne le puis croire,
> Si je ne vois sur vous un rayon de sa gloire.
> On vous a vus tous deux sortir d'un même flanc,
> Ayez mêmes honneurs ainsi que même sang. (231–38)

> Be willing to look at what path you must take, Sire,
> If you wish to spare me the shame of marrying down.
> With all my heart I prefer you to your fortunate rival:
> If you want me to be all yours, become his equal.
> You say he loves you, but I cannot believe it,
> Unless I see a ray of his glory reflected onto you.
> We all know you were borne by the same mother,
> Have the same honors as he, just as you have the same blood.

Domitie continues to be blunt about Domitian's inferiority and her unwillingness to "marry down" ("la honte de descendre"), but she does not present his younger-brother status as dooming the couple's love. Rather, she emphasizes the potential equality of the two brothers, which could salvage it: "If you want me to be all yours, become his equal"; "Have the same honors as he." This might seem contradictory: if primogeniture is in effect, how can a younger brother gain the same honors as his father's heir?[4]

In *Nicomède*, Attale emulates his heroic older brother; in *Tite et Bérénice*, Domitian, for all that he admires Tite, competes with him by making use of undignified sentiments like spitefulness and lust that his brother resists but cannot eliminate. Not the least Racinian aspect of the drama is the persistence of jealousy even in characters who do not love those of whom they feel possessive. For example, Tite's affection for Domitie is purely a product of obligation, yet he is incensed when Domitian informs him Domitie has long been in love with the younger brother (545–46), and when she makes the mistake of appearing onstage, Tite addresses her in these terms:

> On dit que cette foi ne vous donne pas toute,
> Que ce coeur reste ailleurs. Parlez en liberté,
> Et n'en consultez point cette noble fierté,
> Ce digne orgueil du sang que mon rang sollicite:
> De tout ce que je suis ne regardez que Tite,
> Et pour mieux écouter vos désirs les plus doux,
> Entre le Prince et moi ne regardez que vous. (564–70)

> I've heard your promise does not give you all to me,
> That your heart is not mine. Speak freely
> And do not listen to your noble pride,
> That pridefulness of blood impressed by my lofty position:
> Of all that I am, think only of Tite,
> And in choosing between the Prince and me, think only of yourself,
> All the better to heed your sweetest desires.

If one had no knowledge of the situation, one might believe Tite desperately in love with Domitie and see this as a *Rodogune*-style moment of reckoning between brothers who are rivals in love. But there is great irony in this activation of Tite's jealousy over a woman he does not love.[5] Tite is hoisted on his own petard: accepting Domitie as his intended because of duty rather than passion, he is displeased that she returns the favor.

Domitian, a vindictive lover, stirs up the resentment of others in an attempt to compensate for his lack of power. Rejected by Domitie because of her ambitious marriage, he revels in the idea of punishing her by rekindling Tite's love for Bérénice: "Qu'elle serait confuse, et que j'aurais de joie!" (307) [How mortified she would be, what joy I'd feel!]. When Domitie tells him to find another woman, he takes her at her word and courts Bérénice, then punishes his former lover by stating he loves the Judean queen as much as he has to in order to torment Domitie ("Autant qu'il faut l'aimer pour vous faire un supplice" [1264]). This kind of emotional reckoning — I love another only to punish you — is more readily associated with Racine than with Corneille. Similarly, the contradictory nature of Domitie's possessive feelings toward the suitor she has rejected echoes the deluded amorous revisionism of Hermione in Racine's *Andromaque*:

DOMITIAN:
Vous m'avez commandé de quitter qui me quitte,
Vous le savez, Madame, et si c'est vous trahir,
Vous m'avouerez aussi que c'est vous obéir.
DOMITIE:
S'il échappe à l'amour un mot qui le trahisse,
A l'effort qu'il se fait veut-il qu'on obéisse? (776–80)

DOMITIAN:
You know you ordered me to leave you, as you left me,
Madam, and if that means I have betrayed you,
You must confess I have also obeyed you.
DOMITIE:
If love lets out a traitorous command,
Does it want its command to be obeyed?

Domitie's statement that she did not really want to be obeyed is reminiscent of Hermione's reaction when Oreste follows her orders to kill Pyrrhus: "Ne devais-tu pas lire au fond de ma pensée? / Et ne voyais-tu pas, dans mes emportements, / Que mon coeur démentait ma bouche à tous moments?" (*Andromaque*, 1546–48) [Wasn't it up to you to read my mind? / And couldn't you see, in the midst of my fury, / That at every moment my heart gave the lie to my lips?].[6]

If Domitian is mercenary in his dealings with Domitie, he rightly observes that she is as capable of such a thing as he:

N'attendez-vous de Tite, et n'avez-vous pour Tite
Qu'une stérile ardeur qui s'attache au mérite?
De vos destins aux siens pressez-vous l'union
Sans vouloir aucun fruit de tant de passion? (1223–26)

Do you expect nothing more from Tite, and feel nothing more for him
Than a sterile passion swayed only by worthiness?
Do you call for the union of your two fates
And ask nothing in return for so much love?

Domitian does not shy away from calling Domitie on her double standard: after all, is her love for the emperor disinterested? Exploiting Domitian when she needs him as much as Racine's Hermione uses Oreste, Domitie does not rule out the possibility of rewarding him, but she thinks of such a reward less as a wage than as a tip: "Et laissez à mon choix l'effet de votre espoir: / Que ce soit une grâce et non pas un devoir" (1249–50) [And leave the outcome of your hopes up to me: / Let it be a favor, not a duty].

Domitie is a kind of mediating figure between the two brothers and the values they represent. There is little doubt that glory is more important to her than love, and to that extent she might be seen as a throwback to first-generation figures like Don Diègue. But her inconvenient love for Domitian persists even after she has settled on marriage with his brother, and at times she feels obliged to couch her opportunistic relationship with the emperor in terms of love. Her status as a hinge figure is especially clear in a speech about love that she makes during her final appearance onstage (5:2):

> A l'amour vraiment noble il suffit du dehors,
> Il veut bien du dedans ignorer les ressorts,
> Il n'a d'yeux que pour voir ce qui s'offre à la vue,
> Tout le reste est pour eux une terre inconnue,
> Et sans importuner le coeur d'un souverain,
> Il a tout ce qu'il veut quand il en a la main. (1557–62)

> A truly noble love is quite satisfied with appearances,
> It is willing to ignore the heart's inner workings,
> And sees only what is available to the eyes,
> Since everything else is uncharted territory,
> And it does not fret about capturing the king's heart,
> But is perfectly content to possess his promise.

Domitie uses the vocabulary of preciosity, particularly the phrase "une terre inconnue,"[7] but the message of her words is closer in spirit to Don Diègue in *Le Cid* than to Clélie in Madeleine de Scudéry's novels. When one is dealing with love among the ruling classes ("l'amour vraiment noble"), one need not go into all the eccentricities of the heart: appearances, while they may well be deceptive, are good enough.[8]

Bérénice: A Hard Act to Follow

Throughout the groveling, hypocrisy, and posturing that constitute the play's action, Bérénice remains above the fray. The drama's only true hereditary monarch — as we have seen, in succeeding his father as emperor, Tite is quite exceptional — Bérénice is the only Cornelian figure in a play that owes a great deal to Racine and to the evolution of mores that his theater reflects.[9] Bérénice reaffirms feudal values over market values, and hereditary monarchy over Empire: she values tradition and the continuation of the lineage over individual happiness, freedom of choice, and political manipulation. Serge Doubrovsky notes this retrograde aspect of a character for whom "love is once again the locus of a *test of strength*, as in [Corneille's] great tragedies."[10]

By a *coup de théâtre*, Bérénice refuses to marry Tite just as the Senate votes to allow the union by adopting her: "D'une commune voix Rome adopte la Reine" (1672) [Rome adopts the Queen with a single voice]. Her reason for rejecting this solution, she tells Tite, is her desire to set a good example:

> D'autres sur votre exemple épouseraient des reines
> Qui n'auraient pas, Seigneur, des âmes si romaines,
> Et lui [Rome] feraient peut-être avec trop de raison
> Haïr votre mémoire et détester mon nom.
> Un refus généreux de tant de déférence
> Contre tous ces périls nous met en assurance. (1703–8)

> Others would use your example to marry queens
> Who might not have such Roman souls, Sire,
> And would make Rome hate your memory
> And loathe my name, perhaps with good reason.
> A generous refusal of such accommodation
> Keeps us safe from all those perils.

In stark contrast to the mathematics of love that pervades the play, Bérénice's "refus généreux" is a return to feudal values in several ways. Perhaps both Bérénice and Domitie love Tite because he is an emperor, but Domitie's love is a kind of social investment, a search for increased value, while Bérénice's love is simply predicated on the absolute worth of the love object.

For Domitie love may garner value, but for Bérénice love presupposes value. Were Tite to act unworthily, Bérénice would stop loving him: "Daigne me préserver le ciel . . . / De voir tant de faiblesse en une si grande âme! / Si j'avais droit par là de vous moins estimer, / Je cesserais peut-être aussi de vous aimer" (1643–46) [May the heavens spare me . . . / From seeing so much weakness in such a great soul! / If it gave me the right to think less of you, / Perhaps I would also stop loving you]. Marriage to a foreign queen, by setting a dangerous example, would be unworthy of Tite and must be avoided at all cost. We return in spirit to the world of Chimène and Rodrigue.

Another way that Bérénice's generous refusal represents a return to feudal values is that it escapes the drama's market economy of love. Bérénice says to Tite, "Epousez Domitie: il ne m'importe plus / Qui vous enrichissiez d'un si noble refus" (1729–30) [Marry Domitie: I no longer care / Whom you enrich by such a noble refusal]. That Bérénice's love is qualitatively different from the love of the other characters allows her to feel indifferent to Tite's future attachments. Her use of the economic term "enrichir" summarizes the economy of love that she herself rises above. Following the queen's example, Tite vows to match her noble refusal with one of his own:

> Un si noble refus n'enrichira personne.
> J'en jure par l'espoir qui nous fut le plus doux:
> Tout est à vous, Madame, et ne sera qu'à vous,
> Et ce que mon amour doit à l'excès du vôtre
> Ne deviendra jamais le partage d'une autre. (1744–48)

> Such a noble refusal will enrich no one.
> I swear it in the name of what was our dearest hope:
> It is all yours, Madam, and will never be another's,
> And the least my love owes yours, which is so great,
> Is never to be shared by a woman other than you.

Tite withdraws from the economy of love as well: Bérénice cannot return his love and he recognizes his "debt" to her love ("ce que mon amour doit") as nontransferable. What Tite is announcing here is his refusal to take a wife and produce an heir.

A final component of Bérénice's return to feudal values is her defense of inheritance. She not only refuses to accept the possibility of legitimation through her adoption by Rome, but also counters Tite's announcement that he will not marry with a reminder of the importance of producing an heir:

Le mien [love] vous aurait fait déjà ces beaux serments,
S'il n'eût craint d'inspirer de pareils sentiments:
Vous vous devez des fils, et des Césars à Rome,
Qui fassent à jamais revivre un si grand homme. (1749–52)

My love would have already sworn never to marry
Had it not feared that you might follow suit:
To yourself you owe sons, and to Rome you owe Caesars
Who will keep such a great man alive forever.

If the curtain rises on Tite's decision to follow his father's ethical legacy, it falls on his refusal to carry on the lineage:

Pour revivre en des fils nous n'en mourons pas moins,
Et vous mettez ma gloire au-dessus de ces soins.
Du levant au couchant, du More jusqu'au Scythe,
Les peuples vanteront et Bérénice et Tite,
Et l'histoire à l'envi forcera l'avenir
D'en garder à jamais l'illustre souvenir. (1753–58)

Even if we live on in our sons, we die nonetheless;
And you put my glory above these concerns.
From east to west, from the Moors' lands to the Scythians',
Nations will sing the praises of Bérénice and Tite,
And history will force the admiring future
To preserve our illustrious memory through the ages.

Bérénice's lesson is a paradoxical one, for if she is a figure of feudal values and ultimately provides an example of those values for Tite, both rulers foreswear marriage and the producing of an heir; Tite names his brother as his successor: "Prince, après mon trépas, soyez sûr de l'Empire. / Prenez-y part en frère, attendant que j'expire" (1759–60) [Prince, after my death, be assured of the Empire. / And until I die, share in it as a brother]. In *Tite et*

Bérénice, Pierre Corneille undermines feudal values, reaffirms them, and finally relegates them to the realm of tragic heroism, of exemplary figures with no progeny and of models one admires but does not wish to follow.[11]

Racine's *Bérénice*: "A Nobler Theater"?

The sober atmosphere of Racine's *Bérénice* is partly a function of his competition with Corneille and his wish to revive, if only temporarily, "un plus noble théâtre"[12] by avoiding the kinds of delirious scenes that enliven his two previous plays, *Andromaque* and *Britannicus*. But while Racine superficially presents a Corneille-style drama about duty conquering love, his characterizations of Titus and Bérénice gain a new coherence if we see them in the light of the conflict between the two generations. Titus and Bérénice claim to share a powerful *amour par inclination* uninfluenced by their identities or their positions within their respective societies. But I contend that in a remarkable reversal of values that dramatizes how far we have come from the first generation of tragedy, they are embarrassed to admit that their love for each other is at least partially motivated by ambition. Whereas *amour par inclination* was frequently a source of shame in the first generation of tragedy because of its potential for undermining duty and reputation, Titus' and Bérénice's love, which I interpret as having a veiled component of *amour par estime*, is now couched in terms of pure passion to escape the humiliating confession that their love is not, in fact, completely disinterested.

Although Racine does not choose to incorporate the character of Titus' brother in his version of the story, *Bérénice* has an important younger-brother figure in Antiochus. Like a younger brother, Antiochus is a less powerful version of Titus: Bérénice says that her pleasure in taking Antiochus as the principal confidant of her love for Titus is "entretenir Titus dans un autre lui-même" (272) [To converse with Titus in another form of himself]. Whether or not Antiochus is actually younger than Titus, his wish to marry Bérénice was foiled by the arrival of Titus just as in *Tite et Bérénice* Domitian's plan to marry Domitie was compromised by the arrival of Tite:

> Madame, il vous souvient que mon coeur en ces lieux [of Bérénice's birth]
> Reçut le premier trait qui partit de vos yeux.
> J'aimai. J'obtins l'aveu d'Agrippa votre frère;
> Il vous parla de moi. Peut-être sans colère

Alliez-vous de mon coeur recevoir le tribut;
Titus, pour mon malheur, vint, vous vit, et vous plut. (189–94)

Madam, you remember that in the land of your birth
My heart received the first arrow your eyes propelled.
I was smitten. I obtained your brother Agrippa's consent;
He told you of my feelings. Perhaps without displeasure
You would have received my heart's homage;
Titus, for my misfortune, came, saw you, and was pleasing to you.

It would be rude for Antiochus to say Bérénice once loved him, but if the "first arrow" of her eyes pierced his heart, they may have initially looked upon him with favor.[13]

Gérard Defaux interprets the relation of Antiochus and Titus in Girardian terms reminiscent of the relation between an older and a younger brother:

It has often been noted that Racine, in his plays, was fascinated by what René Girard calls mimetic rivalry and the theme of the double, whether doubles are joined together by hatred, admiration, or envy. . . . In *Bérénice*, Antiochus is . . . the "faithful" and reliable friend who is able to "speak from the heart" (138), the ideal, reticent, and discreet representative to whom the two lovers unhesitatingly confide their most intimate secrets, . . . living constantly in the shadow cast by the couple, . . . less an actor in the drama of doubles than an understudy. . . . Antiochus hates Titus as much as he loves and admires him: blindly. The desire that dominates and torments him is to equal Titus, to be Titus, to appropriate everything Titus possesses: grandeur, splendor, glory, and of course Bérénice. At the same time, he is certain, with a truly tragic and despairing certainty, that no matter what he does he will never reach the goal he has set for himself.[14]

To this I would add that Antiochus' desire to take Bérénice away from Titus is complicated by the fact that in a structure typical of Racine, Titus originally took Bérénice away from Antiochus.[15]

Far more problematic than Antiochus' feelings for Bérénice are hers for him. Bérénice's first words onstage, spoken to her former suitor, suggest a certain coyness:

Enfin je me dérobe à la joie importune
De tant d'amis nouveaux que me fait la fortune;
Je fuis de leurs respects l'inutile longueur,
Pour chercher un ami qui me parle du coeur.

Il ne faut point mentir: ma juste impatience
Vous accusait déjà de quelque négligence.
Quoi? cet Antiochus, disais-je, dont les soins
Ont eu tout l'Orient et Rome pour témoins,
. . . .
Ce même Antiochus, se cachant à ma vue,
Me laisse à la merci d'une foule inconnue? (135–48)

At last I can escape the cumbersome pleasure
Of all my new fair-weather friends;
I have left those well-wishers droning on,
To seek out a friend who speaks to me from [or of] the heart.
I must not lie: I was impatient, justifiably,
And was already accusing you of being somewhat neglectful.
What? Antiochus, I said to myself, whose attentions
Were witnessed by the Orient and Rome,
. . . .
That same Antiochus, keeping out of my sight,
Leaves me at the mercy of a crowd of strangers?

Bérénice seeks a friend who speaks from (or of) the heart. The ambiguity of the phrase is suggestive, as if a part of her wanted to hear the very amorous discourse she has forbidden. Her impatience to see Antiochus, her accusations of neglect, and her allusions to his earlier attentions suggest the charming reproaches of a pouting lover.[16]

When Antiochus announces his abrupt decision to leave Rome and explains he can no longer endure the silencing of his love, Bérénice's reply is equally ambiguous:

Seigneur, je n'ai pas cru que, dans une journée
Qui doit avec César unir ma destinée,
Il fût quelque mortel qui pût impunément
Se venir à mes yeux déclarer mon amant.
Mais de mon amitié mon silence est un gage:
J'oublie en sa faveur un discours qui m'outrage. (259–64)

Sire, I would not have believed that on a day
Which is to see my destiny joined to Caesar's,
There existed a mortal man who without reprisal

Could profess his love for me right to my face.
But my silence is a mark of my affection:
Because of it I shall forget your outrageous speech.

It is always flattering to be courted, even when one has declared one's disinterest, but when Bérénice wonders aloud how on such a momentous day a man other than Titus could declare his love for her, we may wonder the same thing. Bérénice's use of the word "silence" is also evocative. She says that silence is proof of her "amitié" or friendship, that she thinks so highly of Antiochus that she will let his gaffe pass without further comment, but a second meaning attaches to her words: in the Classical period "amitié" is a frequent euphemism for "amour." Bérénice's silence matches Antiochus' silence; perhaps, by implication, her love matches his love.

The possibility that Bérénice loves or once loved Antiochus is supported by a telling exchange between Bérénice and Phénice, her confidante, after Antiochus has confessed that he is still smitten with her. To Phénice's question, "Ne le plaignez-vous pas?" (287) [Do you not pity him?], Bérénice enigmatically replies: "Cette prompte retraite / Me laisse, je l'avoue, une douleur secrète" (287–88) [His sudden departure / Leaves behind a secret pain in me, I confess]. Gordon Pocock underscores the difficulty of explaining Bérénice's confession of a secret pain: "In naturalistic terms, this could only mean either that Bérénice really loves Antiochus (which is nonsense) or that she is obliged to conceal her pity for him (which hardly seems more reasonable, as she is now alone with her confidante). But if we listen to it as part of the poetic pattern, it makes very good sense: it expresses once more the theme of concealment / revelation."[17] Perhaps it is "nonsense" that Bérénice might love Antiochus, but such nonsense is the stuff of Racinian love, and as Pocock himself admits, there really is no sensible explanation of Bérénice's words here.

Another line that points to a subtext of troubled love is Bérénice's statement that she must erase Antiochus from her memory. When Phénice pragmatically suggests that her mistress should not be so quick to let Antiochus sail away, Bérénice responds: "Qui? moi? le retenir? / J'en dois perdre plutôt jusques au souvenir" (289–90) [Who, I? keep him from leaving? / On the contrary, I must erase his very memory from my mind]. The news that Antiochus still loves her can hardly be so traumatic as to demand a protective amnesia. If, on the other hand, she is trying to wipe away her memories of her own repressed love for Antiochus, her statement can be read as a prefiguration of similar lines in other plays of Racine in which the dangers of involuntary, irrational love are vainly relegated to the domain of obscurity and forgetfulness.[18]

But why would Bérénice feel obliged to hide her love for Antiochus if in fact she did love him? In *Tite et Bérénice*, Domitie says plainly that she prefers the older to the younger brother because it makes sense to do so and it will get her the object of her ambitions, the title of empress. Perhaps in spite of the Hebrew queen's disclaimers in Racine's play, there is something similar going on in her mind and heart. Phénice's advice to her mistress that until Titus has formalized his intention of marrying her she would be a fool to discourage Antiochus (292–96) assumes that love is a practical matter. Bérénice's rejoinder is not that she loves Titus but rather that he loves her and will surely marry her now that his father has died: "Le temps n'est plus, Phénice, où je pouvais trembler. / Titus m'aime, il peut tout, il n'a plus qu'à parler" (297–98) [The time has passed, Phénice, when I had something to fear. / Titus loves me, he can do anything, he has only to speak up].

This interpretation of a Bérénice whose *amour par inclination* for Antiochus is preempted by an *amour par estime* for Titus is diametrically opposed to what the character repeats ad nauseam, but perhaps the lady doth protest too much. After all, she herself correctly suspects that Titus' need to reassure her by an oath of undying fidelity is a bad sign: "Hé quoi? vous me jurez une éternelle ardeur, / . . . / Pourquoi même du ciel attester la puissance? / Faut-il par des serments vaincre ma défiance?" (589–92) [Why are you swearing to love me forever? / . . . / Why call in the heavens as a witness to your love's power? / Must you conquer my suspicions with an oath?]. The myth of Bérénice's disinterested love for Titus is a persistent leitmotif throughout the drama:[19]

> Jugez de ma douleur, moi dont l'ardeur extrême,
> Je vous l'ai dit cent fois, n'aime en lui que lui-même,
> Moi qui, loin des grandeurs dont il est revêtu,
> Aurais choisi son coeur et cherché sa vertu. (159–62)

> Judge what pain I feel, I whose great passion,
> As I've told you a hundred times, loves him only for himself,
> I who, far from the trappings of greatness that he wears,
> Would have chosen his heart and sought out his virtue.

Why should we doubt Bérénice's sincerity when she says that she would have loved Titus far from the trappings of greatness ("loin des grandeurs"), that in him she loves only "himself" — as if "himself" could be magically extracted from his power and social standing? On the other hand, why should we automatically trust her simply because she spends an inordinate amount of time assuring Titus she does not love him for his title? Why should we trust her, given that in a speech describing Titus' enormous prestige, she speculates that even if he had been born in total obscurity, he was fated to be the master of the world ("peut-on le voir sans penser comme moi / Qu'en quelque obscurité que le sort l'eût fait naître, / Le monde en le voyant eût reconnu son maître?" [314–16])? Does this vision of a Titus destined for greatness not make any discussion of what he might have been like "loin des grandeurs" a disingenuous exercise?

Many passages support the hypothesis that Bérénice's love for Titus is a result of admiration as much as inclination. Antiochus, who has nothing to gain by loving Bérénice, interprets her love for Titus in this way:

> Titus, pour mon malheur, vint, vous vit, et vous plut.
> Il parut devant vous dans tout l'éclat d'un homme
> Qui porte entre ses mains la vengeance de Rome.
> La Judée en pâlit. Le triste Antiochus
> Se compta le premier au nombre des vaincus. (194–98)

> Titus, for my misfortune, came, saw you, and was pleasing to you.
> He appeared before you with the brilliance of a man
> Who carries Rome's revenge in his two hands.
> Judea paled. Unhappy Antiochus
> Counted himself the first of his conquests.

This passage plays with the idea of Titus' "conquering" Bérénice's heart, but suggests that this conquest did not take place. The series of verbs in the *passé simple*, "vint, vous vit, et vous plut," differs from Caesar's famous "Veni, vidi, vinci" only in the final term, "plut" rather than "vaincut," the latter verb being applied to Antiochus, not to Bérénice, four lines later. What Antiochus believes attracted Bérénice to Titus is precisely his "éclat" as a Roman conqueror: if Judea paled at his arrival, there is nothing to indicate that its queen blushed at it.

It is hard to reconcile Bérénice's claim of disinterested love with her depiction of Titus as a source of glory and political clout. In one breath she reiterates for the hundred-and-first time ("Je vous l'ai dit cent fois") that she loves "only himself" in Titus (159–60); in the next she waxes poetic about the new territories he is convincing the Senate to give her (169–72). Bérénice pushes Antiochus' upsetting confession of love out of her memory by dwelling not on Titus' charming person, but rather on the charming memory ("souvenir charmant" [317]) of his glorious coronation:

> De cette nuit, Phénice, as-tu vu la splendeur?
> Tes yeux ne sont-ils pas tout pleins de sa grandeur?
> Ces flambeaux, ce bûcher, cette nuit enflammée,
> Ces aigles, ces faisceaux, ce peuple, cette armée,
> Cette foule de rois, ces consuls, ce sénat,
> Qui tous de mon amant empruntaient leur éclat;
> Cette pourpre, cet or, que rehaussait sa gloire,
> Et ces lauriers encor témoins de sa victoire;
> Tous ces yeux qu'on voyait venir de toutes parts
> Confondre sur lui seul leurs avides regards;
> Ce port majestueux, cette douce présence . . .
> Ciel! avec quel respect et quelle complaisance
> Tous les coeurs en secret l'assuraient de leur foi! (301–13)

> Did you see the splendor of this night, Phénice?
> Are your eyes not filled with his greatness?
> The torches, the pyre, the fiery night,
> The eagles, the fasces, the people assembled, the army,
> The crowd of kings, the consuls, the senate,
> Who all borrowed their brilliance from my lover;
> The purple, the gold, heightened by his glory,
> And the laurels, other witnesses to his victory;
> All those eyes that could be seen converging from all directions
> And focusing their eager looks on him alone;
> The majestic bearing, the gentle presence . . .
> Heavens! with what respect and desire to be pleasing
> Each heart secretly assured him of its fidelity!

Bérénice's admiration for Titus' powerful position belies her claim that none of her love for him derives from his place in the world. Bérénice loves in Titus many things other than "lui-même": this famous speech could be used as a textbook example of triangulated love. What Bérénice loves in Titus is not only the glorious symbols of Roman power—"Ces flambeaux, ce bûcher," "Ces aigles, ces faisceaux"—but also others' admiration for the new emperor, as her own eyes fix on theirs: "ces yeux qu'on voyait venir de toutes parts," "leurs avides regards," "Le monde en le voyant." It is difficult to believe that Bérénice is looking only at Titus "lui-même" when she spends so much time looking at others who are looking at him.

Similar doubts about the nature of Titus' love for Bérénice may also be raised. Roland Barthes goes as far as to question Titus' love for Bérénice altogether,[20] but even if we accept Titus' claims to love Bérénice, he himself admits that his love is essentially a form of gratitude for all Bérénice has done for him: not simply "amour par inclination," but also a combination of "amour par estime" and "amour par reconnaissance."

> Que dis-je? Cette ardeur que j'ai pour ses [glory's] appas,
> Bérénice en mon sein l'a jadis allumée.
> Tu ne l'ignores pas: toujours la renommée
> Avec le même éclat n'a pas semé mon nom.
> Ma jeunesse, nourrie à la cour de Néron,
> S'égarait, cher Paulin, par l'exemple abusée
> Et suivait du plaisir la pente trop aisée.
> Bérénice me plut. Que ne fait point un coeur
> Pour plaire à ce qu'il aime, et gagner son vainqueur! (502–10)

> What am I saying? This passion I feel for glory's charms,
> Bérénice was the one who kindled it in my breast.
> You know full well that renown has not always
> Surrounded my name with the brilliance it has today.
> In my youth, as I was raised at Nero's court,
> I was misguided, dear Paulin, deceived by bad examples,
> And I let myself coast down pleasure's easy slopes.
> Bérénice was pleasing to me. What is a heart not capable of doing
> To be pleasing to what it loves, and to win over its conqueror!

This important passage indicates that for Titus, the very source of virtue is Bérénice. His choice between Roman values and Bérénice is complicated by the fact that his nobility comes as much from Bérénice as from Roman models.[21] The court of Nero, which in Racine's previous tragedy, *Britannicus*, is about to fall into decadence and decay, is here represented as a place of debauchery rather than the formative influence of Titus' "Roman" glory. Ironically, Titus becomes a "true" Roman thanks to his love for the very woman Rome will not allow him to marry, a paradoxical debt Titus summarizes by saying, "Je lui dois tout, Paulin. Récompense cruelle! / Tout ce que je lui dois va retomber sur elle" (519–20) [I owe her everything, Paulin. Cruel reward! / Everything I owe her will come crashing down on her head].

Thus, in his competition with Corneille, Racine pays tribute to his illustrious elder in several ways. He creates two characters whose love owes a greater debt to the values of the first generation of tragedy than the love of most of his creations, and yet who are embarrassed to admit it: I submit that Bérénice and Titus are essentially Cornelian lovers parading as Racinian lovers. Antiochus is the only authentic Racinian lover in the play, and even he is made to maintain a dignity more typical of Corneille by refusing to run Racine's usual gauntlet of emotionally violent scenes.

Titus asks Antiochus to inform Bérénice of his decision not to marry her: what a dream of amorous revenge! Antiochus hasn't the heart, and does his best to get out of delivering the message: "Est-ce à moi, / Arsace, à me charger de ce cruel emploi?" (833–34) [Is it up to me, / Arsace, to take on this cruel task?]; "L'aimable Bérénice entendrait de ma bouche / Qu'on l'abandonne?" (836–37) [Should lovely Bérénice hear from my own lips / That she is being abandoned?]; "Et ne la crois-tu pas assez infortunée / D'apprendre à quel mépris Titus l'a condamnée, / Sans lui donner encor le déplaisir fatal / D'apprendre ce mépris par son propre rival?" (843–46) [Don't you think she is already unfortunate enough / To find out what scorn Titus has condemned her to withstand, / Without adding to that displeasure the unbearable pain / Of learning of her lover's scorn from his rival's lips?]. Other Racinian lovers would not be so reticent to inform those who have spurned them that they have in turn been spurned. Similarly, in his function as go-between, Antiochus could tell Bérénice whatever he wanted about Titus, and yet he paints a falsely rosy picture of a man devoted to her: "pour la consoler je le [Titus] faisais paraître / Amoureux et constant, plus qu'il ne l'est peut-être" (939–40) [to console her I made Titus appear / In love with her and faithful, perhaps more than he actually is].

In this head-to-head competition between two literary brothers, the question of who wins is ultimately less interesting than the question of how the competition affects the nature and quality of each man's work.[22] Just as *Tite et Bérénice* reaffirms feudal values of inheritance through the heroic character of Bérénice, only to conclude with a stance of nongenerativity, *Bérénice* may be read in the wake — or, to be exact, as the wake — of first-generation tragedy. Although it dramatizes the successful transmission of a paternal inheritance, that inheritance is so painful that the play leaves us not with a feeling of an obstacle gloriously overcome, but rather with a sense of a fundamental loss that the protagonists will spend the rest of their lives mourning. Gordon Pocock writes: "There is no Cornelian joy in a conflict surmounted, no surge of liberated energy; only the painful recognition of inevitability."[23] If *Bérénice* starts out being about a paternal inheritance, its opening phrase, "Arrêtons un moment" [Let us stop a moment] ends up being an appropriate description of Racine's entire enterprise here. Even more fundamentally than Pierre Corneille's staging of an inheritance passing from older to younger brother in *Tite et Bérénice*, Racine's exploration of the conflicts underlying a single moment of tragic conflict, a unit (or unity) of time, undermines any possibility of continuity through inheritance.

A Tale of Two Sisters

Thomas Corneille's *Ariane* and
Racine's *Phèdre*

Thomas Corneille's *Ariane* (1672), a play about the rivalry between Phèdre and her older sister, Ariane, for the love of Thésée, and Racine's *Phèdre* (1677) form as inevitable a pairing as the two sisters whose stories they treat. The intertextual links between the two dramas, with their close thematic and chronological connections—*Ariane* takes place only a handful of years before *Phèdre*—have not received the kind of critical attention one might expect, all the more so as *Ariane* was a very successful and popular play that likely remained in the memories of the theater-going public when *Phèdre* was staged five years later. Sociohistorically, *Ariane* and *Phèdre* can be read in tandem as the tragedy of primogeniture and competition; as protopsychological dramas, they are the tragedies of the older and the younger sister. *Ariane* records the triumph of the competitive younger sister, Phèdre, over the older sister, Ariane, whereas *Phèdre* depicts the symbolic revenge of the older sister, and of the system of entitlement she embodies, from beyond the grave. Taken together, the two plays exemplify the very conflict that is the subject of the present study: they suggest that neither the older sister, with her advantages, nor the younger sister, with her resourcefulness, can have it all.

Ariane is worthy of Racine in the simplicity of its situation.[1] The play tells the story of the two daughters of the Cretan king, Minos, and their shared love for the young Thésée, sent to Crete as a sacrificial victim for the Minotaur. Helped by Ariane to exit from the labyrinth after putting the creature to death, Thésée is then forced to take flight before Minos' wrath, and Ariane, in love with Thésée and in danger of severe punishment by her father, flees with the Greek prince. Thésée, beholden to Ariane for saving his life, promises to marry her, but he is actually in love with her sister, Phèdre. The threesome flees to Naxos, where the local king, Oenarus, becomes smitten with Ariane and Thésée postpones the wedding, hoping she will eventually return her new suitor's affections, thus freeing Thésée from his commitment and leaving him free to marry Phèdre. This does not happen, and the play culminates in Ariane's sad realization that her sister has betrayed her by fleeing with Thésée, leaving her without even the satisfaction of a confrontation with this sisterly Benedict Arnold.

Ariane and Phèdre: The Narcissist and her Echo

Unlike Thomas Corneille's earlier tragedy about sibling rivalry, *Persée et Démétrius*, *Ariane* is a play in which the birth order of the two siblings is not foregrounded, but this does not make the issue any less important to an understanding of the drama. Although we are never told directly that Ariane is the older sister, a clear indication of that fact is given by Ariane, speaking to Thésée:

> Pour te sauver le jour dont ta rigueur me prive,
> Ai-je pris à regret le nom de Fugitive?
> La Mer, les vents, l'exil ont-ils pu m'étonner?
> Te suivre, c'était plus que me voir couronner?
> (3:4; *Poëmes dramatiques* 4:558)

> To save your life, did I shy away from assuming the title of Fugitive
> For you who would deprive me of your presence?
> The Sea, the winds, exile, did any of that stop me?
> Was following after you better than seeing myself crowned?

Later in the same scene Ariane reiterates that she gave up the throne to follow Thésée: "Pour toi, pour m'attacher à ta seule personne, / J'ai tout abandonné, repos, gloire, Couronne" (3:4; 4:559) [For you, just so that I could be close to you, / I abandoned everything, a peaceful life, glory, the Crown]. It is thus safe to assume that Ariane is the heir to the throne of Crete, and hence the older of Minos' daughters.[2]

Once we have established this crucial fact, the dynamics of the sisterly bond are visible in a completely different light than one might expect from the events of the play. Ariane is a presumptuous, domineering older sister who believes that all good things are owed her, and that her younger sister's raison d'être is to be her unquestioning audience. Ariane's inability to see what is happening under her very eyes is a function not only of Phèdre's duplicity, but also of Ariane's supreme sense of entitlement. On the surface Ariane might be taken as the trusting, idealistic sister betrayed by the very sister she has so ingenuously counted on. But Phèdre's betrayal of Ariane might also be seen as a kind of retribution for her sister's treatment of her: that is to say, Ariane's presupposition that Phèdre is but an understudy to the "star" sibling, herself.

Ariane treats Phèdre as an annex to herself from the very beginning of the drama, never once demonstrating the slightest self-awareness of her own imperiousness. When Ariane hatches a plan to marry Phèdre off to Thésée's best friend, Pirithoüs, in order to consolidate her own union with Thésée, she has no qualms about suiting her sister's future to her own needs, as she explains to Thésée:

> Apprenez un projet de ma flamme.
> Pour m'attacher à vous par de plus fermes noeuds,
> J'ai dans Pirithoüs trouvé ce que je veux.
> Vous l'aimez chèrement; il faut que l'hyménée
> De ma Soeur avec lui joigne la destinée,
> Et que nous partagions ce que pour les grands coeurs
> L'amour et l'amitié font naître de douceurs.
> Ma Soeur a du mérite, elle est aimable et belle,
> Suit mes conseils en tout, et je vous réponds d'elle.
> Voyez Pirithoüs, et tâchez d'obtenir
> Que par elle avec nous il consente à s'unir. (2:4; 4:542-43)

> Hear the plan that my passion has formed.
> I wanted to tie myself to you with stronger bonds,
> And found what I was seeking in the person of Pirithoüs.
> He is your dear friend; his marriage to my Sister
> Must join together her destiny and his,
> So that we can share the gentle benefits
> That love and friendship plant in great hearts.
> My Sister is deserving, she is lovely and beautiful,
> She follows my advice in all matters, you can leave her to me.
> Go see Pirithoüs, and do your best to get him to consent
> To join in union with us through her intermediary.

Ariane treats Phèdre as nothing more than a nubile cipher. She assumes her sister will follow her advice so slavishly that she can vouch for her ("you can leave her to me") even in a matter as important as marriage. She is un-abashed about arranging Phèdre's marriage merely in order to cement her own union with Thésée.

The finest example of Ariane's haughtiness comes when, suspicious about Thésée's repeated postponement of the wedding, she asks Phèdre to spy on various women at court to discover whom he secretly loves. The scene paints a chilling portrait of the older sister as an unwitting narcissist:

ARIANE:
Je feins de consentir à l'hymen de Thésée [with someone else];
A savoir son secret j'intéresse le Roi.
Pour l'apprendre, ma Soeur, travaillez avec moi,
Car je ne doute pas qu'une amitié sincère
Contre sa trahison n'arme votre colère,
Que vous ne ressentiez tout ce que sent mon coeur.
PHÈDRE:
Madame, vous savez . . .
ARIANE:
                    Je vous connais, ma Soeur;
Aussi c'est seulement en vous ouvrant mon âme,
Que dans son désespoir je soulage ma flamme.
Que de projets trahis! Sans cet indigne abus,
J'arrêtais votre hymen avec Pirithoüs,
Et de mon amitié cette marque nouvelle
Vous doit faire encor plus haïr mon infidèle. (4:3; 4:569)

ARIANE:
I'll pretend to consent to Thésée's marriage with someone else;
I'll get the King interested in his secret.
To find it out, work with me, Sister,
For I have no doubt that your sincere affection
Makes you furious as well about his betrayal,
That you feel everything my own heart feels.
PHÈDRE:
Madam, you know . . .
ARIANE:
                    I know you, Sister;
So it is only when I bare my soul to you
That I can relieve my passion's despair.

So many plans betrayed! Were it not for this lowly action,
I had decided on your marriage to Pirithoüs,
And this fresh mark of my affection
Must make you hate my fickle boy even more.

The scene is designed to send shivers of irony shooting up the spectators' spines: "you feel everything my own heart feels" obviously makes one
think of Phèdre's love for Thésée rather than, as Ariane intended, sisterly
empathy. But the irony does a double flip if we consider that at some level
Ariane is simply being paid back for her arrogance in assuming she knows
her sister's feelings, as if her sister's role were limited to being her confidante and helpmate. Ariane presents her earlier marriage plans for Phèdre
as "this fresh mark of my affection" rather than a selfish attempt to use
Phèdre to consolidate her own position.

What separates Ariane and Phèdre, is, in a word, awareness.[3] Ariane is
conscious neither of her own systematic treatment of Phèdre as an underling nor of the possibility that Phèdre might have her own needs or desires.
It might be objected that Ariane has no idea of her sister's feelings because
Phèdre hides them from her, but the play establishes such a strong pattern
of presumptuousness on Ariane's part that she appears not to recognize
Phèdre as an autonomous being. When Ariane expresses the wish that
Phèdre might know love in order to commiserate more fully with her own
dilemma — "Hélas! et plût au Ciel que vous sussiez aimer, / Que vous
pussiez savoir par votre expérience, / Jusqu'où d'un fort amour s'étend la
violence!" (2:7; 4:550) [Alas! if only the Heavens had allowed you to know
love, / And to be able to know by your own experience, / How far the
violence of a powerful love can go!] — the irony generated by the lines may
distract us from wondering why she is so secure in assuming Phèdre does
not know love, or from observing that yet again Phèdre's situation is important to Ariane only insofar as it may help or hinder her own. Ariane's only
act of generosity toward Phèdre is an unintentional, ironic one: the ploy she
hits upon for discovering the object of Thésée's affections is to tell him to
marry the woman he loves, after which she, Ariane, will agree to marry
Oenarus. At last Ariane has conceded something to her sister, a shocking
case of *lèse-aînesse*: she has unknowingly offered to let her younger sister
marry before she does.

The best example of Ariane's obtuseness, yet again hidden beneath an
explosion of irony, comes in the final act, when she muses that she wishes
Phèdre were the woman Thésée had fallen in love with:

Que n'a-t-il pu l'aimer? Phèdre l'aurait connu,
Et par-là mon malheur eût été prévenu.
De sa flamme par elle aussitôt avertie,
Dans sa première ardeur je l'aurais amortie.
Par où vaincre d'ailleurs les rebuts de ma Soeur? (5:1; 4:578)

Why couldn't he have fallen in love with her? Phèdre would have
    known it,
And I would have been spared all this unhappiness.
She would have warned me instantly of his passion,
And I would have nipped it in the bud.
But how could I have taken up with my Sister's cast-offs?

Even more ironic than the fact that Ariane's fantasy is true is the reason she cannot see that it is true: once again she views her sister from the same blindered perspective. If Thésée had loved Phèdre, of course Phèdre would have stepped aside; of course Ariane would have been able to put a stop to the whole thing. The only question in her mind is whether or not she would have stooped to consorting with her sister's rejects ("les rebuts de ma Soeur").

Phèdre apparently does not have the same compunctions about recycled suitors, but in light of Ariane's systematic dismissal of her, her willingness to be wooed by her sister's fiancé does not put her at as great an ethical disadvantage as one might assume. And even if it did, Phèdre has other qualities that her sister lacks. Phèdre is a typical younger sibling in her heightened understanding of the dynamics of power and betrayal. Her awareness of her own dark thoughts gives her a perceptiveness about others as well as about herself that are in sharp contrast with her sister's obtuse complacency.

The best that can be said of this lopsided relationship is that the two sisters agree on one thing: only Ariane and her needs are of any importance. If Phèdre is generous in her assessment of Ariane, it is undoubtedly because she feels a typical younger-sibling gratitude for any kind of attention, whatever the motivation: "Elle se fie à moi cette Soeur, elle m'aime. / C'est une ardeur sincère, une tendresse extrême, / Jamais son amitié ne me refusa rien" (4:5; 4:575) [She trusts me and loves me, this Sister of mine. / She has a sincere attachment to me, a great tenderness, / Her affection has never refused me anything]. Perhaps Ariane has never refused Phèdre anything, but has it ever occurred to Phèdre to ask her for anything? Ariane and

Phèdre have complementary attitudes toward each other: Ariane demands Phèdre's utter devotion and support and dismisses Phèdre's own feelings and perspective. Phèdre expects nothing from Ariane and inteprets her demands as true friendship.

Phèdre has another ability that comes more easily to younger siblings than to their seniors: looking at an issue from several points of view. This is apparent in the lucid doubts she expresses to Thésée about her own future security with a man who has demonstrated his untrustworthiness by abandoning her sister:

> Et perdant une Soeur, si j'ose encor le dire,
> Vous la laissez dans Naxe en proie à ses douleurs,
> Votre légèreté me peut laisser ailleurs.
> Qui voudra plaindre alors les ennuis de ma vie
> Sur l'exemple éclatant d'Ariane trahie? (4:5; 4:576)

> And you've destroyed my Sister, if I may bring it up once more,
> You're leaving her in Naxos, besieged by her grief,
> Your fickleness might leave me somewhere else.
> Who will take pity then on my life of sorrow
> With the shining example of my betrayal of Ariane?

Phèdre perfectly understands the ramifications of her betrayal. If Thésée stabbed Ariane in the back, what, she inquires of him, protects her from the same treatment? "Et qui me répondra que vous serez fidèle?"; "Ma Soeur l'avait reçue [your promise] en fuyant avec vous" (4:5; 4:574) [And what will vouchsafe your faithfulness to me? My Sister received your promise when she fled with you]. Phèdre's doubts about Thésée, in spite of her passion for him, demonstrate not only perceptiveness, but also a certain humility, both of which traits her sister lacks. Is Phèdre not implicitly asking, with as much intelligence as brute realism, why she should end up better off than Ariane, and on what shaky moral ground she will be if she, a traitor, is in turn betrayed?

Love and Duty (The Sequel)

Given the dynamics of the relation between older and younger sister, it is difficult to read the love between Thésée and Phèdre other than as a rebellion by both parties against Ariane. Thésée's attractiveness to Phèdre is surely heightened by her wish to make her sister sit up and take notice, while Thésée's rejection of Ariane and his love for Phèdre also reflect the distinct positions of older and younger sister. From Thésée's point of view, what is important is not the individual differences between the women; rather, it is what loving the younger as opposed to the older sister represents.

Although *Ariane* is not technically about primogeniture — Ariane is disinherited by her father for her scandalous conduct[4] — the birth order of the sisters in the love triangle is not coincidental. For Thésée, loving the older sister is a duty, while loving the younger sister stands for individual choice. The union of Thésée and Ariane smacks of a "suitable," arranged marriage, as if in spite of the severance of the older sister's inheritance she still retained vestiges of a legacy of obligation. Marriage with Phèdre is a revolt against that obligation, an exercise in the pursuit of personal happiness. The woman Thésée loses his heart to is not Phèdre, but Ariane's younger sister.

From the start Thésée's relationship with Ariane is tainted by necessity. In this version of the story even his initial confrontation with the Minotaur is thrust upon him:

Qui l'eût cru, que, du Sort le choix illégitime
L'ayant au Minotaure envoyé pour victime,
Il dût par un triomphe à jamais glorieux
Affranchir son pays d'un tribut odieux? (1:2; 4:527)

Who would have believed that, sent to the Minotaur
As a victim by the illegitimate choice of Fate,
He would have to free his country from a hateful tribute
In a glorious victory that will be remembered always?

Thésée does not volunteer to fight the Minotaur; rather, "the illegitimate choice of Fate" sends him to Crete as one of the monster's victims. Thésée turns his doom into a triumph; still, he has no real choice. Once he is picked by fate — "Sort" probably refers to a lottery, as in the choice of which brother will rule first in Racine's *La Thébaïde*[5] — his entire relation with Ariane is set into motion. He must fight the Minotaur if he does not want to be eaten by it. He must accept Ariane's help to emerge from the labyrinth. Once she has saved his life, he owes her his allegiance, his protection, and his heart.

If Thésée's heart leaps at the sight of Ariane's sister, her most appealing feature may be that he owes her nothing. Thésée explains his feelings to Phèdre in this way:

L'emmener [Ariane] avec moi fut un coup nécessaire.
Il fallait la sauver de la fureur d'un Père,
Et la reconnaissance eut part seule aux serments
Par qui mon coeur du sien paya les sentiments.
Ce coeur violenté n'aimait qu'avec étude;
Et quand il entrerait un peu d'ingratitude
Dans ce manque de foi qui vous semble odieux,
Pourquoi me reprocher un crime de vos yeux?
L'habitude à les voir me fit de l'inconstance
Une nécessité dont rien ne me dispense. (4:5; 4:574–75)

Taking Ariane away with me was a hard necessity.
I had to save her from her Father's fury
And gratitude was the only reason for the promises
With which my heart repaid her feelings for me.
My heart, so set upon, only appeared to be in love;
And even if my lack of good faith, which you find so hateful,
Might be considered somewhat ungrateful,
Why take me to task for a crime your eyes committed?
Once I was accustomed to seeing them, inconstancy became
A simple necessity that nothing could save me from.

This speech hinges on two kinds of necessity: the need to save Ariane from her father ("un coup nécessaire") and the torment of Phèdre's irresistible eyes ("Une nécessité dont rien ne me dispense"). The first is, if not exactly political, at least politic:[6] how can Thésée maintain a good reputation if he fails to repay Ariane for her assistance? What choice does he have but to take her along? The second, on the contrary, is an example of the delicious necessity of the heart, the compulsion one does not so much resist as postpone, like a kind of foreplay designed not to prevent but rather to prolong the pleasure of abandonment.

Thus, if Thésée's entire misadventure with Ariane is colored by constraint, from his selection as the Minotaur's victim to the debt he must repay his savior, Phèdre is bathed in the provocative light of personal whim. What seduces Thésée is the fact that when he looks at the two sisters together, all he can think of is that he has been forced to choose Ariane, while he is free to choose Phèdre:

Vous [Phèdre] voyant auprès d'elle, et mon amour extrême
Ne pouvant avec vous s'expliquer par vous-même,
Ce que je lui disais d'engageant et de doux,
Vous ne saviez que trop qu'il s'adressait à vous. (4:5; 4:575)

When I saw you next to her, and knew my great love
Could not be expressed directly to you,
All the sweet engaging things I said to her,
You knew perfectly well they were meant for you.

This love triangle of communication—Thésée woos Phèdre under the guise of courting Ariane—is worthy of Racine's universe of displaced desire: *Bajazet*, in which the sultaness falls in love with the younger-brother hero in a similarly vicarious manner, for a time alternated with *Ariane* at the Hôtel de Bourgogne.[7]

Perhaps the truth Ariane ultimately learns about Phèdre is applicable to younger siblings in general: that those cut off from a sense of entitlement must resort to cunning in their fight against the obscurity to which they appear destined. If Phèdre's love is not easily discerned, the reason is largely Ariane's lack of discernment: Thésée accurately characterizes his fiancée as "cette crédule Soeur" (4:5, 4:575) [that gullible Sister]. When the two lovers, masters of dissimulation to the end, scurry off, Ariane's main cry of reproach to her sister has to do not with Phèdre's love for Thésée, but with her refusal to reveal herself to a sister whose own love life was an open, if boring, book:

La Rivale sur qui tombe cette fureur,
C'est Phèdre, cette Phèdre à qui j'ouvrais mon coeur.
Quand je lui faisais voir ma peine sans égale,
Quand j'en marquais l'horreur, c'était à ma Rivale.
La perfide abusant de ma tendre amitié,
Montrait de ma disgrâce une fausse pitié,
Et jouissant des maux que j'aimais à lui peindre,
Elle en était la cause, et feignait de me plaindre.
C'est là mon désespoir; pour avoir trop parlé,
Je perds ce que déjà je tenais immolé. (5:5; 4:584)

The Rival that is the object of my fury
Is Phèdre, the same Phèdre to whom I bared my heart.
While I was letting her see my extreme despair,
While I showed her its horror, she was my Rival.
The traitor took advantage of my tender affection,
Pretended to commiserate with my disgrace,
And took pleasure in the troubles I reveled in describing,
She was their cause, her pity was a fake.
That is the source of my despair; because I spoke too much,
I have lost the revenge I held in my two hands.

This moment marks the cataclysmic tragic recognition of the older sibling who realizes at last that her sister has never viewed her as she has viewed her sister. Ariane never filters herself with Phèdre as she is presenting her with the spectacle of herself: only too late does she realize that she has spoken too much ("trop parlé"). Ariane's discovery is the difficult lesson siblings can teach best: how to recognize when others are getting tired of listening to you; when, if you keep talking, they start holding it against you and vow to find a way to turn the tables, however many years that might take.

Ariane's Revenge: Racine's *Phèdre*

It would be possible to read or see *Phèdre* any number of times without even registering that it is the drama of a younger sister.[8] The play takes place some time after the death of Ariane, which the conclusion of Corneille's tragedy hints at. Racine's Phèdre does mention Ariane by name, but only once,[9] just before she confesses her love for Hippolyte to Oenone: "Ariane, ma soeur, de quel amour blessée / Vous mourûtes aux bords où vous fûtes laissée!" (253–54) [Ariane, my sister, what love wounded you / And how you were left to die on the shores where you were abandoned!]. Racine's Phèdre, as selective about what she does and does not discuss as Corneille's, prudently decides not to dwell on the circumstances of her sister's abandonment and death; the point of mentioning Ariane's abysmal end is simply to suggest that her own love for Hippolyte should be viewed with compassion as well as horror, for she comes from a family with a long history of doomed love. But with *Ariane* fresh in the audience's memories, the allusion must certainly have resonated.

How might a reading of *Phèdre*, the most scrutinized tragedy in the entire Classical canon, be affected by a juxtaposition of Racine's masterpiece with Corneille's? There is no dearth of similarities between the plays, but the most interesting point of contact is the portrayal of Phèdre. *Ariane* dramatizes not only its titular heroine's downfall, but also the coming of age and temporary triumph of her younger sister. *Phèdre* stages the defeat of the younger sister who in spite of her earlier victory goes to her doom *as a younger sister*. Being a younger sister informs Phèdre's character in both plays: it is the source of both her heroic attempt at transcending the disadvantage of her birth and her ultimate defeat at the hands of a character who, as we shall see, is a figure of her older sister and an agent of Ariane's revenge.

Phèdre's heroism in Racine's play is an extension of the conflict between Ariane and Phèdre in Corneille's. As we have seen, the individualistic Thésée rejects Ariane as a figure of duty and constraint and associates Phèdre with freedom of choice. Similarly, Racine's Phèdre is not only a heroine by choice, but a heroine of choice. She is the epitome of the heroism of the second generation in that hers is not an inherited or natural heroism. Although she is by necessity an aristocrat, she is not born to privilege so much as she is born into a family curse; she experiences all the drawbacks of family origins with few of the advantages. She is a heroine by a pure act of will, because in spite of the odds, she chooses to be a heroine. All heroes must prove themselves worthy, but as a representative of a rising ethic of individual self-determination and enterprise, Phèdre might be said to be a self-made heroine.

Unlike the heroes and heroines of the first generation of tragedy presented by Pierre Corneille during the waning years of Louis XIII's rule, Phèdre is a heroine in spite of her essence. For her, heroism consists not of revealing an innate superiority, but of keeping hidden an innate worthlessness, of putting on a good front. For Rodrigue, heroism demands the externalization and revelation of what the hero knows to be his extraordinary nature, even before he has been tested. In order to be a hero, he must simply appear to be what he knows himself to be. For Phèdre, on the contrary, heroism is based on never exposing what she knows all along to be her inadequacy. It depends on not revealing what she is and on appearing to be what she is not.[10]

How is Phèdre's status as a representative of second-generation heroism related to her position as a younger sister? Being a younger sibling, like being the sort of hero Phèdre is, is based upon an internal paradox, a contradiction, a balancing act that attempts to mediate between the advantages and disadvantages of two opposing systems. On the one hand, in terms of feudal values, Phèdre as a younger sibling has no inherent worth. She can be and is fundamentally overlooked by Ariane; in effect, she is her lady-in-waiting. On the other hand, from the perspective of market or capitalistic values, she has the advantage of needing to struggle from birth, the goad of having to overcome difficulties, and the competitive edge that comes of not expecting life to be easy. Phèdre is born not with a silver spoon, but with the bitter pill of younger siblinghood in her mouth, but the disadvantage of her birth becomes transformed into an asset in that it pushes her to rid herself of its unpleasant aftertaste.

What, then, is the problem? Can Phèdre not simply be a hero of individual enterprise, living proof that, family curses and overbearing sisters notwithstanding, life is what you make of it? She cannot, and this is where the psychology of birth order enters the picture. Who is better off, a person with a strong sense of self-worth from a very early age who feels no need to be exceptional, or one who compensates for feelings of self-doubt by aspiring to be extraordinary? There is no simple answer to that question. Perhaps being the heir apparent, psychological or otherwise, is a padded cell from which one can never escape to discover one's desires and potential. Perhaps it is a fortress of comfort and protection from which one happily views those who are down below, striving to overcome their position of inferiority.

Phèdre has both the advantages and the disadvantages of the younger sibling, and this is shown by her heroic resistance to her unwanted passion. Her various strategies in resisting her desire for Hippolyte (279–96) demonstrate her resourcefulness. She builds a temple to Venus, passes laws that persecute her nemesis, even drives Thésée to exile his son. Nothing works. Her decision to die is indeed heroic, for it proves that she will go to any lengths not to reveal her inferior essence to the world.[11]

The figure opposed to Phèdre, the Ariane figure, the woman who feels she is owed everything but has done nothing to get it, is Aricie.[12] Despite his disclaimers, the character is largely invented by Racine,[13] purportedly so that Hippolyte would be rendered fallible by his forbidden love,[14] but in reality so that he would not appear effeminate, which a courtly audience might find him to be if he spurned Phèdre's advances without having another woman in mind.[15] The name "Aricie" is suggestive of "Ariane," and also, given Aricie's status as the play's bluest blood, "aristocrate": as we shall see, the character of Aricie is a throwback to feudal values.

In addition to being a psychological drama of love and incest, *Phèdre* is also a dynastic tragedy of succession in which Aricie alone has full blood rights to inherit the throne of Athens. When Thésée is believed dead, the succession may conceivably go to three parties, as Hippolyte explains to Aricie: "Du choix d'un successeur Athènes incertaine / Parle de vous, me nomme, et le fils de la reine [Phèdre]" (485–86) [Athens, uncertain of the choice of a successor / Has spoken of you and named me and the queen's son]. Racine has used the complex mythological background of the story to create a veritable hierarchy of legitimacy; Aricie is at its summit. In ascending order of legitimacy we have the children of Phèdre and Thésée; Hippolyte, the son of Thésée and an Amazon; and Aricie. Let us examine the claims to legitimacy in that order.

Phèdre herself has no blood claim to the throne. She is a foreigner, the daughter of a king, yes, but of a foreign king and, as we have seen, his younger daughter. Her sons by Thésée might stake a claim to the throne through their father, but Hippolyte is also Thésée's son and is older than his half-brothers. As if to emphasize to what extent Phèdre's heroism consists of turning her position of dispossession to her advantage, Racine makes Phèdre's son the chosen successor to the throne. When Hippolyte's tutor, Théramène, informs him Athens has chosen Phèdre's son to succeed Thésée — "Son fils est roi, Seigneur" (727) [Her son is king, Sire] — and Hippolyte incredulously replies, "Dieux, qui la connaissez, / Est-ce donc sa vertu que vous récompensez?" (727–28) [Gods, you who know her, / Is it her virtue, then, you are rewarding?], his error is in believing that Phèdre has been divinely chosen; in Racine's Christian view, this would imply an interior knowledge of her essence. But in reality she has been chosen by the will of the Athenians, who know her only from the outside, and her outside is virtuous. It is not simply that the Athenians do not know "who Phèdre is," but that she has conducted herself with such dignity, whatever her inner turmoil, that she has been deemed worthy to be the mother of the new king. From a genealogical perspective, Phèdre's son has the weakest claim to be the successor to the throne. From a behavioral point of view, Phèdre is judged suitable to be the mother of a future royal lineage.

As for Hippolyte, if his mother is also a foreigner, the Amazon Antiope, he is convinced, even before he knows of Phèdre's shameful love, that he has a better claim to the throne than her sons. He mentions this in his first scene with Aricie:

La Grèce me reproche une mère étrangère.
Mais si pour concurrent je n'avais que mon frère [Phèdre's son],

Madame, j'ai sur lui de véritables droits
Que je saurais sauver du caprice des lois. (489–92)

Greece takes me to task for my foreign mother.
But if my only competitor were my brother,
Madam, I have indisputable rights over him
That I would be able to protect against legal manipulation.

Hippolyte is undoubtedly referring to his *droit d'aînesse*, which might well
come into play since the legitimacy of both Phèdre's son and Hippolyte
comes from their father.

Nonetheless, in Racine's version of the story Thésée's own claim is
weaker than Aricie's, as Hippolyte points out to the captive princess:

Je vous cède, ou plutôt je vous rends une place,
Un sceptre que jadis vos aïeux ont reçu
De ce fameux mortel que la terre a conçu.
L'adoption le mit entre les mains d'Egée.
Athènes, par mon père accrue et protégée,
Reconnut avec joie un roi si généreux,
Et laissa dans l'oubli vos frères malheureux. (494–500)

I am giving my place up to you, or rather back to you,
A scepter that your ancestors once received
From the famous mortal that the earth conceived.
Adoption put it into Aegeus' hands.
Athens, augmented and protected by my father,
Joyfully recognized that king's nobility,
And overlooked your unfortunate brothers.

Aricie is the only surviving descendant of Erechtheus, the legendary founder
of Athens, for Racine has followed a tradition attested to by Apollodorus[16]
whereby Aegeus, Theseus' father, is the adoptive son of Erechtheus' son,
Pandion, whereas Pallas, Aricie's father, is Pandion's son by blood. As the
architect of Athens' civic institutions, Thésée is recognized as "un roi si
généreux," but the adjective retains its usual Classical associations with the
Latin *generosus*, "of noble birth," as if to remind us obliquely that Thésée is
not in fact a direct descendant of the founder of the city. Threatened by
Erechtheus' descendants, Thésée kills Aricie's brothers and subsequently

emprisons Aricie, forbidding her from marrying and producing bother-some potential heirs to the throne:

> Tu sais, depuis leur [Aricie's brothers'] mort, quelle sévère loi
> Défend à tous les Grecs de soupirer pour moi:
> On craint que de la soeur les flammes téméraires
> Ne raniment un jour la cendre de ses frères. (427–30)

> You know, since my brothers' deaths, what a harsh law
> Has forbidden any Greek man from asking for my hand:
> The fear is that the sister's bold passions
> Might one day rekindle her brothers' ashes.

Aricie, the bothersome sister that Thésée does his best to rid himself of so that he and Phèdre can rule in peace; Aricie, the holder of a lost birthright who retains a strong sense of entitlement in spite of her straitened circumstances; Aricie, the tiresome problem that won't go away. At every turn Aricie echoes the figure of Ariane. When Aricie is discussing the object of her affections, Hippolyte, and her chief persecutor, Thésée, how can we help but think of Ariane?

ARICIE:
Hippolyte demande à me voir en ce lieu?
Hippolyte me cherche, et veut me dire adieu?
Ismène, dis-tu vrai? N'es-tu point abusée?
ISMÈNE:
C'est le premier effet de la mort de Thésée.
Préparez-vous, Madame, à voir de tous côtés
Voler vers vous les coeurs par Thésée écartés. (367–72)

ARICIE:
Hippolyte is asking to see me in this place?
Hippolyte seeks me out, and wants to bid me farewell?
Ismène, are you telling the truth? Are you not confused?
ISMÈNE:
It is the immediate result of Thésée's death.
Prepare yourself, Madam, to see hearts flocking to your side
From every direction, now that Thésée cannot keep them away.

Like her Cornelian counterpart, Aricie expresses openly her love for the
same man Phèdre loves covertly: Aricie's anaphoric repetition of "Hippolyte" in her first two lines onstage contrasts sharply with Phèdre's extreme
reticence even to hear the name. And like Ariane, Aricie has been thwarted
in love by Thésée.

When Aricie contrasts her heroic love for Hippolyte with Phèdre's
facile love for Thésée, one can almost hear the voice of Phèdre's original
rival in love, as if a revisionist Ariane had sent Aricie back to give her own
unhappy love a favorable spin:

> Phèdre en vain s'honorait des soupirs de Thésée:
> Pour moi, je suis plus fière et fuis la gloire aisée
> D'arracher un hommage à mille autres offert,
> Et d'entrer dans un coeur de toutes parts ouvert. (445–48)

> Phèdre took empty pride in Thésée's sighs of love:
> But I am more difficult than that and want none of the easy glory
> Of securing the attentions a man pays to a thousand others,
> Or of penetrating a heart open to all comers.

Aricie rightly observes that Thésée was not a difficult catch in the same way
Hippolyte is—the challenge with Thésée is not getting him into the net,
but keeping him from jumping back into the water—but once we have
heard the echo of Ariane's voice resonating beneath Aricie's words, this
speech begins to sound like the vindictive retort of a haughty older sister
making light of and devaluing her little sister's conquest.

With the cruel events of *Ariane* in mind, should we be surprised that
Aricie balks at Hippolyte's proposal of fleeing Trézène and the wrath of his
father without the benefit of marriage?

> Hélas! qu'un tel exil, Seigneur, me serait cher!
> Dans quels ravissements, à votre sort liée,
> Du reste des mortels je vivrais oubliée!
> Mais n'étant point unis par un lien si doux,
> Me puis-je avec honneur dérober avec vous? (1376–80)

> Alas! how I would cherish such an exile, Sire!
> What delight it would be, bound up with your fate,
> To live forgotten by the rest of humankind!

But since we are not united by such a sweet bond,
How can I run away with you and save my honor?

Even if Hippolyte's nascent resemblance to his father is hinted at, nothing in the play suggests he will betray Aricie. Once again, this is the ghost of Ariane speaking, the leery voice of a woman who fled her homeland and the king's anger only to discover that the man who claimed to love her and promised to marry her was a traitor.[17]

Aricie's confrontation with Thésée in act 5 is not a lull in the action before the final cataclysm of the report of Hippolyte's death, the revelation of his innocence, and Phèdre's suicide, but rather the climax of Ariane's revenge, her symbolic day in court.

ARICIE:
Seigneur, je ne vous puis nier la vérité:
De votre injuste haine il [Hippolyte] n'a pas hérité;
Il ne me traitait point comme une criminelle.
THÉSÉE:
J'entends; il vous jurait une amour éternelle.
Ne vous assurez point sur ce coeur inconstant,
Car à d'autres que vous il en jurait autant.
ARICIE:
Lui, Seigneur?
THÉSÉE:
                    Vous deviez le rendre moins volage:
Comment souffriez-vous cet horrible partage?
ARICIE:
Et comment souffrez-vous que d'horribles discours
D'une si belle vie osent noircir le cours?
Avez-vous de son coeur si peu de connaissance? (1419–29)

ARICIE:
Sire, I cannot hide the truth from you:
Hippolyte has not inherited your unfair hatred;
He did not treat me as if I were a criminal.
THÉSÉE:
You mean he swore his eternal love to you.
Don't let yourself feel secure in this untrustworthy heart,
For he was swearing the very same thing to others.

ARICIE:
He was, Sire?
THÉSÉE:
                    You should have made him less unfaithful:
How could you bear sharing him in that horrible way?
ARICIE:
And how could you bear using such horrible words
To sully the course of such a fine life?
Have you really such little knowledge of his heart?

This entire exchange can be read as harkening back to Thésée's betrayal of Ariane. "Hippolyte has not inherited your unfair hatred; / He did not treat me as if I were a criminal"; translation: You think Hippolyte is your heir, but he is nothing like you. He does not hate me and make me suffer. "You should have made him less unfaithful [i.e. than me]: / How could you bear sharing him in that horrible way?"; translation: What makes you think he'll be any more reliable than I was? "Have you really such little knowledge of his heart?"; translation: You have been cruel and unfair; he is kind and just. He is not your heir. You don't know the first thing about your son or about love.[18]

Thésée's adoption of Aricie at the end of *Phèdre* is the climax of the vexed problem of inheritance that permeates French Classical tragedy. Thésée has lost one blood descendant, Hippolyte, but he still has sons by Phèdre. If he wished, he could make them his heirs, or he could remarry.[19] But in homage to the beloved, misunderstood nonheir of a son he has just lost, he opts for adoption:

Allons, de mon erreur, hélas! trop éclaircis,
Mêler nos pleurs au sang de mon malheureux fils!
Allons de ce cher fils embrasser ce qui reste,
Expier la fureur d'un voeu que je déteste.
Rendons-lui les honneurs qu'il a trop mérités,
Et pour mieux apaiser ses mânes irrités,
Que malgré les complots d'une injuste famille
Son amante aujourd'hui me tienne lieu de fille! (1647–54)

Let us go, with open eyes, alas! that see my mistake all too well,
Mix our tears with the blood of my unlucky boy!

One last time I'll embrace what remains of my dear son,
And pay the price for my furious wish — how I loathe it.
We shall give him the honors he so richly deserved,
And so that his angry shade might be better laid to rest,
Let his mistress, in spite of her family's conniving,
Take the place of my daughter from this day forward!

Thésée's adoption of Aricie, signaling the ultimate dispossession of Phèdre's sons by Thésée, marks Phèdre's final failure as the heroine of choice.
The adoption can be read as an expression of the need to pay tribute to a
past ethic — an ethic not of choice, but of predetermination and the faithful
replication of the models of the past — embodied by Aricie.

As *Phèdre* and Racine's theater draw to a close, Thésée does what he
can to acquit a debt to the sole remaining descendant of the founders of his
land. He adopts the scion of the first family that two generations earlier had
adopted him. This enigmatic doubled adoption marks a double separation
from the land and its original masters that is as much a return to origins as a
further distancing from origins. Thésée's final action may well be to choose
an heir to the throne,[20] but he chooses the very woman whose blood ties to
the land would have designated her as the heir even if Thésée had not been
there to make his choice. Thésée thus "chooses" an heir who seems to have
been predetermined by a system that does not require or even allow one to
choose one's heir. This paradoxical action may be read as the consummate
expression of the encounter between two systems of value that generates
Classical tragedy.

Notes

Preface

1. Michel de Certeau, *L'Ecriture de l'histoire* (Paris: Gallimard, 1975), 148, translation mine.

Introduction

1. Frank J. Sulloway, *Born to Rebel: Birth Order, Family Dynamics, and Creative Lives* (New York: Pantheon Books, 1996), 260.
2. Sulloway, *Born to Rebel*, 45–46.
3. Erik H. Erikson, "The Human Life Cycle," in *A Way of Looking at Things: Selected Papers from 1930 to 1980*, ed. Stephen Schlein (New York: W. W. Norton, 1987), 607.
4. Erik H. Erikson, "Human Strength and the Cycle of Generations," in *Insight and Responsibility: Lectures on the Ethical Implications of Psychoanalytic Insight* (New York: W. W. Norton, 1964), 131–32.
5. See Francesco Orlando, *Toward a Freudian Theory of Literature*, trans. Charmaine Lee (Baltimore: Johns Hopkins University Press, 1978); Mitchell Greenberg, *Corneille, Classicism, and the Ruses of Symmetry* (Cambridge: Cambridge University Press, 1986) and *Subjectivity and Subjugation in Seventeenth-Century Drama and Prose: The Family Romance of French Classicism* (Cambridge: Cambridge University Press, 1992).
6. Marc Augé in preface to Anne Gotman, *Hériter* (Paris: Presses Universitaires de France, 1988), vii, trans. mine.
7. As we shall see, in one of Pierre Corneille's tragedies, *Nicomède*, a younger brother is portrayed as his older brother's rather than his father's spiritual heir.

Chapter 1. Primogeniture and Its Discontents in Early Modern France

1. Pierre Maranda, *French Kinship: Structure and History* (The Hague: Mouton, 1974), 125. See also Philippe Ariès, *L'Enfant et la vie familiale sous l'Ancien Régime* (1960; rpt. Paris: Seuil, 1973), 261–62.
2. There were certain *coutumes* that allowed eldest daughters and sometimes nephews to inherit in the absence of sons, although this was not widespread. See Roland Mousnier, *Les Institutions de la France sous la monarchie absolue 1598–1789* (Paris: Presses Universitaires de France, 1974), 1:66.

3. Frederick E. Greenspahn, *When Brothers Dwell Together: The Preeminence of Younger Siblings in the Hebrew Bible* (New York and Oxford: Oxford University Press, 1994), 38.

4. Ariès, *L'Enfant et la vie familiale*, 262. Unless otherwise noted, all translations are my own. Even though primogeniture was not done away with in France until the Revolution, during the seventeenth and eighteenth centuries its power is mitigated by other, more egalitarian forces.

5. The North-South division was not systematic, however, and the West, particularly Britanny and Anjou, also tended toward more egalitarian inheritance practices than the East. See Alain Collomp, "Le Statut des cadets en Haute-Provence avant et après le Code civil," in *Les Cadets*, ed. Georges Ravis-Giordani and Martine Segalen (Paris: CNRS, 1994), 158. By contrast, the region of the Alps, an area of relatively small farms, made extensive use of primogeniture. See Dionigi Albera, "La Maison des frères," in *Les Cadets*, 169–70.

6. Mousnier, *Les Institutions de la France*, 1:65. In England, primogeniture held sway even longer than it did in France; see Didier Lancien, "Le Sort des cadets dans les grandes familles de l'aristocratie et de la bourgeoisie britanniques (1890–1920)," in *Les Cadets*, 241. In England parents nonetheless had greater freedom to choose their heir: "Frequently also, the last will and testament is used to disfavor an undeserving elder son to the advantage of a more intelligent younger one, who would be likelier to use his inheritance wisely." René Pillorget, *La Tige et le rameau: Familles anglaise et française XVIe-XVIIIe siècle* (Paris: Calmann-Lévy, 1979), 100.

7. Pillorget, *La Tige et le rameau*, 101–2. See also Christian Biet, "Le Cadet, point de départ des destins romanesques dans la littérature française du XVIIIe siècle," in *Les Cadets*, 301 n.2.

8. Although the large and important issue of gender inequalities in inheritance practices is beyond the scope of this study, it should be pointed out that gender inequalities often surpassed inequalities related to birth order, as Alain Collomp explains: "If we examine the laws governing the distribution of estates in the absence of a will, we discover that the inequality between older and younger siblings is less dramatic than the inequality between sons and daughters" ("Le Statut des cadets," 158).

9. Beatrice Gottlieb, *The Family in the Western World from the Black Death to the Industrial Age* (New York: Oxford University Press, 1993), 213.

10. Pillorget, *La Tige et le rameau*, 100, unattributed quotation cited in the original English.

11. Mousnier, *Les Institutions de la France*, 1:151.

12. Christian Biet, "Le Cadet, point de départ des destins romanesques," 292.

13. Martine Segalen, "La Notion d'avantage dans les sociétés égalitaires," in *Les Cadets*, 195.

14. Furetière's *Dictionnaire* of 1690 says that the word is becoming old-fashioned ("le mot vieillit"). Jean-Louis Flandrin points out that the notion of lineage is limited to juridical language as early as the mid-sixteenth century. *Familles: Parenté, maison, sexualité dans l'ancienne société* (Paris: Hachette, 1976), 20.

15. Mousnier, *Les Institutions de la France*, 1:503.

16. For a discussion of the evolution of the concept of kingship from one that

sees the kingdom as the personal patrimony of the king to one that distinguishes it as a special case to which the feudal laws of inheritance do not apply, see Herbert H. Rowen, *The King's State: Proprietary Dynasticism in Early Modern France* (New Brunswick, N.J.: Rutgers University Press, 1980), chapter 1, "Proprietary Dynasticism in Ancient and Medieval Times," 5–26.

17. Greenspahn, *When Brothers Dwell Together*, 69–70.

18. Norbert Elias, *The Court Society*, trans. Edmund Jephcott (Oxford: Basil Blackwell, 1983), 177.

19. In fact this is a difficult issue to present in terms of simple causality, because the various threats to the old landed aristocracy also led to a retrenchment, with an increased emphasis on lineage. I will return to this question later in the chapter.

20. Chris Harman, "From Feudalism to Capitalism," *International Socialism* 45 (Winter 1989): 57. Harman provides an excellent overview of theories of the development of capitalism.

21. Harman, "From Feudalism to Capitalism," 37.

22. Michel Foucault, *The Order of Things: An Archaeology of the Human Sciences* (1970; rpt. New York: Vintage Books, 1973), 174–76.

23. It goes without saying that present-day agribusiness is market based rather than strictly land based.

24. See Roland Mousnier, *Les XVIe et XVIIe Siècles* (Paris: Presses Universitaires de France, 1954), 57–58. The specific examples Mousnier gives are of early capitalists and are limited to Germany, Italy, and Spain, but examples of cooperative ventures and partnerships among siblings are not hard to come by in both Europe and America, and at all economic levels.

25. Harman, "From Feudalism to Capitalism," 70.

26. Erica Harth, *Ideology and Culture in Seventeenth-Century France* (Ithaca, N.Y.: Cornell University Press, 1983), 19.

27. In *The Family Romance of the French Revolution* (Berkeley: University of California Press, 1992), Lynn Hunt demonstrates the importance of the rhetoric of brotherhood in the early years of the Revolution, when the beheading of Louis XVI is seen as the killing of the evil father. For a succinct overview of the debate about inheritance laws during the revolutionary period, see Anne Gotman, *Hériter* (Paris: Presses Universitaires de France, 1988), 77–85.

28. Suzanne Desan, "'War Between Brothers and Sisters': Inheritance Law and Gender Politics in Revolutionary France," *French Historical Studies* 20:4 (Fall 1997): 598.

29. Ariès, *L'Enfant et la vie familiale*, 305.

30. Ariès, *L'Enfant et la vie familiale*, 263.

31. Davis Bitton, *The French Nobility in Crisis, 1560–1640* (Stanford, Calif.: Stanford University Press, 1969), 100.

32. Harman, "From Feudalism to Capitalism," 69.

33. Margaret Mead, *Culture and Commitment: A Study of the Generation Gap* (Garden City, N.Y.: Doubleday [Natural History Press], 1970), 34.

34. Gottlieb, *The Family in the Western World*, 213.

35. Mousnier, *Les XVIe et XVIIe Siècles*, 161.

36. Pierre Chevallier, *Louis XIII: Roi cornélien* (Paris: Fayard, 1979), 11 and 8.

The feudalistic nature of the internal challenges to Louis XIII's power has been pointed out by numerous historians. David Hunt stresses that birth and inheritance were so important in "a society where legal and bureaucratic ties were so weak" that Louis XIII's birth was attended by the princes of the blood "as a proof of the legitimacy of the infant." David Hunt, *Parents and Children in History: The Psychology of Family Life in Early Modern France* (New York: Basic Books, 1970), 84.

37. Hélène Himelfarb, "Un journal peu ordinaire," *Nouvelle Revue de Psychanalyse* 19 (Spring 1979): 279.

38. John Wolf reports that when Louis XIV came down with smallpox in 1647, "Several of Gaston of Orléans' intimates had the bad taste to toast 'Gaston I,' for they assumed that Philippe [Louis' younger brother] would follow Louis to an early grave." John B. Wolf, *Louis XIV* (New York: Norton, 1968), 30.

39. Anne undoubtedly had her own interests in mind as well in doing what she could to raise Philippe not to be the threat Gaston had been: she hoped to retain a good deal of power herself even after Louis reached majority.

40. John B. Wolf, "The Formation of a King," in *Louis XIV: A Profile*, ed. John B. Wolf (New York: Hill and Wang, 1972), 3–4.

41. A. Lloyd Moote, *Louis XIII, the Just* (Berkeley: University of California Press, 1989), 283.

42. Moote, *Louis XIII*, 193.

43. François Bluche, *Louis XIV*, trans. Mark Greengrass (New York: Franklin Watts, 1990), 359–60.

44. Bluche, *Louis XIV*, 358.

45. Elias, *The Court Society*, 120 and 199. The French quotation can be translated: "The best place of security for a son of France is the king's heart."

46. Mousnier, *Les Institutions de la France*, 1:503–4.

47. Mousnier, *Les Institutions de la France*, 1:31.

48. Hunt, *Parents and Children*, 28–29. Mousnier, for example, speaks of the "centralizing and, to some extent, egalitarian revolution of the absolute monarchy" (*Les XVIe et XVIIe Siècles*, 164).

49. Maranda, *French Kinship*, 41 and 47.

50. Mousnier, *Les Institutions de la France*, 1:39.

51. Elias, *The Court Society*, 94 and 105.

52. Elias, *The Court Society*, 85.

53. Elias, *The Court Society*, 90.

54. Desiderius Erasmus, *The Education of a Christian Prince*, trans. Lester K. Born (New York: Columbia University Press, 1936), 151.

55. Mousnier, *Les Institutions de la France*, 1:101.

56. A notable exception is the work of Mitchell Greenberg, particularly *Subjectivity and Subjugation in Seventeenth-Century Drama and Prose: The Family Romance of French Classicism* (Cambridge: Cambridge University Press, 1992). Erica Harth certainly deals with this crisis in *Ideology and Culture in Seventeenth-Century France*, but her discussion does not extend to theater. John D. Lyons' study, *The Tragedy of Origins: Pierre Corneille and Historical Perspective* (Stanford, Calif.: Stanford University Press, 1996), analyzes five tragedies of Corneille in terms of a historical crisis: the "wrenching dislocation" experienced by audiences who recognize in these plays

the "irreversible transformation" of their own evolving society (xiv). Nonetheless, Lyons' framing questions are very different from my own.

57. Jonathan Dewald, *Aristocratic Experience and the Origins of Modern Culture: France, 1570–1715* (Berkeley: University of California Press, 1993), 9.

58. Dewald, *Aristocratic Experience*, 77.

59. Jean Starobinski, "Sur Corneille," in *L'Oeil vivant* (Paris: Gallimard, 1961), 64–65.

60. Mead, *Culture and Commitment*, 1–2.

61. Mead, *Culture and Commitment*, 32–33.

62. Elias, *The Court Society*, 194–95.

63. An individual of any social class may, of course, be enterprising, and as Jonathan Dewald observes, the interaction between the constraints and duties of lineage and individual ambition is one of the central contradictions of the French aristocracy during the early modern period (*Aristocratic Experience*, 15). Nevertheless, I believe it is not unreasonable to view this conflict as a product, in part, of the basic differences in outlook fostered by feudalism and capitalism.

64. It is interesting to note that tragedy also flourished in England at roughly the same time primogeniture was beginning to be challenged in that country. According to Joan Thirsk, challenges to primogeniture in England began in the sixteenth century, which roughly corresponds to the great period of Elizabethan tragedy. Joan Thirsk, "The European Debate on Customs of Inheritance," in *Family and Inheritance: Rural Society in Western Europe, 1200–1800*, ed. Jack Goody, Joan Thirsk, and E. P. Thompson (Cambridge: Cambridge University Press, 1976), 177.

65. Georg Wilhelm Friedrich Hegel, "Philosophy of Right," trans. T. M. Knox, in *On Tragedy*, ed. Anne and Henry Paolucci (New York: Harper and Row, 1962), 237.

Chapter 2. Psychological Primogeniture

1. Nancy Chodorow, *The Reproduction of Mothering: Psychoanalysis and the Sociology of Gender* (Berkeley: University of California Press, 1978), 12.

2. Anne Gotman, *Hériter* (Paris: Presses Universitaires de France, 1988), 112. Unless otherwise noted, all translations are my own.

3. Pierre Bourdieu, *La Distinction: Critique sociale du jugement* (Paris: Minuit, 1979), 83.

4. Stephen P. Bank and Michael D. Kahn, *The Sibling Bond* (New York: Basic Books, 1982), 301. Subsequent references will be given in the body of the text.

5. Such is the implication of Brian Sutton-Smith and B. G. Rosenberg, co-authors of *The Sibling* (New York: Holt, Rinehart and Winston, 1970), who use a rather elaborate code to indicate on the title page of their book that they are, respectively, the secondborn of two children and the fourthborn of five children, and who dedicate their work to "our older siblings who will undoubtedly regard this as just another form of harassment" (v).

6. Frank J. Sulloway, *Born to Rebel: Birth Order, Family Dynamics, and Creative Lives* (New York: Pantheon, 1996), 56. Subsequent references to this work will be given in the body of the text.

7. Freud actually had half-siblings who were a generation older than he, but they were apparently a completely distinct family and had no impact on his upbringing.

8. See Philip Rieff, *Freud: The Mind of the Moralist* (1959; 3rd ed. Chicago: University of Chicago Press, 1979); Heinz L. Ansbacher, "The Significance of Socio-economic Status of the Patients of Freud and of Adler," *American Journal of Psychotherapy* 13 (1959): 376–82; and H. C. Dechêne, *Geschwisterkonstellation und psychische Fehlentwicklung* (Munich: Barth, 1967).

9. Karl König, *Brothers and Sisters: A Study in Child Psychology* (Blauvelt, N.Y.: St. George Books, 1963), 59.

10. Stephen Bank and Michael Kahn point out, "Neither Freud nor his followers described the sibling relationship in its own right" (Bank and Kahn, 162).

11. In her synthesis of the history of the bias toward parental influence in the field of developmental psychology, Judith Rich Harris points out the pervasive influence Freud had from this point of view even on branches of psychology that reacted against him. See *The Nurture Assumption: Why Children Turn Out the Way They Do* (New York: Free Press, 1998), 4–8. According to Harris, while Freud constructed "an elaborate scenario in which all the psychological ills of adults could be traced back to things that happened to them when they were quite young and in which their parents were heavily implicated" (4), the behaviorism that arose in the mid-twentieth century largely in reaction to Freudian theory "threw out the script of Freud's psychodrama but retained its cast of characters. The parents still get leading roles" (5).

12. Judy Dunn and Carol Kendrick, *Siblings: Love, Envy and Understanding* (London: Grant McIntyre, 1982), 86–87.

13. Alfred Adler, *What Life Should Mean to You*, ed. Alan Porter (Boston: Little, Brown, 1931), 148.

14. Alfred Adler, *Understanding Human Nature*, trans. Walter Béran Wolfe (Garden City, N.Y.: Garden City Publishing, 1927), 150.

15. The economic corollary of the principle of spiritual heir is the distinction, described by Martine Segalen, between inheritance and succession: "In an egalitarian system, the heir and the successor are quite distinct. In principle all children by right inherit an equal portion, but they cannot all be chosen to succeed their fathers as heads of the family business." "La notion d'avantage dans les sociétés égalitaires," in *Les Cadets*, ed. Georges Ravis-Giordani and Martine Segalen (Paris: CNRS, 1994), 197.

16. Judy Dunn and Robert Plomin, *Separate Lives: Why Siblings Are So Different* (New York: Basic Books, 1990), 79.

17. Even a recent critic of birth-order effects in general and Sulloway's work in particular, Judith Rich Harris, concedes that birth-order effects do exist within the strict context of the family, although she believes that there is no systematic carryover between behavior within the family and behavior outside of the family for children in different birth-order positions: "The patterns of behavior that are acquired in sibling relationships neither help us nor hinder us in our dealings with other people. They leave no permanent mark on our character. . . . At home there are birth order effects, no question about it. . . . If you see people with their parents or

their siblings, you do see the differences you expect to see. The oldest does seem more serious, responsible, and bossy. The youngest does behave in a more carefree fashion." *The Nurture Assumption*, 61.

18. Simone de Beauvoir, *Mémoires d'une jeune fille rangée* (Paris: Folio, 1958), 59–60.

19. Adler, *What Life Should Mean to You*, 147.

20. Lucille K. Forer, *Birth Order and Life Roles* (Springfield, Ill.: Charles C. Thomas, 1969), 34.

21. König, *Brothers and Sisters*, 39.

22. Christian Biet, "Le Cadet, point de départ des destins romanesques dans la littérature française du XVIIIe siècle," in *Les Cadets*, 302 n.13.

23. Bernard Barc, "Aîné et cadet dans la Bible," in *Les Cadets*, 50–51.

24. All quotations from *Les Femmes savantes* are taken from Molière, *Oeuvres complètes* (Paris: Seuil, 1962); line numbers are given in the body of the text. All translations are mine.

Chapter 3. Médée

1. Mitchell Greenberg, *Corneille, Classicism, and the Ruses of Symmetry* (Cambridge: Cambridge University Press, 1986), 20.

2. This and all other references to and quotations from Pierre Corneille's theater indicate line numbers in the body of the text. The edition used throughout this study is Pierre Corneille, *Oeuvres complètes*, ed. André Stegmann (Paris: Seuil, 1963).

3. In Euripides' play the children's bodies are actually displayed. Seneca goes even further than his Greek predecessor: he has Medea kill one of the two children before Jason's eyes. Marc Fumaroli, who speaks of "the murder of Jason's children under his very eyes," is either speaking figuratively or else is mistaken in assuming the same thing happens in Corneille's play. "Melpomène au miroir: La Tragédie comme héroïne dans *Médée* et *Phèdre*," *Saggi e ricerche di letteratura francese* 19 (1980): 186. Unless otherwise indicated, all translations are my own.

4. In other versions of the story, Medea unsuccessfully attempts to have Aegeus, the king of Athens, put his own son, Theseus, to death.

5. I use the term "class" for lack of a better one; the problem with the word "estate" is that the *tiers état* comprises many different groups. For a good overview of the sociological ramifications of applying the term "class" to a society predating the industrial revolution, see Robert Mandrou, *Introduction à la France moderne, 1500–1640* (1961; rpt. Paris: Albin Michel, 1989), 141–45.

6. Given the fact that the rejuvenation of Aeson was not invented by Corneille but rather is part of the myth that he inherited, it might seem contradictory to interpret this element of the story in a sociohistorical perspective. Nonetheless, playwrights choose the mythic material they use even if they do not invent it, and they may choose it for the same complex reasons — sociohistorical, psychological, aesthetic, etc. — that they choose to execute a given myth in their own particular way.

7. Although the daughters' mysterious goal is never explained, the passage is heavy with sexual overtones: "Les soeurs crient miracle et chacune ravie / Conçoit pour son vieux père une pareille envie" (73–74) [The sisters exclaim that it is a miracle and each of them, delighted, / Conceives a similar desire for her elderly father].

8. "It is in order to assure his reduplication, and thus his 'immortality,' that Créon (without male descent) desires and agrees to the divorce of Jason and Médée. He wants Jason to marry his own daughter and assure him a progeny" (Greenberg, *Corneille*, 20).

9. In addition to Mitchell Greenberg, a number of scholars and critics of recent years, stressing the centrality of *Médée* to Corneille's subsequent tragedies, have read Médée as a heroic figure. See, for example, André de Leyssac, "Pour une reprise de 'Médée,'" *Revue d'histoire du théâtre* 36:1 (1984): 180–84; John E. Jackson, "Corneille: Du triomphe de la vengeance à l'instauration de la loi," *Dix-septième siècle* 155:2 (April-June 1987): 155–72; and Hélène Domon, "Médée (ou) L'autre," *Cahiers du dix-septième* 1:2 (Fall 1987): 87–102. Marc Fumaroli speaks of the "obvious complicity between Corneille as a playwright and the character of Médée, upon whom he can project his powerful poetic will acting upon people's souls through the lure of his words." *Héros et orateurs: Rhétorique et dramaturgie cornéliennes* (Geneva: Droz, 1990), 502.

10. See in particular Mitchell Greenberg's otherwise subtle and perceptive reading of the play. In his schematization of the play along gender lines, it seems to me that Greenberg overlooks the ironic portrayal of Jason as inferior to his wife. He claims, for example, that "Despite his failings, Jason represents the superiority of ideality over materiality, of reason over passion, of men over women" (*Corneille*, 29).

11. See *Oeuvres complètes*, 175 n.6.

12. Christian Delmas observes that the play "constantly flirts with tragicomedy and even comedy." "Médée, figure de la violence dans le théâtre français du XVIIe siècle," *Pallas* 45 (1996): 224.

13. See *Trésor de la langue française*, 16 vols. (Paris: Gallimard, 1971–1994), 7:1244.

14. Only Médée's opening soliloquy in act 1 is longer.

15. Créon is also physically afraid of Médée. When the two meet onstage for the first time, Créon has his guards restrain her: "Ses yeux ne sont que feu, ses regards que menace. / Gardes, empêchez-la de s'approcher de moi" (378–79) [Her eyes are fire, her glance a threat. / Guards, keep her away from me].

16. William O. Goode, "Médée and Jason: Hero and Nonhero in Corneille's *Médée*," *French Review* 51 (May 1978): 812.

17. Holly Tucker observes that in his relation to love, Jason is quite the opposite of Corneille's subsequent heroes, "for whom passion stands as an *obstacle* to their *gloire*"; for Jason passion is "a valuable tool for fulfilling his overriding desire for power." "Corneille's *Médée*: Gifts of Vengeance," *French Review* 69:1 (October 1995): 2.

18. Even Pollux's exit line at the end of the first scene of the play may be read ironically. Jason, ever the nervous lover, says he cannot escort his friend to his

audience with the king because he is waiting for Créuse, to which Pollux rejoins: "Adieu, l'amour vous presse / Et je serais marri qu'un soin officieux / Vous fît perdre pour moi des temps si précieux" (158–60) [Farewell, love is on your mind / And I would hate for such a demanding task / To make you waste so much precious time].

19. The examples are: "he undertook [il a entrepris] the furnishing of food for such and such a price" and "this Architect undertook [a entrepris] the construction of a building for a certain sum of money." *Le Dictionnaire de l'Académie françoise* (Paris: Jean Baptiste Coignard, 1694), 2:313. "Entrepreneur" apparently has at least some economic connotations as early as 1611. See *Trésor de la langue française*, 7:1246.

20. Neither in Euripides' nor in Seneca's play does Jason commit suicide. The fact that Jason gives up the fight against Médée at the end of Corneille's drama caps the unheroic evolution the French playwright has made his masculine protagonist undergo.

Chapter 4. Horace, *or How to Kill Friends and Influence People*

1. Sabine first appears in 1:1 and Camille in 1:2. Curiace arrives onstage in 1:3, Horace in 2:1.

2. One of the difficulties of reading *Horace* as a pure and simple reaffirmation of patriarchal authority — however strongly Tulle's ultimate verdict in Horace's trial may send that sort of message — is that along the way the drama is quite evenhanded in its portrayal of male and female characters: the distinction between Romans and Albans is ultimately more meaningful than the distinction between men and women.

3. *Critique des tragédies de Corneille et de Racine par Voltaire*, ed. B. Bonieux (1866; rpt. Geneva: Slatkine, 1970), 88. Unless otherwise noted, all translations are my own.

4. Of course this is partly explainable in terms of le Vieil Horace's Roman pride: he may be presumptuous enough to assume Curiace will not come back alive. Nonetheless, his touching adieu to Curiace is in striking contrast to both his brusque leave-taking of his own son and to the latter's frigid farewell to his best friend.

5. Octave Nadal, *Le Sentiment de l'amour dans l'oeuvre de Pierre Corneille* (Paris: Gallimard, 1948), 181. One might argue that by this reasoning Horace, who is already married, would seem more mature than Curiace, but marriage played a considerably larger role in a woman's life than in a man's in the seventeenth century, and men were much freer than women to postpone marriage. Hence the fact that Sabine is a married woman while Camille is not is a much more important commentary on the relative positions of these two characters than the corresponding difference between Horace and Curiace. Moreover, although le Vieil Horace expects his daughter to obey his commands — he orders her not to mourn Curiace after he has been killed (4:3) — neither Camille nor Sabine is portrayed as the main bearer of a family tradition or as a potential heir within her family of origin: both have brothers

who take precedence over them. And as is typical of Pierre Corneille's most canonical tragedies, neither the mother of the Curiace brothers nor the wife of the Vieil Horace is ever mentioned.

6. As Jacques Scherer observes, "[Sabine's] strange initial decision to favor the losers is untenable, and she will not ultimately hold to it." *Le Théâtre de Corneille* (Paris: Nizet, 1984), 57.

7. Scherer, *Le Théâtre de Corneille*, 57.

8. This is a very ancient conflict and one that must be addressed by all societies. The issue is already raised in Greek tragedy, which frequently airs the idea that as an outsider to her husband's family of origin, a wife is easily viewed as an intruder or a foreigner in times of conflict. Since the breakdown of extended family relations wrought by the mobility of most postindustrial Western societies, the conflict between family of origin and family of procreation has been driven underground, its overt expressions largely reduced to disputes over which set of parents or grandparents one spends holidays with.

9. Serge Doubrovsky, *Corneille et la dialectique du héros* (Paris: Gallimard, 1963), 137.

10. As social psychologists have pointed out, one of the main peace-making mechanisms within a family is diversification and the development of distinct roles and niches. One might say that Camille and Horace have done this by championing different causes, but when their causes enter into conflict, their apparent differences do not allow them to keep their distance because of the structural similarity of their characters. If harmony within a family depends upon diversity of character — one sibling tense and driven, another easy-going; one serious, another ironic; one extreme and rigid, another open-minded — it makes perfect sense that Camille and Horace should fight bitterly, for they are two of a kind. See Chapter 2.

11. David Clarke, *Pierre Corneille: Poetics and Political Drama Under Louis XIII* (Cambridge: Cambridge University Press, 1992), 182.

12. Harriet Stone, *The Classical Model: Literature and Knowledge in Seventeenth-Century France* (Ithaca, N.Y.: Cornell University Press, 1996), 48.

13. I see Horace's stance as a strategy designed to assure his victory — and by the same token a proleptic rehearsing of his blindered pursuit of the Curiace brothers in battle — rather than as the kind of self-immolation that his rhetoric vaunts as the ultimate heroic gesture. But obviously the play has many levels, and I do not fundamentally disagree with critics like Serge Doubrovsky, who reads Horace's victory over Curiace, a man he loves, as an example of the highest form of self-mastery. See *Corneille et la dialectique du héros*, 148–49.

14. I would extend John D. Lyons' observation about the impersonal nature of Horace's murder of Camille to Horace's defeat of Curiace: "The older claim of the dominant male within the family over the lives of subordinate family members yields, in Horace's own words, to a newly impersonal formulation." *The Tragedy of Origins: Pierre Corneille and Historical Perspective* (Stanford, Calif.: Stanford University Press, 1996), 57.

15. In 2:1 and 2:2, respectively.

16. Robert Brasillach, *Corneille* (1938; rpt. Paris: Fayard, 1961), 129.

17. I disagree with John D. Lyons' interpretation of why "Curiace never de-

fines or exalts an Alban civilization of Alban values" (*The Tragedy of Origins*, 53): "In the nonexistence of an explicitly Alban culture and character we see how history inscribes itself in Corneille's tragedy as a lack or lacuna. Corneille and we cannot imagine the rise of the Alban republic in place of Rome and with that rise the modification of all subsequent history" (54). I read Curiace's lack of dogma as a reflection of his maturity; as the speech quoted here indicates, his perspective is synthetic rather than exclusionary.

18. It is for this reason that I am puzzled by Michel Prigent's characterization of Horace as a wise man ("un sage"). *Le Héros et l'Etat dans la tragédie de Pierre Corneille* (Paris: Presses Universitaires de France [Quadrige], 1986), 131.

19. In Western capitalistic societies, oldest siblings are often highly competitive because competition has become a societal norm. But even today oldest siblings often have a kind of self-assurance lacking in their younger brothers and sisters.

20. "The arrogance manifested by Horace is a mask of grandeur and effectiveness that the Roman hero, identifying his own glory with Rome's, uses in the service of Rome. But underneath this mask one can glimpse what lies within: Horace rises above his love for Sabine, but he has not snuffed it out; he rises above his friendship with Curiace, but he has not turned his back on it. On the contrary, he attempts to transform it into a kind of heroic emulation befitting the circumstances." Marc Fumaroli, *Héros et orateurs: Rhétorique et dramaturgie cornéliennes* (Geneva: Droz, 1990), 338.

21. Even Michel Prigent's generally probing study of Corneille errs on the side of oversimplifying the character of Horace. See *Le Héros et l'Etat dans la tragédie de Pierre Corneille*, 126–38.

22. The centrifugal movement of Camille's curse (1305–12) is clearly one of its main organizing principles. In her vision of Rome's destruction, Camille moves from its neighbors ("voisins"), to all of Italy ("toute l'Italie"), to the Orient, to "a hundred peoples united together from the ends of the universe." In accordance with the old saw that Rome could ultimately fall only at its own hands, Camille concludes with an image of Rome's violence toward itself that is clearly meant to bring us back to her brother's proud self-immolation: "Qu'elle-même sur soi renverse ses murailles / Et de ses propres mains déchire ses entrailles" (1311–12) [May Rome knock down its own ramparts / And rip out its guts with its own hands].

23. Harriet Stone, *Royal DisClosure: Problematics of Representation in French Classical Tragedy* (Birmingham, Ala.: Summa, 1987), 21.

24. Many critics read the character of Horace quite narrowly, as if his self-identification with Rome necessarily precluded other motivations. John D. Lyons escapes this trap by observing that "Both of these enemy siblings place domestic concerns ahead of the state" (*The Tragedy of Origins*, 55).

25. "J'ai même défendu, par une expresse loi, / Qu'on osât prononcer votre nom devant moi" (*Phèdre* 603–4) [I even had a law passed / To prevent anyone from uttering your name in my presence].

26. I am grateful to Kennedy Schultz for pointing out the infrequency with which Horace says the name "Curiace." By contrast, Curiace, who is onstage a much shorter time than Horace, says the name "Horace" three times (354, 420, 536). In Valère's description of the death of Curiace and his brothers (1101–40), the Albans'

family name is avoided, to the point of confusion (1115–18), while Horace is mentioned by name twice (1113, 1124).

Chapter 5. The End of an Era, or The Death of Pomp(ey)

1. Auguste Dorchain goes as far as to call *La Mort de Pompée* "the most magnificent portrayal of politics and history that Corneille ever composed," surpassing other historical dramas in that it makes us "live through a crucial moment of Roman politics and world history: the moment when the Republic crumbles and the Empire is about to be built." *Pierre Corneille* (Paris: Garnier Frères, 1918), 245. Unless otherwise noted, all translations are my own.

2. Michel Prigent, *Le Héros et l'Etat dans la tragédie de Pierre Corneille* (Paris: Presses Universitaires de France [Quadrige], 1986), 193.

3. See, for example, Serge Doubrovsky, *Corneille et la dialectique du héros* (Paris: Gallimard, 1963), 549, n.232.

4. Rumor attributed Louis XIII's demise to a slow-acting poison mysteriously administered by Richelieu before his own death. It would appear from two lines in the sonnet Corneille wrote to commemorate Louis' death that he himself may have believed that Richelieu was somehow responsible for the king's death: "Son tyran et le nôtre [Richelieu] à peine perd le jour, / Que jusque dans sa tombe il le force à le suivre" [His tyrant and our own has hardly closed his eyes / When he forces him to follow him to the grave] (*Oeuvres complètes*, 872).

5. David Clarke, *Pierre Corneille: Poetics and Political Drama Under Louis XIII* (Cambridge: Cambridge University Press, 1992), 253–54.

6. "Paradoxically, it would appear that pomp is conjured up by the name of Pompée." Jacques Scherer, *Le Théâtre de Corneille* (Paris: Nizet, 1984), 76. In his 1660 "Examen," Corneille himself calls *La Mort de Pompée* "les vers les plus pompeux que j'aye faits" [the most pomp-laden lines of poetry I have ever composed] (*Oeuvres complètes*, 316).

7. An exception to this is Michel Prigent, who recalls Pompée's role as possessor of the paternal will and observes that his own death is therefore "an internal affair of the Egyptian dynasty" (*Le Héros et l'Etat*, 192). Nevertheless, Prigent's analysis does not explore the question of inheritance.

8. As César puts it in one of his final speeches to Cléopâtre, "par cette mort [de Ptolomée] l'Égypte est toute à vous" (1784) [by Ptolomée's death, all Egypt belongs to you]. In his 1660 "Examen," Corneille himself points out that in fact Cleopatra did not rule alone, but married her younger brother.

9. Even though *La Mort de Pompée* ends with the victory of the older sibling over the younger, it would be foolhardy to read the play simply as a triumph for primogeniture. Cléopâtre is a woman, and ancient Egyptian inheritance practices aside, for a seventeenth-century French audience this would disqualify her, in the presence of a brother, from being considered as simply her father's heir. Moreover, the reason the elder Ptolemy chose to write his daughter into his will is not her seniority, but her past service to him during a time of political upheaval. In her first confrontation with her brother (1:3), Cléopâtre reminds Ptolomée that she her-

self is the reason that both Pompée and César helped to reestablish her father's shaky power after the latter's dethronement (289–312). When her deposed father brought her and her younger brother, the present king, to Rome to stir up the Senate's sympathy for the ousted family, César lost his heart to her, which led him to give the unfortunate Egyptians financial help and elicit for them the aid of his then ally, Pompée. The elder Ptolemy, duly recrowned, drafted a will that expressed his gratitude toward his daughter. Nevertheless, as we shall see, the relation between the older and younger siblings is developed in such a way as to foreground Cléopâtre's connections to a traditional, indeed, a conservative ethic.

10. Serge Doubrovsky points this out in his analysis of *La Mort de Pompée*. *Corneille et la dialectique du héros*, 277.

11. To this extent I disagree with David Clarke's otherwise enlightening analysis, which creates too stark a polarity between Pompée as a model of a past ethic and all the other characters, lumped together, who are said to be "governed solely by ambition." Clarke sees Cléopâtre as "competing under an appearance of honour with a foolish and dishonourable King of Egypt in a sorry scramble for power which spells the end of an older order of justice and heroic devotion." *Pierre Corneille*, 253.

12. "I have made Ptolomée older, so that he could be an active character and live up to his official title as king. Even though the historians and the poet Lucan generally call him *rex puer*, the child-king, he was not so much of a child that he would have been unable to follow his father's orders and marry his sister" (*Oeuvres complètes*, 316).

13. *Horace*, 131–34.

14. By contrast, both of the play's female characters, Cléopâtre and Cornélie, are quite similar to Chimène. All that is missing in order for Cornélie, often described as one of Corneille's noblest heroines, to be in a situation analogous to Chimène's is for her and César to fall in love. He has already pursued and fought someone she loves; she swears to exact revenge from him. And César and Cornélie both give voice to a certain admiration for each other. Her grudging compliment to him ("O ciel, que de vertus vous me faites haïr" [1072] [O heavens, how many virtues you make me despise]) is matched by his surprise at her fortitude ("Son courage m'étonne" [1425] [Her courage astonishes me]).

15. See *Le Cid*, 237–250; *Horace*, 1559–72.

16. Doubrovsky, *Corneille et la dialectique du héros*, 276.

17. A number of critics have understood that Achorée's comment about Ptolomée's death being worthy of a king—"il est mort . . . avec toutes les marques / Que puissent laisser d'eux les plus dignes monarques" (1633–34) [he died . . . leaving an impression of grandeur / That only the worthiest of kings can give]—is scathingly ironic. By an extraordinary oversight, Georges Couton reads the line straight: "in the end [Corneille] redeems Ptolomée by means of a glorious death." *Oeuvres complètes*, vol. 1, ed. Georges Couton (Paris: Gallimard [Bibliothèque de la Pléiade], 1980), 1722. Even Louis Marin, in an otherwise penetrating analysis of the play, puts forth the idea that Ptolomée "will die nobly, as a king, in combat" (*Des pouvoirs de l'image* [Paris: Seuil, 1993], 148).

18. Prigent, *Le Héros et l'Etat*, 198.

19. The two terms are linked by a phonic rather than an etymological connec-

tion; nonetheless, especially given the seventeenth-century spelling of "tête," "teste," an association between the words might well have been intended.

20. Marin associates what he calls the "objet fétiche," Pompée's truncated head, with the myth of Medusa (*Des pouvoirs de l'image*, 153).

21. Marin, *Des pouvoirs de l'image*, 147.

22. This is not simply a case of ellipsis of the pronoun's referent — that kind of ellipsis being quite widespread in Classical theater — for that construction requires the referent to be clearly inferable from the context. By contrast, in this passage there is a genuine logical hesitation over the referent: is it really Pompée's truncated head that is figured as feeling grief and anger and as having undergone a defeat?

23. Marin points out that Pompée's instantly recognizable trunk is also to be contrasted with the unidentifiable headless trunks lying on the battlefield of Pharsalus described in the play's opening speech (*Des pouvoirs de l'image*, 141).

24. Paul Valéry, *Mauvaises pensées et autres*, in *Oeuvres*, vol. 2, ed. Jean Hytier (Paris: Gallimard [Bibliothèque de la Pléiade], 1960), 895. Georges Couton is completely mistaken in suggesting that Valéry exaggerated the grotesqueness of this description. See Corneille, *Oeuvres complètes*, vol. 1, ed. Couton, 1728.

25. David Clarke's overly bleak reading of the play's conclusion seems to me to overlook the importance of ritual as a potential source of redemption. He writes, "there is little to reassure the spectator in these tragic obsequies of traditional order abandoned and betrayed, where Pompée's ashes seem to be revered only as the symbol of a legitimacy embattled or even lost for ever" (*Pierre Corneille*, 250–51). I am basically in agreement with Clarke's interpretation of the play, but given the play's movement between an unceremonious lack of a funeral at the beginning and a solemn state funeral at the end, I believe the final action of consecrating Pompée's ashes and crowning Cléopâtre can be seen as a wistful affirmation of past values.

Chapter 6. A Sibling Rivalry over Sibling Rivalry

1. If *Rodogune* can be labeled a "problem play," as Derek Watts has called it, this may be because it heightens our awareness of the problematic nature of inheritance without offering any solutions. As Watts points out, it is unlikely Cléopâtre, the twins' mother, could have withheld the information about the brothers' birth order for so long. Derek A. Watts, "A Further Look at 'Rodogune,'" in *Ouverture et dialogue: Mélanges offerts à Wolfgang Leiner*, ed. Ulrich Döring, Antiopy Lyroudias, and Rainer Zaiser (Tübingen: Gunter Narr, 1988), 447 and 451. More recently Hélène Merlin has written that "the dénouement [of *Rodogune*] short-circuits the issue of the hereditary principle of the monarchy" ("*Cinna, Rodogune, Nicomède*: Le Roi et le *moi*," *Littératures* 37 [Autumn 1997]: 79; all translations, unless otherwise noted, are my own).

2. It goes without saying that while this reasoning may be superficially true, Corneille could have found a way of clearly establishing the brothers' birth order.

3. I disagree with Harriet Ray Allentuch's interpretation of the play's dénouement, which is not untypical of literal-minded discussions of the issue of birth order in *Rodogune*: "A widowed queen has borne twin sons, but clasping power to herself,

refuses to identify her first born and yield him the throne. Providence intervenes to crush her and crown the sacred blood." "Sacred and Heroic Blood and the Religion of Monarchy on the Cornelian Stage," in *Homage to Paul Bénichou*, ed. Sylvie Romanowski and Monique Bilezikian (Birmingham, Ala.: Summa, 1994), 49. This reading overlooks the numerous problems left unresolved by the play, including the question of whether Antiochus' inheritance of the throne is in fact legitimate.

4. "She [Cléopâtre] had two sons by Démétrius [Nicanor], the older of whom, Séleucus, she shot and killed with an arrow as soon as he had assumed the throne upon his father's death, either because she feared he might want to take revenge on her or because the same rage pushed her to commit yet another kin-murder. He was succeeded by his brother Antiochus, who forced this unnatural mother to take the poison she had prepared for him" (Corneille, *Oeuvres complètes*, 416–17).

5. This is not the only time in the play that Séleucus "prévient" or comes before his brother. When Cléopâtre pays Séleucus the dubious honor of killing him before she does away with his brother — something she makes clear is not a coincidence — she resembles a monstrous caricature of a mother quicker to mete out punishment to her older, more responsible son: "Mais déjà l'un [Séleucus] a vu que je les veux punir: / Souvent qui tarde trop se laisse prévenir" (1493–94) [But already Séleucus has seen that I wish to punish them: / When one puts things off too long, others get to them first]. As Jacques Scherer explains, Corneille's historical sources attribute the order of the mother's attacks to the sons' age difference. *Le Théâtre de Corneille* (Paris: Nizet, 1984), 85.

6. One of the most interesting ways Corneille has transformed the material from his Spanish source for *Le Cid*, Guillén de Castro's *Las Mocedades del Cid*, is that in that play Rodrigo is the eldest of three brothers, and Diego first hesitates to ask him rather than his younger brothers to avenge the insult he has received because he is afraid Rodrigo, his heir, might be killed. It is true that Corneille already had his hands full with the material he did select for his drama, but nonetheless the elimination of the theme of sibling rivalry from the most famous early French Classical play goes along with Pierre Corneille's general emphasis on vertical family relations in his early theater.

7. Michel Prigent, *Le Héros et l'Etat dans la tragédie de Pierre Corneille* (Paris: Presses Universitaires de France [Quadrige], 1986), 240.

8. See, for example, Rodogune's assessment of them: "Comme ils ont même sang avec pareil mérite, / Un avantage égal pour eux me sollicite" (355–56) [Since they have the same blood and the same merit, / An equal advantage speaks to me in their favor]; "L'un et l'autre fait voir un mérite si rare / Que le souhait confus entre les deux s'égare" (431–32) [Both of them show such unusual merit / That it is difficult to know how to choose between them]. As Ullrich Langer puts it, "Given so few 'natural' differences between the brothers, only a willful instance of authority can distinguish between them." *Perfect Friendship: Studies in Literature and Moral Philosophy from Boccaccio to Corneille* (Geneva: Droz, 1994), 226.

9. Prigent, *Le Héros et l'Etat*, 223.

10. Mitchell Greenberg is quite right in associating Antiochus with earlier female protagonists of Corneille: "Antiochus' refusal to look, his refusal to see the

truth, his constant refuge in tears and sighs, places him squarely within the traditional camp of femininity in the Cornelian universe." *Subjectivity and Subjugation in Seventeenth-Century Drama and Prose: The Family Romance of French Classicism* (Cambridge: Cambridge University Press, 1992), 98. Serge Doubrovsky sees in the reversal of traditional feminine and masculine roles in *Rodogune* a trend that will dominate Corneille's subsequent theater. *Corneille et la dialectique du héros* (Paris: Gallimard, 1963), 292.

11. Gordon D. MacGregor, "*Rodogune, Nicomède*, and the Status of History in Corneille," *Stanford French Review* 11:2 (Summer 1987): 149.

12. Gordon D. MacGregor attributes Corneille's preference for *Rodogune* and *Nicomède* "above all his other dramatic progeny" to the "relative independence of preexisting models, be they historical or theatrical." "*Rodogune, Nicomède*, and the Status of History in Corneille," 138.

13. Greenberg, *Subjectivity and Subjugation*, 97.

14. In spite of the lack of resemblance between Antiochus and his mother, I agree with Harriet Stone's observation that Antiochus does maintain a troubling sort of identification with Cléopâtre even after he has realized she attempted to kill him. Stone speaks of Antiochus' "sustained identification with Cléopâtre" and states that "mother and son exchange roles without ever acknowledging their obliqueness to the Father." Harriet Stone, *Royal DisClosure: Problematics of Representation in French Classical Tragedy* (Birmingham, Ala.: Summa, 1987), 45.

15. The fact that the paternal heritage is purely affective, that what Nicanor passes on to his sons is nothing but his love for Rodogune, is made explicit later on by Cléopâtre in an apostrophe to Antiochus: "Reste du sang ingrat d'un époux infidèle, / Héritier d'une flamme envers moi criminelle, / Aime mon ennemie, et péris comme lui" (1515–17) [Remains of the ungrateful blood of a faithless mate, / Heir to a passion I consider a crime, / Love my enemy, and die like your father].

16. If we think back a scant seven years, to *Le Cid*, it is quite startling to see how sharply the sons' reticence to avenge their father's death contrasts with Rodrigue's willingness to sacrifice his love for a mere insult done to Don Diègue. It is true that Nicanor purportedly threatened to dispossess his sons in favor of the children he might have had with Rodogune, but this is not presented as the sons' motivation for not avenging their father's death, and indeed Corneille modifies his historical sources such that in his drama Nicanor and Rodogune were not yet married when Cléopâtre did away with Nicanor, which makes the dispossession motif somewhat less immediate. See Jacques Scherer, *Le Théâtre de Corneille*, 85.

17. All quotations from Thomas Corneille's theater are taken from Thomas Corneille, *Poëmes dramatiques*, 5 vols. (Paris: Guillaume Cavelier, 1722). Since this edition does not give line numbers, references will be given to act and scene numbers, followed by volume and page numbers. I have taken the liberty of modernizing the spelling so as to conform with quotations from the works of Pierre Corneille and Racine. I have not modified punctuation or capitalization.

18. See, for example, my discussion of Pierre Corneille's *La Mort de Pompée* in Chapter 5. For examples of Rome's mistrust of hereditary monarchy one could also cite Pierre Corneille's *Nicomède* and Racine's *Bérénice*, among other plays.

19. Démétrius' popularity is in fact identified as one of the possible sources of his

brother's resentment of him: "Il est aimé du Peuple, et peut-être en ces lieux, / Qui s'en peut faire aimer, fait bien des envieux" (2:1; 3:333) [He is loved by the People, and perhaps in this place / Being loved by them makes others envious of him].

20. Andromaque's first lines onstage include her ironic response to Pyrrhus' report of the threatening sense of alarm in the Greek camp: "[Astyanax,] Digne objet de leur crainte! / Un enfant malheureux qui ne sait pas encor / Que Pyrrhus est son maître, et qu'il est fils d'Hector" (*Andromaque*, 270–72) [Astyanax, what a worthy object of their fear! / A miserable child who does not yet know / That Pyrrhus is his master, and that he is Hector's son].

21. In his confrontation with Didas over the question of marriage with his daughter, Démétrius also becomes as violent as is allowed by *bienséance*, that is to say that he cuts the scene short with a furious threat: "Peut-être aurez-vous lieu de craindre ma colère. / C'est à vous d'y penser" (2:5; 3:347) [Perhaps you will have occasion to fear my anger. / Think about it].

22. The edition of reference for this book mistakenly labels the last scene of the play as act 5, scene 6, whereas it should be numbered as scene 7. Subsequent editions of the play correct this error, as have I.

23. John D. Lyons calls *Rodogune* a play "dominated by nostalgia." *The Tragedy of Origins: Pierre Corneille and Historical Perspective* (Stanford, Calif.: Stanford University Press, 1996), 76.

Chapter 7. The Brother as Father, the Father as Brother

1. Gordon D. MacGregor characterizes the central difference between the two plays in terms of their very different portrayals of the dominant brother: "If in [*Rodogune*] the stronger, more perspicacious of the brothers drastically departs from the weaker one's static position, with tragic consequences all round, in *Nicomède* it is the weaker brother who finally comes to espouse the monumental and unbudging position of the stronger." "*Rodogune, Nicomède,* and the Status of History in Corneille," *Stanford French Review* 11:2 (Summer 1987): 153.

2. Although it seems likely that the reestablishment of a clear age hierarchy between the two brothers in *Nicomède*, as compared with the uncertainty that reigns in *Rodogune*, does to some extent reflect Corneille's essentially conservative stance during the Fronde, it is interesting that he does not go so far as to present paternal authority in a positive light in this play. Certainly Prusias is less monstrous than Cléopâtre in *Rodogune* — and, as we shall see, less monstrous toward Nicomède than his historical analogue — but he is far from being an adequate ethical model.

3. To this extent Alain Couprie's observation about *Nicomède* is far more applicable to *La Mort d'Annibal*: "Nicomède's situation has its own uniqueness. Nicomède is recognized by all as the perfect, noble heir . . . of Annibal." Alain Couprie, "Le Moi, le double et le dédoublement," in *Lectures de Corneille:* Cinna, Rodogune, Nicomède, ed. Daniel Riou (Rennes: Presses Universitaires de Rennes, 1997), 93. All translations, unless otherwise noted, are my own.

4. Georges Couton, *Corneille et la Fronde* (Clermont-Ferrand: Bussac, 1951), 62–63.

5. In its "adoption" of the younger brother, Rome fulfills a function analogous to the Church of Rome in the seventeenth century: it provides refuge for a younger sibling, taking him off his parents' hands for a price: "Ce grand nom de Romain est un précieux titre; / Et la Reine et le Roi l'ont assez acheté / Pour ne se plaire pas à le voir rejeté" (192–94) [The great name of a Roman is a precious title; / And the Queen and the King have paid dearly enough for it / Not to want to see it cast off].

6. Serge Doubrovsky, *Corneille et la dialectique du héros* (Paris: Gallimard, 1963), 324.

7. 1:2–1:3, 3:6, and 4:4. In act 4, scene 4, the crucial scene in which Prusias names his younger son as his universal heir, Attale is present but says nothing.

8. Carlo François characterizes Nicomède as a man of such inborn privilege that he simply cannot fail, a hero "destined to incarnate the paradox by which reason is an innate faculty that one need not develop . . . , a privilege belonging to the highest elite." *Raison et déraison dans le théâtre de Pierre Corneille* (York, S.C.: French Literature Publications, 1979), 83.

9. Terence Cave sees this as one of Corneille's "conversion scenes" similar to the climactic scene in *Cinna. Recognitions: A Study in Poetics* (Oxford: Clarendon, 1988), 324. I would simply add that there is a certain irony in the fact that it is not a father figure like Auguste who offers the model of *générosité* here, but rather an older brother.

10. Jacques Scherer is quite right to stress the openendedness of the play's conclusion rather than its harmoniousness: "Does Nicomède triumph in the end? Nothing could be less certain. . . . In his final appearance Nicomède is in his glory and has made up with everyone, but he is not married. The situation is basically the same as it was before. Nicomède has not been defeated. But neither has he defeated anyone else." "Les Intentions politiques dans 'Nicomède,'" in *Pierre Corneille: Actes du colloque de Rouen*, ed. Alain Niderst (Paris: Presses Universitaires de France, 1985), 498–99.

11. Corneille reduces the motif of Prusias' murderous intentions toward his son to a single sentence. When Prusias is threatened by a population infuriated by Nicomède's being sent to Rome as a hostage, he proposes decapitating Nicomède: "du haut d'un balcon pour calmer la tempête, / Sur ses nouveaux sujets faisons voler sa tête" (1587–88) [from high up on the balcony, let us calm the storm / By pitching his head onto his new subjects].

12. Michel Prigent characterizes Prusias by stating that "the lack of authority leads to authoritarianism and tyranny." *Le Héros et l'Etat dans la tragédie de Pierre Corneille* (Paris: Presses Universitaires de France [Quadrige], 1986), 299.

13. Auguste Dorchain's quick description of Prusias says it all: Prusias is "jealous of the exploits of a son who bears so little resemblance to him and to whom he finds it burdensome to owe so much." *Pierre Corneille* (Paris: Garnier Frères, 1918), 327.

14. MacGregor, "*Rodogune, Nicomède*, and the Status of History," 155.

15. It is true that in his role as past kingmaker for his father, Nicomède bears some resemblance to Rodrigue, the dynamic "arm" assuring the authority of his

father as head of the lineage and rescuing the kingdom for his monarch, and the logic of primogeniture as a form of family continuity frequently tolerates this kind of partial substitution of the son for the father even before the latter's death. If Prusias is bitter in sounding the theme of the debt he owes his heir as guarantor of his country's security (373–78; 413–22), it is that *Nicomède* goes much further than a simple replacement or representation of the governing function by the warrior function.

16. Hélène Merlin, "*Cinna, Rodogune, Nicomède*: Le Roi et le *moi*," *Littératures* 37 (Autumn 1997): 76.

17. The only instance of Nicomède's following his father's example is an ironic one. When Prusias gives Nicomède the option of either inheriting his four kingdoms or marrying Laodice, and Nicomède chooses love over political duty, Nicomède deflates the indignant Prusias by pointing out that he is simply following his father's lead: "Je crois que votre exemple est glorieux à suivre. / Ne préférez-vous pas une femme à ce fils / Par qui tous ces Etats aux vôtres sont unis?" (1344–46) [I believe your example is a glorious one to follow. / Don't you yourself prefer your wife to your son, / Who conquered all these Lands for you?].

18. Mitchell Greenberg's reading of the end of *Nicomède* as a restoration of patriarchy seems to me to overlook the irony of the status of inheritance at the end of the drama. See *Corneille, Classicism, and the Ruses of Symmetry* (Cambridge: Cambridge University Press, 1986), 150.

19. David Clarke explains the feeling of almost untragic reconciliation that ends plays like *Nicomède* as indicative of Corneille's stretching the limits of tragedy: "Certain of Corneille's plays, like *Cinna, Polyeucte* and *Nicomède*, are undoubtedly closer to heroic drama than tragedy in so far as they show how the hero may finally . . . transform the social order in which he establishes his identity through a celebration of a providential harmony between heroic initiative and the values which govern its larger contexts." *Pierre Corneille: Poetics and Political Drama Under Louis XIII* (Cambridge: Cambridge University Press, 1992), 261.

20. In *Nicomède* Annibal's death before the action begins greatly lessens the dramatic impact of the relation between Nicomède and his spiritual father. By contrast, Annibal's appearance as a character in Thomas' tragedy is all the more powerful.

21. Nicomède actually appears in the fewest number of scenes of all the play's protagonists.

22. David A. Collins, *Thomas Corneille: Protean Dramatist* (The Hague: Mouton, 1966), 139.

23. Collins, *Thomas Corneille*, 139.

24. The play could also be read as an attack upon the injustices of excessive government controls, but I do not believe a play like *La Mort d'Annibal* can be reduced to a clear-cut sociopolitical allegory in which, for example, Rome might be taken to be the rising absolutist monarchy of Louis XIV working to undermine the power of the hereditary aristocracy. Not the least problem raised by such a scheme would be to find a coherent counterpart for Annibal, who opposes both Rome and the system of primogeniture that Rome itself calls into question.

Chapter 8. Degenerating Inheritance

1. "Racine himself invited comparison with Corneille in the choice of subject for his first play. Corneille had given a version of the Oedipus story in his *Oedipe*. Five years later Racine challenged Corneille with *La Thébaïde*." David Maskell, *Racine: A Theatrical Reading* (Oxford: Clarendon, 1991), 178.

2. Without going as far as to say that *Oedipe* is directly influenced by *Timocrate*, Jacques Scherer observes that in his *Oedipe* Pierre adapts "to the new public that had just applauded his brother's *Timocrate*." *Le Théâtre de Corneille* (Paris: Nizet, 1984), 112. Unless otherwise noted, all translations are my own.

3. If Timocrate's two identities are viewed as mutually exclusive, the play is a tragedy, whereas if they are seen to be reconcilable to some degree, it is closer to comedy or tragicomedy. But in either case, what is important is the identities themselves and the relation between them.

4. Auguste Dorchain scathingly summarizes the bizarre embellishments that Corneille has given to the famous plot: "The main point of the drama seems to be to find out whether Thésée . . . will or will not be allowed to marry Dircé . . . , whence a series of conjugal squabbles that already keep us at a vast distance from the main subject. But that's nothing: Corneille will also find a way . . . to lead us down three garden paths which take us even further away from it. . . . In the end it appears that the entire dark tale — Oedipe's patricide, Jocaste's incest, the plague decimating the city, and all the rest of it — has been dragged onstage merely to postpone and thus make us eagerly await the happiness of the two lovers!" *Pierre Corneille* (Paris: Garnier Frères, 1918), 365–66.

5. Also indicative of Corneille's view that this play initiates a new stage of life for him are the prefatory verses dedicated to his patron Nicolas Fouquet, himself a fine representative of the upstart spirit of the second generation in that he is a member of the *noblesse de robe* and a *nouveau riche*:

> Oui, généreux appui de tout notre Parnasse,
> Tu me rends ma vigueur lorsque tu me fais grâce,
> Et je veux bien apprendre à tout notre avenir
> Que tes regards bénins ont su me rajeunir.
> Je m'élève sans crainte avec de si bons guides:
> Depuis que je t'ai vu, je ne vois plus mes rides,
> Et plein d'une plus claire et noble vision,
> Je prends mes cheveux gris pour cette illusion.

> Yes, generous support of our entire Parnassus,
> You give me back my life force when you favor me,
> And I shall do my best to teach all our posterity
> That your kindly eyes have made me young again.
> With such fine guides I rise up without fear:
> Since first seeing you, I no longer see my wrinkles,
> And full of a clearer and nobler vision,
> I take my gray hair as an illusion. (*Oeuvres complètes*, 565)

Corneille's rhetorical claim that Fouquet has rejuvenated him is reminiscent of his first tragedy, *Médée*, in which the sorceress has the power to do just that. See Chapter 3.

6. Another reason for this embellishment of the myth is undoubtedly to hold the interest of the women in the audience with a prominent female character as well as a love interest—Corneille's Dircé is engaged to be married to her cousin, but is in love with Thésée, the king of Athens. One might argue that the role of Jocaste could have been expanded to the same end, along with the theme of her love for Oedipe, which is actually touched upon in the play, but because Dircé is a character of his own invention, Corneille is free to make her more conventionally heroic than Jocaste could be, given the constraints of the myth.

7. Lucien Goldmann calls Corneille's confection of Dircé as a double for Oedipe a "metaphysical and dramatic sleight of hand" ("ce tour de passe-passe dramatique et métaphysique"). *Le dieu caché* (Paris: Gallimard, 1959), 339. Jean Schlumberger laments, "As if the kinship bonds were not already complicated enough in this Theban family, Corneille adds a daughter of Jocaste and Laïus; and you can just imagine how much Corneille enjoys the ensuing chaos, in which no one knows who he is or who the others are." *Plaisir à Corneille* (Paris: Gallimard, 1936), 192.

8. In fact Dircé is the opposite of Chimène in every way. She glories in the possibility that she might meet a heroic death as her father's daughter. She actively competes with Thésée, refusing to accept his claim that as her long lost brother—an identity he falsely assumes to save her life—he, not she, should die to save the city. Dircé will have none of it:

> Souffrez que pour la gloire une chaleur égale
> D'une amante aujourd'hui vous fasse une rivale.
> Le ciel offre à mon bras par où me signaler:
> S'il ne sait pas combattre, il saura m'immoler. (699–702)

> Accept that an eagerness for glory equal to yours
> Makes your mistress into your rival on this day.
> The heavens give my valorous arm a chance to prove my worth:
> If I cannot use it to fight, I can sacrifice myself.

It is Dircé, not Thésée, who is given the same sort of "stances" as Rodrigue in *Le Cid*, yet another reversal:

> Je meurs l'esprit content, l'honneur m'en fait la loi,
>   Mais j'aurais vécu plus contente,
>   Si j'avais pu vivre pour toi. (826–28)

> I die with contentment, honor tells me what is right,
>   But I would have lived with greater contentment
>   If I had been able to live for you.

9. The second half of the seventeenth century is a time of great scientific debate over the precise mechanisms involved in procreation, and especially the question of the contribution made by each of the parents. For a succinct discussion of the discoveries and beliefs of the period in this domain, see Jacques Roger, *Les Sciences de la vie dans la pensée française du XVIIIè siècle: La Génération des animaux de Descartes à l'Encyclopédie* (1963; rpt. Paris: Albin Michel, 1993), 256–67.

10. Here again the character of Dircé is a forerunner of Racine's Iphigénie, whose idealization of her father, Agamemnon, is also constitutive of her own identity. In the case of Iphigénie, the daughter's idealization is also undermined or ironicized, in that case by the existence of Iphigénie's double, the malcontent Eriphile.

11. Susan Read Baker, while she recognizes that the prominence of Dircé and Thésée draws attention away from Oedipe, reads this distraction as harmful to Oedipe's standing in the eyes of the audience: "Dircé, Oedipe's sister and the proper heiress of the throne which he has usurped, forms an alliance with her suitor, Thésée. Because this ideologically correct royal pair has Corneille's political sympathy, attention is constantly sapped away from Oedipe and empathy with his role is made impossible." *Dissonant Harmonies: Drama and Ideology in Five Neglected Plays of Pierre Corneille* (Tübingen: Gunter Narr, 1990), 19. I would simply add that the prominence of Dircé also makes empathy with Oedipe's role less crucial than it might otherwise be, since the shocking pathos of his situation is partially absorbed by the complications created by his sister's role.

12. Gordon Pocock is correct in his assessment of *Oedipe* as yet another example of Corneille's attempt to adapt his art to evolving tastes and styles: "[In *Oedipe*], he abandons the attempt at tragic intensity . . . [and] develops a wider range of interesting elements — misunderstandings, mistaken identities, political interests, an added love-story, philosophical speeches, oracles, miracles and realism — a confection of rich ingredients skillfully combined." *Corneille and Racine: Problems of Tragic Form* (Cambridge: Cambridge University Press, 1973), 138.

13. Jocaste is an important character in *La Thébaïde*, but not really an influential one. She commits suicide onstage practically without being noticed by her two squabbling sons, as is indicated by her daughter Antigone's horrified reaction to Jocaste's death: "Madame . . . O ciel! que vois-je? Hélas! rien ne les touche!" (1191) [Madam . . . Heavens! what do I see? Alas! nothing touches them!].

14. It is in fact possible that one of the reasons Racine made the brothers into twins is that two ancient sources disagree about which brother is the older. See *Oedipus at Colonus,* 374–76, in Sophocles, *Fabulae,* ed. A. C. Pearson (1924; rpt. Oxford: Clarendon, 1975); and *Phoenissae,* 71–72, in Euripides, *Fabulae,* vol. 3, ed. Gilbert Murray (1909; rpt. Oxford: Oxford University Press, 1975).

15. See Chapter 6.

16. To the extent that Racine leaves aside the question of birth order in his treatment of this material, he might be said to be returning to the spirit of Greek tragedy, in which, as Suzanne Saïd has pointed out, there is relatively little concern for birth-order issues. See "Couples fraternels dans la tragédie grecque ou le cadet introuvable," in *Les Cadets,* ed. Georges Giordani and Martine Segalen (Paris: CNRS, 1994), 67–75. Didier Pralon extends the Greeks' disinterest in birth order to their entire mythology: "The rules and behaviors of primogeniture, . . . which must have

existed in reality, did not . . . disturb the ancient Greeks to the point of giving rise to important myths." "L'Invention des cadets: la faute exemplaire," in *Les Cadets*, 59.

17. All quotations from and references to Racine's theater are taken from Jean Racine, *Théâtre complet*, ed. Jacques Morel and Alain Viala (Paris: Garnier Frères, 1980). Line numbers will be given in the body of the text.

18. Mitchell Greenberg succinctly characterizes the kind of negative inheritance that permeates Racine's theater: "The origin of familial guilt, of familial retribution, is never actually attributable to the person in question but loses itself in a former crime, committed in a more remote time, by an ancestor." *Subjectivity and Subjugation in Seventeenth-Century Drama and Prose: The Family Romance of French Classicism* (Cambridge: Cambridge University Press, 1992), 158.

19. As Georges Poulet puts it, "Racine's drama in its entirety is presented as the intrusion of a fatal past, a predetermining past, a causative past, into a present that desperately seeks to free itself of the past." "Notes sur le temps racinien," in *Racine*, ed. Wolfgang Theile (Darmstadt: Wissenschaftliche Buchgesellschaft, 1976), 100.

20. "Instead of the image of love as union that Jocaste would have [Etéocle and Polynice] reflect to each other . . . when each looks at his own (br)other he sees the image of his own negation, of his own death." Greenberg, *Subjectivity and Subjugation*, 160.

21. Terence Cave hypothesizes that the brothers are identical twins. *Recognitions: A Study in Poetics* (Oxford: Clarendon, 1988), 328. Jacques Scherer also implies that Etéocle and Polynice are identical. *Racine et / ou la cérémonie* (Paris: Presses Universitaires de France, 1982), 192.

Chapter 9. The Younger Brother Comes into His Own

1. Terence Cave, *Recognitions: A Study in Poetics* (Oxford: Clarendon, 1988), 332.

2. Georges May, "L'Unité de sang chez Racine," *Revue d'histoire littéraire de la France* 72 (1972): 227. Unless otherwise noted, all translations are my own.

3. Jean Racine, *Théâtre complet*, ed. J. Morel and A. Viala (Paris: Garnier Frères, 1980), 848 n.15.

4. Volker Schröder, "Politique du couple: amour réciproque et légitimité dynastique dans *Britannicus*," *Cahiers de l'Association Internationale des Etudes Françaises* 49 (May 1997): 478–79.

5. *Annales* 12:69, in Cornelius Tacitus, *Annales*, ed. Pierre Wuilleumier (Paris: Les Belles Lettres, 1974), 3:352.

6. See Chapter 10.

7. For a discussion of the role of adoption in the Roman political system, see Marcel-Henri Prevost, *Les Adoptions politiques à Rome sous la République et le Principat* (Paris: Sirey, 1949); and Jérôme Carcopino, "L'Hérédité dynastique chez les Antonins," *Revue des études anciennes* 51 (1949): 262–321.

8. Agrippine's confidante calls her "Vous qui, déshéritant le fils de Claudius, / Avez nommé César l'heureux Domitius" (17–18) [You who, by disinheriting Claudius' son / Named fortunate Domitius as Caesar].

9. Schröder, "Politique du couple," 467 and 485.

10. Junie perhaps indirectly alludes to this fact when, after Britannicus has been murdered, she addresses the statue of Augustus and calls Britannicus "Le seul de tes neveux qui te pût ressembler" (1734) [The only one of your descendants (nephews) who might have resembled you]. Even though in the Classical period the word "neveu" is generally used in the etymological sense of the Latin *nepos*, "grandson or descendant," Junie's words may be a veiled allusion to the fact that Britannicus, unlike Néron, is actually a distant nephew of Augustus. Volker Schröder ingeniously reads this line as Junie's establishment of Britannicus, after his death, as a direct descendant of Augustus. See "Politique du couple," 485.

11. May, "L'Unité de sang," 221.

12. Harriet A. Stone, "Authority and Authorship: Néron's Racine," in *Relectures raciniennes: nouvelles approches du discours tragique*, ed. Richard L. Barnett (Paris: Biblio 17, 1986), 167–68.

13. See Tacitus, *Annales* 11:11, 12:26, 13:17. Tacitus' narration of the adoption ceremony does not condemn Nero, and the historian speculates that the sympathy felt by some for Britannicus was merely a result of his dangerous situation.

14. Philip Lewis, "L'Adoption dans le théâtre de Racine," *Dix-septième siècle* 185 (October-December 1994): 773.

15. Georges Couton, "*Britannicus* tragédie des cabales," in *Mélanges d'histoire littéraire (XVIe-XVIIe siècle) offerts à Raymond Lebègue* (Paris: Nizet, 1969), 276.

16. Jacques Scherer, *Racine et /ou la cérémonie* (Paris: Presses Universitaires de France, 1982), 94–95.

17. Racine, *Théâtre complet*, 696. As Jean Morel's notes to *Athalie* indicate, this event is ironically foreshadowed by Joad's wish that Joas and his adoptive brother might always be on good terms: "Enfants, ainsi toujours puissiez-vous être unis!" (*Athalie*, 1416) [Children, may you always be so united!].

18. The other play is *Phèdre*, in which Ariane, Phèdre's older sister who has been dead for several years, is an important shadow presence. See Chapter 11.

19. The historical Amurat had an older brother, Osman II, who was overthrown in 1622 and succeeded by Amurat. Racine does not allude to this figure. See Jean Racine, *Oeuvres complètes*, vol. 1, ed. Georges Forestier (Paris: Gallimard [Bibliothèque de la Pléiade], 1999), 1511 (note 2 to p. 562).

20. The question of whether or not Amurat has children by other women in his harem is never brought up, nor is any mention made of an heir to the throne. Given Racine's emphasis on Amurat's unprecedented decision to grant Roxane the title of sultaness before she has borne him an heir, it is fair to conclude Bajazet would be Amurat's only logical successor if the sultan were to be killed in battle.

21. Racine, *Théâtre complet*, 854 n.21.

22. Atalide's noble birth is precisely the reason Acomat plans to marry her after Roxane has been married off to Bajazet and Amurat has been deposed: "J'aime en elle [Atalide] le sang dont elle est descendue" (182) [I love in Atalide the blood from which she descends].

23. Roland Barthes, *Sur Racine* (Paris: Seuil, 1963), 96.

24. Barthes calls her a "plebeian" (*Sur Racine*, 97).

25. "*Mithridate* is the last play in which the theme [of fraternal conflict] appears." In Racine, *Théâtre complet*, 444.

26. In fact the play opens with Xipharès' assertion of his authority over the country in which the action takes place, and thus it has the potential of being a territorial dispute between the surviving sons of a recently deceased king, a potential blocked by Mithridate's return.

27. In a paper given at the twenty-ninth conference of the North American Society for Seventeenth-Century French Literature, Victoria, British Columbia, April 1997.

28. Racine might as well have called his tragedy *La Mort de Mithridate*: in his preface to the play, he says that "[Mithridate's] death is the action of my tragedy" (*Théâtre complet*, 448).

29. See Chapter 5.

30. The problem that opens *La Mort de Pompée*, that of death left shockingly unavenged by the family members of the deceased — "Ces montagnes de morts privés d'honneurs suprêmes, / Que la nature force à se venger eux-mêmes" (*La Mort de Pompée*, 9–10) [The mountains of corpses, deprived of the last rites, / Forced by nature to take their own revenge] — may well be echoed by a later speech by Xipharès: "Qui sait si . . . / [Mithridate] Dans ses propres Etats privé de sépulture, / Ou couché sans honneur dans une foule obscure, / N'accuse point le ciel qui le laisse outrager, / Et des indignes fils qui n'osent le venger?" (299–306) [Who knows if . . . / Mithridate, deprived of burial in his own Lands, / Or lying without honor on some obscure pile, / Is not accusing the heavens that allow this outrage, / And the worthless sons who dare not avenge him?].

31. Racine, *Théâtre complet*, 443.

32. Even if Monime was born the year of her father's death, she would be fifty-one years older than Mithridate. Given that the historical Mithridates died at the age of sixty-nine and that this age is consistent with Racine's characterization of Mithridate at the time of his death, Monime would be 120 years old.

Chapter 10. An Older Brother's Loss

1. As Gordon Pocock observes, Racine's story line rather demands that Titus' younger brother be mentioned, since Titus himself threatens suicide: "Here we have an emperor threatening to kill himself, and not a word is said about the succession; Domitian is not mentioned in the play." *Corneille and Racine: Problems of Tragic Form* (Cambridge: Cambridge University Press, 1973), 209.

2. That the issue driving the action of the play is marriage reflects its status as a "comédie héroïque," as Corneille calls it, rather than a tragedy. In spite of this comic structure, based on the question of who ought to marry whom, the play's conclusion, as we shall see, has a strong element of tragedy: the reconciliation between the brothers and the projected marriage of Domitie and Domitian cannot be viewed as a simple reaffirmation of societal norms and values, as is generally the case in comedy.

3. In Pierre Corneille, *Oeuvres complètes*, ed. André Stegmann (Paris: Seuil, 1963), 743 n.19. Unless otherwise noted, all translations are my own.

4. The issue of primogeniture is complicated by the fact that in *Tite et Bérénice*, as in other plays of the period, there is a certain degree of conflation between the ancient Roman and the contemporary French political systems. As we have seen, the

Roman Empire was not a hereditary monarchy; Titus and his brother are the only emperors in the span of almost two centuries who inherited the title of emperor, each in his turn, directly from their biological father. This issue is crucial to my reading of Racine's *Britannicus* (see Chapter 9). The kind of jockeying for position and advantage that Domitie seems to be referring to in her exhortation to Domitian to become his brother's equal is not limited to any particular political system: as we have seen, even in seventeenth-century France, where royal succession strictly followed the law of primogeniture, Louis XIII was repeatedly challenged by his younger brother.

5. Similarly, Domitie, whose claims to be genuinely in love with Tite ring hollow, is nevertheless jealous of Tite's attraction to Bérénice: "Est-elle plus charmante, ai-je moins de mérite? / Suis-je moins digne qu'elle enfin du coeur de Tite?" (699–700) [Is she more charming, am I less deserving? / Am I really less worthy of Tite's heart than she?].

6. The similarity of Domitie's lines and Hermione's demonstrates how close the supposed madness of Racine's character is to undecorous self-interest; Hermione's "insanity" may be nothing more than a refusal to respect the conventions and artifices required by the values of the previous generation. Hermione's immediately preceding lines are, of course, much more famous — "Pourquoi l'assassiner? Qu'a-t-il fait? A quel titre? / Qui te l'a dit?" (*Andromaque*, 1542–43) [Why murder him? What did he do? For what reason? / Who told you to do it?] — and are often given as evidence of her complete mental breakdown. But in light of the lines that follow, which are expressive of a lover's egotistical tyranny rather than her loss of a sense of reality, Hermione's deludedness is somewhat difficult to distinguish from the kind of unbridled narcissism that Domitie expresses without any suggestion of being detached from reality.

7. André Stegmann points this out in *Oeuvres complètes*, 749 n.31.

8. The same idea is expressed by Domitie earlier when she is confronted by the two brothers and asked which one she prefers: "il n'importe du coeur quand on sait son devoir" (610) [the heart does not matter when one knows one's duty]; "de vos pareils les hautes destinées / Ne le [le coeur] consultent point sur ces grands hyménées" (611–12) [the high destinies of such as you / Do not consult the heart about these great marriages].

9. That the clearest proponent of old-style Cornelian heroism is neither a man nor a European may be taken as an indication of the marginal position to which this ethic has been relegated. As both a heroic and an archaic figure belonging to an ancient culture, Bérénice is placed in a similar position to Racine's Andromaque.

10. Serge Doubrovsky, *Corneille et la dialectique du héros* (Paris: Gallimard, 1963), 403.

11. The brevity of Bérénice's role may be related to this idea that she stands for an ideal difficult to maintain — the same could be said of Racinian characters like Andromaque and Britannicus. Serge Doubrovsky observes that Bérénice's first onstage appearance at the end of act 2 is nearly as late as Tartuffe's entrance in act 3 of Molière's play, one of the latest first appearances for a title character in all of Classical theater. *Corneille et la dialectique du héros*, 401.

12. The phrase is placed in the mouth of Titus — "je me propose un plus noble

théâtre" (356) [I aspire to a nobler theater] — whose condemnation of the "the-ater" of Nero's court is an intertextual allusion to Racine's most recent play before *Bérénice, Britannicus.*

13. The love between Antiochus and Bérénice is reminiscent of the love of Britannicus and Junie in *Britannicus*, a drama that premiered less than a year before *Bérénice*. Roland Barthes gives it as an example of "Eros sororal," love between two people who have grown up in close proximity and are of similar backgrounds, as op-posed to "amour immédiat," unmediated passion. See Roland Barthes, *Sur Racine* (Paris: Seuil, 1963), 16. I disagree with the starkness of Barthes' distinction between the two forms of love: it seems to me that he overlooks the fact that even "amour immédiat" is always triangulated in Racine and hence mediated by some other person or factor. Just as, according to my reading, Bérénice sees Rome in Titus, Phèdre sees in Hippolyte the idealized, expurgated version of Thésée that she has tried to create for herself since marrying the once-fickle Athenian hero; in Junie, Néron sees the lover of his rival, Britannicus; in Bajazet, Roxane finds a vulnerable younger brother with whom she can reverse the cruel power structure whereby she has been completely dependent upon the whims of the older brother.

14. Gérard Defaux, "The Case of *Bérénice*: Racine, Corneille, and Mimetic Desire," *Yale French Studies* 76 (1989): 224–25.

15. Two other plays in which the older sibling and / or father tries to take away the younger sibling's lover are *Britannicus* and *Mithridate*. See Chapter 9.

16. Bérénice's playful reproach to Antiochus is in fact echoed by her opening speech to Titus — "Votre deuil est fini, rien n'arrête vos pas, / Vous êtes seul enfin, et ne me cherchez pas!" (565–66) [Your mourning is over, nothing keeps you away, / You're alone, and you do not seek me out!] — which draws further attention to her coquettishness with both men.

17. Pocock, *Corneille and Racine*, 201.

18. For example, Oreste vainly tries to forget Hermione: "Mais quand je me souvins que parmi tant d'alarmes / Hermione à Pyrrhus prodiguait tous ses charmes, / Tu sais de quel courroux mon coeur alors épris / Voulut en l'oubliant punir tous ses mépris" (*Andromaque*, 49–52) [But when I recalled that in the midst of the disorder / Hermione paraded her charms before Pyrrhus' eyes, / You know how fiercely my inflamed heart / Wished to punish her disdain by forgetting her]. Hippolyte tries to forget Thésée's scandalous past: "Heureux si j'avais pu ravir à la mémoire / Cette indigne moitié d'une si belle histoire!" (*Phèdre*, 93–94) [How happy if only I could have plucked from my memory / That unworthy half of such a fine story!]. And Oenone tries to soothe Phèdre's torment about her mother's bestial passions: "Oublions-les Madame, et qu'à tout l'avenir / Un silence éternel cache ce souvenir" (*Phèdre*, 251–52) [Forget them, Madam, and for all time / May an eternal silence hide this memory]. These are all cases of forgetfulness as a protec-tion from passions seen as unacceptable.

19. Titus: "Je connais Bérénice, et ne sais que trop bien / Que son coeur n'a jamais demandé que le mien. / . . . / Sans avoir en aimant d'objet que son amour" (529–33) [I know Bérénice, and I know all too well / That her heart has never asked for anything but mine. / . . . / Having no object in loving other than love itself]. Bérénice (to Titus): "Depuis quand croyez-vous que ma grandeur me

touche? / Un soupir, un regard, un mot de votre bouche, / Voilà l'ambition d'un coeur comme le mien" (575–77) [Since when have you believed that greatness is what I crave? / A sigh, a glance, a word from your lips, / That is the ambition of a heart like mine].

20. Barthes, *Sur Racine*, 88.

21. I believe that Harriet Stone, in an otherwise fine and subtle interpretation of *Bérénice*, does not take sufficient account of this essentially moral role played by Bérénice. See her analysis in *The Classical Model: Literature and Knowledge in Seventeenth-Century France* (Ithaca, N.Y.: Cornell University Press, 1996), 77–93.

22. Among the various discussions of the competition between Racine and Corneille, Gérard Defaux' analysis is perhaps the most compelling: "The rivalry with Corneille played a role that can hardly be overestimated. . . . Corneille dictate[d] to Racine the very principles of his art, defining for him, through *fuite* rather than *suite*, the theoretical bases upon which his oeuvre would be *consciously* constructed. . . ." "The Case of *Bérénice*," 214. To this I would add that I do not see Racine's relation to Corneille as simple enough to be characterized by pure "fuite."

23. Pocock, *Corneille and Racine*, 211.

Chapter 11. A Tale of Two Sisters

1. In fact, the situation in *Ariane* is far simpler than it is in *Phèdre*, partly because the prehistory of *Phèdre* includes the events dramatized in *Ariane*, as well as their aftermath, and partly because *Phèdre* dwells on the mythological background of the story and the family at much greater length than *Ariane*.

2. It is true that in the context of this scene Ariane also declines the opportunity of receiving a throne by marrying the king of Naxos — "Qu'ai-je affaire du Trône et de la main d'un Roi?" (3:4; 4:559) [What do I care about the Throne and marriage with a King?] — but the chronology of events is such that the crown she refused by leaving home with Thésée can only be the crown she would have inherited from her father. Unless otherwise noted, all translations are my own.

3. It would be possible to extend to oldest-sibling heirs and their junior counterparts Terence Cave's observations about the differences between the way male and female characters experience the phenomenon of recognition. See Terence Cave, *Recognitions: A Study in Poetics* (Oxford: Clarendon, 1988), 494–95.

4. It should be added that Ariane takes pains to reject out of hand the whole dynastic issue by claiming that she has no desire to be queen: "Trône, Sceptre, grandeurs, sont des biens superflus; / Thésée étant à moi, je ne veux rien de plus" (2:5; 4:545) [Throne, Scepter, and greatness are superfluous benefits; / If Thésée is mine, I want nothing more].

5. As Jocaste says to Etéocle, "Le sort vous appela le premier à l'empire" (*La Thébaïde*, 88) [Your lot was to come to power first]. In this case the word is also ambiguous: it probably suggests the choice was made by lottery, but might possibly mean it was made by destiny. See Chapter 8.

6. The relation between politics and love is, of course, one of the moving forces behind many of the tragedies of this period, not only thematically — tragic

conflicts often hinge on the choice between love and political expediency, or the use of love for political purposes—but also lexically. The ascendancy of preciosity and the novel in the period between the two generations of tragedy is reflected by the ubiquity of love in Racine's theater, for example, but also by the transferral of the vocabulary of political power into the domain of love. This certainly starts to occur in the first generation of tragedies, but it becomes even more widespread in the second generation. In *Ariane*, for instance, Oenarus does not wish to "tyrannize" Ariane by forcing himself on her: "En la tyrannisant toucherais-je son âme?" (1:1; 4:526) [By tyrannizing her, would I touch her soul?].

7. In *Bajazet*, Atalide, Bajazet's secret lover, speaks for him in his meetings with Roxane, the problem being that Bajazet himself is unable to convince Roxane that he loves her (which in fact he does not). But while the dynamics of the vicarious love-triangle are different in *Bajazet* and in *Ariane*, the role of mediated communication is similar. For a more detailed analysis of the relation between Bajazet and his older brother, see Chapter 9.

8. Indeed, it is not surprising that critics have focused on parent-child relations, both in this drama and in other plays of Racine. As Mitchell Greenberg has pointed out, both Roland Barthes and Charles Mauron emphasize the importance of patricide as a seminal Racinian theme. See Mitchell Greenberg, *Subjectivity and Subjugation in Seventeenth-Century Drama and Prose: The Family Romance of French Classicism* (Cambridge: Cambridge University Press, 1992), 142. By the same token, Greenberg himself orients his analysis of Racinian tragedy around the parent-child axis as well.

9. Hippolyte also mentions Ariane in his inventory of Thésée's dastardly sexual exploits: "Ariane aux rochers contant ses injustices" (89) [Ariane reciting her unfair treatment to the cliffs].

10. Roland Barthes goes even further by reversing the cause-and-effect relation between guilt and interiority: "*Phèdre* posits an identification of interiority with guilt; in *Phèdre*, things are not hidden because they are guilty . . . ; things are guilty because they are hidden." *Sur Racine* (Paris: Seuil, 1963), 116.

11. Voltaire sees Phèdre as "always excusable, always worthy of pity, however guilty she might appear." *Critique des tragédies de Corneille et de Racine par Voltaire*, ed. B. Bonieux (1866; rpt. Geneva: Slatkine, 1970), 236.

12. The fact that I see Aricie as a figure of Phèdre's older sister is independent of the ages of Phèdre and Ariane in Racine's play; at any rate, their relative ages are impossible to determine.

13. See Roy C. Knight, *Racine et la Grèce* (1951; rpt. Paris: Nizet, 1974), 355–57.

14. As Racine puts it in his preface to the play, "I thought I had to give [Hippolyte] some form of weakness that would make him somewhat guilty toward his father. . . . I call the involuntary passion he feels for Aricie a weakness, for she is the daughter and sister of his father's mortal enemies." *Théâtre complet*, ed. J. Morel and A. Viola (Paris: Garnier Frères, 1980), 577.

15. Roy C. Knight writes, "The public's taste absolutely demanded that Hippolyte not be immune to love." *Racine et la Grèce*, 355.

16. See Jean Racine, *Théâtre complet*, 860, n.16.

17. Given the very real dynastic concerns that permeate this tragedy, not to mention the subtext of Ariane's abandonment by Thésée, it is difficult to take seriously Lucien Goldmann's dismissal of Aricie's preoccupation with marriage as a sign of the character's insubstantiality. "Structure de la tragédie racinienne," in *Racine*, ed. Wolfgang Theile (Darmstadt: Wissenschaftliche Buchgesellschaft, 1976), 291.

18. These are obviously very ironic words, since Hippolyte is Thésée's psychological heir *malgré lui*.

19. As Jacques Scherer observes, the fate of Phèdre's children is not mentioned in the play's final scene: "When [Phèdre] reappears just before her death, she does not say a word about her children. Phèdre's children can no longer be protected by anyone. . . . Phèdre has failed as a mother. The maternal function is not what is essential to her." *Racine et / ou la cérémonie* (Paris: Presses Universitaires de France, 1982), 158.

20. It is perfectly possible to read Thésée's last words as indicative of a more general acceptance of Aricie and an intention to stop persecuting her, rather than as a designation of Aricie as his political heir; Thésée can certainly adopt Aricie without naming her as heir apparent. I merely wish to emphasize the great irony of Thésée's "choosing" to recognize at least some of the rights of a character who believes that her rights do not depend on his recognition.

Bibliography

Adam, Antoine. *Grandeur and Illusion: French Literature and Society, 1600–1715.* Trans. Herbert Tint. London: Weidenfeld and Nicholson, 1972.
———. *Histoire de la littérature française au XVIIe siècle.* 5 vols. Paris: Domat, 1948–1956.
Adler, Alfred. *Understanding Human Nature.* Trans. Walter Béran Wolfe. Garden City, N.Y.: Garden City Publishing, 1927.
———. *What Life Should Mean to You.* Ed. Alan Porter. Boston: Little, Brown, 1931.
Albera, Dionigi. "La Maison des frères." In *Les Cadets.* Ed. Georges Ravis-Giordani and Martine Segalen. Paris: CNRS, 1994.
Allentuch, Harriet Ray. "Sacred and Heroic Blood and the Religion of Monarchy on the Cornelian Stage." In *Homage to Paul Bénichou.* Ed. Sylvie Romanowski and Monique Bilezikian. Birmingham, Ala.: Summa, 1994.
Ansbacher, Heinz L. "The Significance of Socio-economic Status of the Patients of Freud and of Adler." *American Journal of Psychotherapy* 13 (1959): 376–82.
Ariès, Philippe. *L'Enfant et la vie familiale sous l'Ancien Régime.* 1960. Rpt. Paris: Seuil, 1973.
Armengaud, André. *La Famille et l'enfant en France et en Angleterre du XVIe au XVIIIe siècle.* Paris: Société d'Edition d'Enseignement Supérieur, 1975.
Auden, W. H. "Brothers and Others." In *The Dyer's Hand and Other Essays.* New York: Random House, 1948.
Bach, Ray. "Fatal Identity: Parents and Children in Racine's *Andromaque.*" *Stanford French Review* 16:1 (1992): 9–18.
Baker, Susan Read. *Dissonant Harmonies: Drama and Ideology in Five Neglected Plays of Pierre Corneille.* Tübingen: Gunter Narr, 1990.
Bank, Stephen P., and Michael D. Kahn. *The Sibling Bond.* New York: Basic Books, 1982.
Barc, Bernard. "Aîné et cadet dans la Bible." In *Les Cadets.* Ed. Georges Ravis-Giordani and Martine Segalen. Paris: CNRS, 1994.
Barthes, Roland. *Sur Racine.* Paris: Seuil, 1963.
Beauvoir, Simone de. *Mémoires d'une jeune fille rangée.* Paris: Folio, 1958.
Bénichou, Paul. *Morales du grand siècle.* Paris: Gallimard, 1948.
Biet, Christian. "Le Cadet, point de départ des destins romanesques dans la littérature française du XVIIIe siècle." In *Les Cadets.* Ed. Georges Ravis-Giordani and Martine Segalen. Paris: CNRS, 1994.
Bitton, Davis. *The French Nobility in Crisis, 1560–1640.* Stanford, Calif.: Stanford University Press, 1969.
Bluche, François. *Louis XIV.* Trans. Mark Greengrass. New York: Franklin Watts, 1990.
Bourdieu, Pierre. *La Distinction: Critique sociale du jugement.* Paris: Minuit, 1979.

Brasillach, Robert. *Corneille*. 1938. Rpt. Paris: Fayard, 1961.

Carcopino, Jérôme. "L'Hérédité dynastique chez les Antonins." *Revue des études anciennes* 51 (1949): 262–321.

Castro, Guillén de. *Las Mocedades del Cid*. Letras hispanicas, 72. Madrid: Catedra, 1998.

Cave, Terence. *Recognitions: A Study in Poetics*. Oxford: Clarendon, 1988.

Certeau, Michel de. *L'Ecriture de l'histoire*. Paris: Gallimard, 1975.

Chevallier, Pierre. *Louis XIII: roi cornélien*. Paris: Fayard, 1979.

Chodorow, Nancy. *The Reproduction of Mothering: Psychoanalysis and the Sociology of Gender*. Berkeley: University of California Press, 1978.

Clarke, David. *Pierre Corneille: Poetics and Political Drama Under Louis XIII*. Cambridge: Cambridge University Press, 1992.

Collins, David A. *Thomas Corneille: Protean Dramatist*. The Hague: Mouton, 1966.

Collomp, Alain. "Le Statut des cadets en Haute-Provence avant et après le Code civil." In *Les Cadets*. Ed. Georges Ravis-Giordani and Martine Segalen. Paris: CNRS, 1994.

Corneille, Pierre. *Oeuvres complètes*. 3 vols. Ed. Georges Couton. Paris: Gallimard (Bibliothèque de la Pléiade), 1980–1987.

——. *Oeuvres complètes*. Ed. André Stegmann. Paris: Seuil, 1963.

Corneille, Thomas. *Poëmes dramatiques*. 5 vols. Paris: Guillaume Cavelier, 1722.

Couprie, Alain. "Le Moi, le double et le dédoublement." In *Lectures de Corneille: Cinna, Rodogune, Nicomède*. Ed Daniel Riou. Rennes: Presses Universitaires de Rennes, 1997.

Couton, Georges. "*Britannicus* tragédie des cabales." In *Mélanges d'histoire littéraire (XVIe-XVIIe siècle) offerts à Raymond Lebègue*. Paris: Nizet, 1969.

——. *Corneille et la Fronde*. Clermont-Ferrand: Bussac, 1951.

Dechêne, H. C. *Geschwisterkonstellation und psychische Fehlentwicklung*. Munich: Barth, 1967.

Defaux, Gérard. "The Case of *Bérénice*: Racine, Corneille, and Mimetic Desire." *Yale French Studies* 76 (1989): 211–39.

Delmas, Christian. "Médée, figure de la violence dans le théâtre français du XVIIe siècle." *Pallas* 45 (1996): 219–28.

Desan, Suzanne. "'War Between Brothers and Sisters': Inheritance Law and Gender Politics in Revolutionary France." *French Historical Studies* 20:4 (Fall 1997): 597–634.

Dewald, Jonathan. *Aristocratic Experience and the Origins of Modern Culture: France, 1570–1715*. Berkeley: University of California Press, 1993.

Domon, Hélène. "Médée (ou) L'autre." *Cahiers du dix-septième* 1:2 (Fall 1987): 87–102.

Dorchain, Auguste. *Pierre Corneille*. Paris: Garnier Frères, 1918.

Doubrovsky, Serge. *Corneille et la dialectique du héros*. Paris: Gallimard, 1963.

Duby, Georges. *Les Trois Ordres ou l'imaginaire du féodalisme*. Paris: Gallimard, 1978.

Dunn, Judy and Carol Kendrick. *Siblings: Love, Envy and Understanding*. London: Grant McIntyre, 1982.

Dunn, Judy, and Robert Plomin. *Separate Lives: Why Siblings Are So Different*. New York: Basic Books, 1990.

Elias, Norbert. *The Court Society*. Trans. Edmund Jephcott. Oxford: Basil Blackwell, 1983.

Enriquez, Eugène. *De la horde à l'état: essai de psychanalyse du lien social*. Paris: Gallimard, 1983.

Erasmus, Desiderius. *The Education of a Christian Prince*. Trans. Lester K. Born. New York: Columbia University Press, 1936.

Erikson, Erik H. "The Human Life Cycle." In *A Way of Looking at Things: Selected Papers from 1930 to 1980*. Ed. Stephen Schlein. New York: W. W. Norton, 1987.

——. "Human Strength and the Cycle of Generations." In *Insight and Responsibility: Lectures on the Ethical Implications of Psychoanalytic Insight*. New York: W. W. Norton, 1964.

Flandrin, Jean-Louis. *Familles: parenté, maison, sexualité dans l'ancienne société*. Paris: Hachette, 1976.

Forer, Lucille K. *Birth Order and Life Roles*. Springfield, Ill.: Charles C. Thomas, 1969.

Foucault, Michel. *The Order of Things: An Archaeology of the Human Sciences*. 1970. Rpt. New York: Vintage Books, 1973.

François, Carlo. *Raison et déraison dans le théâtre de Pierre Corneille*. York, S.C.: French Literature Publications, 1979.

Fumaroli, Marc. *Héros et orateurs: rhétorique et dramaturgie cornéliennes*. Geneva: Droz, 1990.

——. "Melpomène au miroir: La Tragédie comme héroïne dans *Médée* et *Phèdre*." *Saggi e ricerche di letteratura francese* 19 (1980): 177–205.

Goldmann, Lucien. *Le Dieu caché*. Paris: Gallimard, 1959.

——. "Structure de la tragédie racinienne." In *Racine*. Ed. Wolfgang Theile. Darmstadt: Wissenschaftliche Buchgesellschaft, 1976.

Goode, William O. "Médée and Jason: Hero and Nonhero in Corneille's *Médée*." *French Review* 51 (May 1978): 804–15.

Gossip, C. J. " 'Le Goût de l'antiquité': Thomas Corneille and the Death of Hannibal." *Forum for Modern Language Studies* 1990 (26:1): 13–25.

Gotman, Anne. *Hériter*. Paris: Presses Universitaires de France, 1988.

Gottlieb, Beatrice. *The Family in the Western World from the Black Death to the Industrial Age*. New York and Oxford: Oxford University Press, 1993.

Greenberg, Mitchell. *Corneille, Classicism, and the Ruses of Symmetry*. Cambridge: Cambridge University Press, 1986.

——. "Racine's Children." In *Actes de Columbus*. Paris: Biblio 17, 1990.

——. *Subjectivity and Subjugation in Seventeenth-Century Drama and Prose: The Family Romance of French Classicism*. Cambridge: Cambridge University Press, 1992.

Greenspahn, Frederick E. *When Brothers Dwell Together: The Preeminence of Younger Siblings in the Hebrew Bible*. New York: Oxford University Press, 1994.

Harman, Chris. "From Feudalism to Capitalism." *International Socialism* 45 (Winter 1989): 35–87.

Harris, Judith Rich. *The Nurture Assumption: Why Children Turn Out the Way They Do*. New York: Free Press, 1998.

Harth, Erica. *Ideology and Culture in Seventeenth-Century France*. Ithaca, N.Y.: Cornell University Press, 1983.

Hegel, Georg Wilhelm Friedrich. "Philosophy of Right." Trans. T. M. Knox. In *On Tragedy*. Ed. Anne and Henry Paolucci. New York: Harper and Row, 1962.

Himelfarb, Hélène. "Un journal peu ordinaire." *Nouvelle Revue de Psychanalyse* 19 (Spring 1979): 269–79.

Hunt, David. *Parents and Children in History: The Psychology of Family Life in Early Modern France*. New York: Basic Books, 1970.

Hunt, Lynn. *The Family Romance of the French Revolution*. Berkeley: University of California Press, 1992.

Jackson, John E. "Corneille: du triomphe de la vengeance à l'instauration de la loi." *Dix-septième siècle* 155:2 (April-June 1987): 155–72.

Knight, Roy C. *Racine et la Grèce*. 1951. Rpt. Paris: Nizet, 1974.

König, Karl. *Brothers and Sisters: A Study in Child Psychology*. Blauvelt, N.Y.: St. George Books, 1963.

Lancaster, Henry Carrington. *A History of French Dramatic Literature in the Seventeenth Century*. Vol. 2. *The Period of Corneille, 1635–1651*. Baltimore: Johns Hopkins University Press, 1932.

Langer, Ullrich. *Perfect Friendship: Studies in Literature and Moral Philosophy from Boccaccio to Corneille*. Geneva: Droz, 1994.

Lévi-Strauss, Claude. *Les Structures élémentaires de la parenté*. 1949. 2nd ed. Paris: Mouton, 1967.

Lewis, Philip. "L'Adoption dans le théâtre de Racine." *Dix-septième siècle* 185 (October-December 1994): 773–85.

Leyssac, André de. "Pour une reprise de Médée." *Revue d'histoire du théâtre* 36:1 (1984): 180–84.

Lyons, John D. *The Tragedy of Origins: Pierre Corneille and Historical Perspective*. Stanford, Calif.: Stanford University Press, 1996.

MacGregor, Gordon D. "*Rodogune, Nicomède*, and the Status of History in Corneille." *Stanford French Review* 11:2 (Summer 1987): 133–56.

Mandrou, Robert. *Introduction à la France moderne, 1500–1640*. 1961. Rpt. Paris: Albin Michel, 1989.

Maranda, Pierre. *French Kinship: Structure and History*. The Hague: Mouton, 1974.

Marin, Louis. *Des pouvoirs de l'image*. Paris: Seuil, 1993.

Maskell, David. *Racine: A Theatrical Reading*. Oxford: Clarendon, 1991.

May, Georges. "L'Unité de sang chez Racine." *Revue d'histoire littéraire de la France* 72 (1972): 209–33.

Mead, Margaret. *Culture and Commitment: A Study of the Generation Gap*. Garden City, N.Y.: Doubleday (Natural History Press), 1970.

Merlin, Hélène. "*Cinna, Rodogune, Nicomède*: Le Roi et le *moi*." *Littératures* 37 (Autumn 1997): 67–86.

Mink, JoAnna Stephens, and Janet Doubler Ward, ed. *The Significance of Sibling Relationships in Literature*. Bowling Green, Ohio: Bowling Green State University Popular Press, 1993.

Molière. *Oeuvres complètes*. Paris: Seuil, 1962.

Moote, A. Lloyd. *Louis XIII, the Just*. Berkeley: University of California Press, 1989.

Mousnier, Roland. *Les Institutions de la France sous la Monarchie absolue, 1598–1789*. 2 vols. Paris: Presses Universitaires de France, 1974.

——. *Les XVIe et XVIIe siècles*. Paris: Presses Universitaires de France, 1954.

Nadal, Octave. *Le Sentiment de l'amour dans l'oeuvre de Pierre Corneille*. Paris: Gallimard, 1948.

Oddon, Marcel. "Les Tragédies de Thomas Corneille: structures de l'univers des personnages." *Revue d'histoire du théâtre* 37:1 (1985): 199–213.

Orlando, Francesco. *Toward a Freudian Theory of Literature*. Trans. Charmaine Lee. Baltimore: Johns Hopkins University Press, 1978.

Pillorget, René. *La Tige et le rameau: familles anglaise et française XVIe-XVIIIe siècle*. Paris: Calmann-Lévy, 1979.

Pocock, Gordon. *Corneille and Racine: Problems of Tragic Form*. Cambridge: Cambridge University Press, 1973.

Poulet, Georges. "Notes sur le temps racinien." In *Racine*. Ed. Wolfgang Theile. Darmstadt: Wissenschaftliche Buchgesellschaft, 1976.

Pralon, Didier. "L'Invention des cadets: la faute exemplaire." In *Les Cadets*. Ed. Georges Giordani and Martine Segalen. Paris: CNRS, 1994.

Prevost, Marcel-Henri. *Les Adoptions politiques à Rome sous la République et le Principat*. Paris: Sirey, 1949.

Prigent, Michel. *Le Héros et l'Etat dans la tragédie de Pierre Corneille*. Paris: Presses Universitaires de France (Quadrige), 1986.

Quinones, Ricardo J. *The Changes of Cain: Violence and the Lost Brother in Cain and Abel Literature*. Princeton: Princeton University Press, 1991.

Racine, Jean. *Oeuvres complètes*, vol. 1. Ed. Georges Forestier. Paris: Gallimard (Bibliothèque de la Pléiade), 1999.

——. *Théâtre complet*. Ed. Jacques Morel and Alain Viala. Paris: Garnier Frères, 1980.

Rank, Otto. *The Incest Theme in Literature and Legend: Fundamentals of a Psychology of Literary Creation*. Trans. Gregory C. Richter. 1912. Rpt. Baltimore: Johns Hopkins University Press, 1992.

Reiss, Timothy J. "*Bérénice* et la politique du peuple." In *Re-lectures raciniennes: nouvelles approches du discours tragique*. Ed. Richard L. Barnett. Paris: Biblio 17, 1986.

Rieff, Philip. *Freud: The Mind of the Moralist*. 1959. 3rd ed. Chicago: University of Chicago Press, 1979.

Roger, Jacques. *Les Sciences de la vie dans la pensée française du XVIIIe siècle: la génération des animaux de Descartes à l'Encyclopédie*. 1963. Rpt. Paris: Albin Michel, 1993.

Rowen, Herbert H. *The King's State: Proprietary Dynasticism in Early Modern France*. New Brunswick, N.J.: Rutgers University Press, 1980.

Saïd, Suzanne. "Couples fraternels dans la tragédie grecque ou le cadet introuvable." In *Les Cadets*. Ed. Georges Giordani and Martine Segalen. Paris: CNRS, 1994.

Scherer, Jacques. "Les intentions politiques dans Nicomède." In *Pierre Corneille: Actes du colloque de Rouen*. Ed. Alain Niderst. Paris: Presses Universitaires de France, 1985.

——. *Racine et / ou la cérémonie*. Paris: Presses Universitaires de France, 1982.

——. *Le Théâtre de Corneille*. Paris: Nizet, 1984.

Schlumberger Jean. *Plaisir à Corneille*. Paris: Gallimard, 1936.

Schröder, Volker. "Politique du couple: amour réciproque et légitimité dynastique dans *Britannicus*." *Cahiers de l'Association Internationale des Etudes Françaises* 49 (May 1997): 455–91.

Segalen, Martine. "La Notion d'avantage dans les sociétés égalitaires." In *Les Cadets*. Ed. Georges Ravis-Giordani and Martine Segalen. Paris: CNRS, 1994.

Simon, Bennett. *Tragic Drama and the Family: Psychoanalytic Studies from Aeschylus to Beckett*. New Haven: Yale University Press, 1988.

Starobinski, Jean. *L'Oeil vivant*. Paris: Gallimard, 1961.

Stone, Harriet A. "Authority and Authorship: Néron's Racine." In *Re-lectures raciniennes: nouvelles approches du discours tragique*. Ed. Richard L. Barnett. Paris: Biblio 17, 1986.

——. *The Classical Model: Literature and Knowledge in Seventeenth-Century France*. Ithaca, N.Y.: Cornell University Press, 1996.

——. *Royal DisClosure: Problematics of Representation in French Classical Tragedy*. Birmingham, Ala.: Summa, 1987.

Sulloway, Frank J. *Born To Rebel: Birth Order, Family Dynamics, and Creative Lives*. New York: Pantheon, 1996.

Sutton-Smith, Brian, and B. G. Rosenberg. *The Sibling*. New York: Holt, Rinehart and Winston, 1970.

Tacitus, Cornelius. *Annales*. Ed. Pierre Wuilleumier. Paris: Les Belles Lettres, 1974.

Thirsk, Joan. "The European Debate on Customs of Inheritance." In *Family and Inheritance, Rural Society in Western Europe, 1200–1800*. Ed. Jack Goody, Joan Thirsk, and E. P. Thompson. Cambridge: Cambridge University Press, 1976.

Trésor de la langue française. 16 vols. Paris: Gallimard, 1971–1994.

Tucker, Holly. "Corneille's *Médée*: Gifts of Vengeance." *French Review* 69:1 (October 1995): 1–12.

Valéry, Paul. "Mauvaises pensées et autres." In *Oeuvres*, vol. 2. Ed. Jean Hytier. Paris: Gallimard (Bibliothèque de la Pléiade), 1960.

Venesoen, Constant. "Le Thème de la fraternité dans l'oeuvre de Racine: un cas de dédoublement." In *L'Age du théâtre en France*. Ed. David Trott and Nicole Boursier. Edmonton: Academic Printing and Publishing, 1988.

Voltaire. *Critique des tragédies de Corneille et de Racine par Voltaire*. Ed. B. Bonieux. 1866. Rpt. Geneva: Slatkine, 1970.

Watts, Derek A. "A Further Look at Rodogune." In *Ouverture et dialogue: mélanges offerts à Wolfgang Leiner*. Ed. Ulrich Döring, Antiopy Lyroudias, and Rainer Zaiser. Tübingen: Gunter Narr, 1988.

Wolf, John B. "The Formation of a King." In *Louis XIV: A Profile*. Ed. John B. Wolf. New York: Hill and Wang, 1972.

——. *Louis XIV*. New York: Norton, 1968.

Acknowledgments

The early stages of research for this book were conducted under the auspices of several grants from the University of Wisconsin-Madison: a Vilas Associate Award in 1992–94 and a Resident Fellowship at the Institute for Research in the Humanities in the fall of 1993. My thanks go to colleagues at the University of Wisconsin who have read parts of the manuscript at various stages and/or heard lectures based on this project and have given me useful suggestions, in particular, Martine Debaisieux, Ullrich Langer, Elaine Marks, Yvonne Ozzello, and Nicholas Rand. I am grateful to Joan DeJean, John Lyons, and Tom Conley for reading the entire manuscript and giving me much needed and much appreciated support, as well as a good number of helpful suggestions. I also wish to acknowledge the support of Faith Beasley, Annette Becker, Jean-Pierre Becker, Christian Biet, Megan Dixon, Mitchell Greenberg, Patricia Hannon, David Harrison, Patrick Litscher, Michèle Longino, Andrew O'Shaughnessy, Jerome Singerman, and Harriet Stone.

Earlier version of parts of the book have appeared in print previously. I wish to thank the publishers for their permission to reprint these materials. From Chapter 2: "Dévier de soi: l'écart spirituel des *Femmes Savantes*," in *Le Labyrinthe de Versailles: Parcours critiques de Molière à La Fontaine à la mémoire d'Alvin Eustis*, ed. Martine Debaisieux (Amsterdam: Rodopi, 1998), 17–31. From Chapter 6: "*Born to Rebel* Revisited: Pierre Corneille's *Rodogune* and Thomas Corneille's *Persée et Démétrius*," in *Actes de Victoria* (Tübingen: Gunter Narr [Biblio 17:111], 1998), 241–55. From Chapter 7: "*Nicomède 1 and 2*: The Fraternal Heritage of Pierre and Thomas Corneille," *Papers on French Seventeenth-Century Literature* 25:48 (1998): 255–65. From Chapter 11: "Thomas Corneille's *Ariane* and Jean Racine's *Phèdre*: The Older Sister Strikes Back," *L'Esprit créateur* 38:2 (Summer 1998): 60–71.

Index